CAPITOL HILL'S
CRIMINAL
UNDERGROUND

THE MOST THOROUGH EXPLORATION
OF GOVERNMENT CORRUPTION EVER PUT IN WRITING

TRILLIONS OF DOLLARS STOLEN
**NO FBI INVESTIGATIONS
NO U.S. ATTORNEY
PROSECUTIONS
NO ACTION BY
THE SEC**

**CIA WIRETAPS
DOJ PAYOFFS
DEATH THREATS**

RICHARD LAWLESS

Medlaw Publishing

All companies, municipalities, government agencies and individuals discussed or named in this book should be consider innocent of all wrongdoing until such time a court of law determines otherwise.

This story is about the Capitol Hill's Criminal Underground: a loose association of bad actors that call Wall Street and Capitol Hill their home. What you are about to read is a true story. No names have been changed and those involved have been identified.

This is a story about one of the longest running government protected, criminal enterprises in the history of our country. It is a story about the successful efforts of a few hucksters to transfer massive amounts of wealth from the hands of tens of millions of innocent Americans into the hands of a few thousand powerful people.

Unlike most books you may read, *Capitol Hill's Criminal Underground* will focus on real events while unmasking those who thrive in the dark corners of the Department of Justice and their "Political Overseers" who use their power and influence to usurp our legal protections.

By reading this book to the end, you will fully understand the roles within this criminal organization and the cooperation between municipal executives, credit rating executives, bankers, government employees and politicians that make it all possible.

There is enough evidence in this book to investigate and prosecute over one thousand high ranking government employees, bankers and politicians.

PREFACE

It was never the intent of our founders to have career politicians in office. In fact, it was quite the opposite. There was a pervasive fear of falling into the trap of another monarchy or some other form of leadership that was not decided on by the citizens. It was supposed to be "a government by the people and for the people".

A hundred years ago, the average senator served five years; today the average is thirteen years. Congressmen now serve an average of nine years and four months. More disturbing is the growing number of politicians who serve for decades and are often content to hold the reins of power until they die in office. The numbers of senators and congressmen serving twenty, thirty or forty years has been growing since the inception of this country.

When one takes a look at the average age of our senators, it is clear that this is a group of people determined not to give up the power and control accumulated over many decades.

You hear all the time that Congress is a mess and they should all be voted out of office. Approval ratings for our Congress and the Senate can't get much lower. This book will blow away the common misconception that many voters believe: "their guy" is okay; it is all the "other people" in government that are the problem.

This investigation will show the readers that it is in fact "their guy" that is the problem. The American people are voting for the very type of government that our founders feared.

It appears these career politicians appoint individuals into powerful positions within government agencies like the Department of Justice and the Securities and Exchange Commission with the implicit understanding that some things are not to be questioned.

This unfortunate journey of discovery has shown that the level of arrogance and contempt our political leaders hold for the American people is boundless. The more we looked, the more evidence of serious criminal activity we found. And why not? The politicians control all the levers of power; their people in the Department of Justice will make sure there are no investigations or prosecutions. Their constituents will vote them back into office with almost absolute certainty.

It is my hope that this story will help change the way people look at our government and more importantly, change the way American's vote.

TABLE OF CONTENTS

CHAPTER ONE
HOW IN THE WORLD DID THIS HAPPEN TO US?

It was 2008, and the United States was in the midst of a financial meltdown. This crisis impacted tens of millions of Americans, and I was one of those indirectly affected.

I was a banker, and it was a tough time for banks in general. After twenty-five years in the industry, this crisis presented an opportunity for me to move on. Banks were in trouble. Commercial real estate values had plummeted, and many of the loans that banks had made now exceeded the value of the properties. All lending activity was likely to slow or stop until the economy turned around. It was the perfect time to retire from banking and move on to a new chapter of my life.

I have always dreamt about starting my own company and building something I could hand off to my family. Like most entrepreneurs, I would need to be willing to risk everything. Everything I built over a lifetime, to make this dream a reality. But right now, it was time to focus on my family. Tragically, this was about the same time that we found out that my wife Karyn had stage four cancer. At age fifty-two, with two daughters still in high school, it was not something we thought was possible.

My wife and I sought out the best treatments possible, but the cancer kept progressing. Out of desperation, we even spent a month in Mexico seeking alternative treatments when the conventional treatments failed. The cancer was unstoppable. The pain increased so much that even heavy doses of morphine had little effect. I can't put into words what it was like to be up night after night with my wife, screaming in pain, begging me to do something to stop it. Finally, the cancer ran its course and my wife passed away. It was a blessing to see her at peace.

My daughters and I were angry and devastated. Many months went by as our family struggled to find a new balance, a new normal. As things slowly improved, we all learned how to move forward. I decided it was time for me to move on as well. Starting a new company would be a welcome distraction and help put all this pain behind us.

In early 2009, I sought out other like-minded individuals and formed a Renewal Energy Development Company. The company would seek out opportunities to develop and build large renewable energy power plants for major electric utility companies. Our specialty would be solar energy, but we would also engage in wind and other forms of renewable energy.

Like most new companies, our team put in a lot of sweat equity and personal resources. The first few years, we perfected our skills and started to build a nice reputation for the company. The projects we worked on for the utilities were twenty to forty megawatts. These projects would span two-hundred to four-hundred acres and could cost anywhere from sixty to two-hundred million dollars. The typical project would take from twelve to eighteen months to complete.

When dealing with projects of this size and cost, the first thing we would do when examining a project opportunity was to check the credit rating of the utility company. Because of the immense cost of developing and building these power plants, it was critical that our lenders were confident that the utility company could pay for the electricity. The credit rating was the largest factor in building our lenders confidence.

In the fourth quarter of 2010, our company attended one of the major renewable energy conferences that are held throughout the year. We use those events to learn about the latest technology, engineering and equipment. We also networked for business opportunities with the vendors at the conferences. As was always the case, we were presented with a number of potential projects; one in particular was a contract to build a two-hundred-acre, twenty- megawatt solar power plant for the Puerto Rico Electric Power Authority (PREPA).

When we returned from the conference, we began our due diligence on all the new projects. The PREPA opportunity was ideal for us and fit perfectly into our skill sets. We first checked the rating on the utility with Moody's, Fitch and S&P, all of which gave the utility an equivalent rating of BBB+. BBB+ is a very good rating for a major utility company. We forwarded the contract to our law firms for review and started to research the utility company. To my surprise, PREPA was the one of the largest government-owned electric utilities in our database. PREPA had a monopoly on electricity in Puerto Rico. The company produced almost 95% of its electricity from oil and was looking to diversify into renewable energy. It was our understanding that the utility was under a federal mandate to add renewable energy production.

Puerto Rico is an Unincorporated Territory of the United States. Puerto Rico uses the U.S. Dollar, the United States Postal Service, and the IRS. It is subject to Federal laws. Most business people in Puerto Rico speak English, but their official language is Spanish. Puerto Rico has its own police force and District Attorney, but they are also overseen by the U.S. Department of Justice (FBI & U.S Attorneys). We believed that doing business in Puerto Rico would be similar to doing business in any other state.

The legal review of the contract came back satisfactory, the credit rating was solid, and the utilities stated desire for alternative energy aligned perfectly with what our company had to offer. Our team approved the project, and we made a one-million-dollar deposit towards the purchase of the project. We committed to paying for all of the development and construction costs of the project.

We selected General Electric Corporation as our equipment partner because they had over one-hundred years' experience in operating in Puerto Rico and already had material projects on the island. General Electric had also expressed an interest in buying the project from us once the construction was complete.

In mid-2011 our company began the expensive and time-consuming development of the project. We secured the land, began designing the project and engineering the transportation of the electricity from our site to the end users. Many millions of dollars were spent, thousands of billable hours were incurred, and tens of thousands of pages of documents were created.

By early 2012, we started to have issues with PREPA. They were slow to respond to our questions, if they responded at all. On technical issues, the utility often seemed lost and had to seek time-consuming, outside consultants to answer some pretty basic questions.

Our company had experience in dealing with major utilities: Southern California Edison, The Tennessee Power Authority, Pacific Gas and Electric and many more. PREPA was actually bigger than most and had been in business for over sixty years. Their behavior was nothing like any of the utilities we had worked for in the past.

By late 2012, all the delays were starting to put increasing financial pressure on our company. These projects normally take twelve to eighteen months, and this project was not on track at all. We expended the money and resources to get into construction mode, and we were now standing still. To add insult to injury, PREPA demanded two unilateral contract changes during this period. These changes added expenses and reduced profitability on all the contracts. You either had to enter expensive, long-term, litigation with them or accept their new terms. Litigation would cost millions and could take five years or more. Like most contract holders, we reluctantly accepted the contract modifications.

What PREPA was doing by late 2012 left all of their contract holders with the distinct feeling that the utility would do whatever they could to avoid building these projects. It was very concerning. It made no business sense for the utility or companies like ours. The projects would save the utility's customers significant money and improve their environment.

PREPA's endless delays and contract changes sent many contract holders to the exit door. I believe the company issued either seventy-five or sixty-three of these contracts, and by 2013 there were fewer than ten of us left. That doesn't happen by accident!

In 2013, we started to read articles in the paper that PREPA was not paying its bills and had some sort of financial problems. By 2014, the Credit Rating Agencies were dropping PREPA's credit ratings rapidly. These credit rating adjustments made it impossible to borrow money for the project's construction.

Our Board of Directors and our creditors were demanding answers. Our founders, creditors and investors were about to lose everything: their homes, their savings, their kid's college funds, and their good credit. Most of these folks were in their late fifties and early sixties. They wondered what they would live on in retirement.

I had two girls in college at this time. How would I be able to continue to pay for that? How could I keep our house when I personally guaranteed all of our Companies debt? *Oh my God, what have I done to my family? How could this be happening? We did everything right, by the book! I don't understand, how could all of this be possible? How do I fix it?*

Puerto Rico finally declared bankruptcy, and our company and its founders lost everything.

What follows is the result of our three-year investigation.

At its core, this is not a story about Puerto Rico. This is a story that begins in Puerto Rico, but the journey will take us from the island nation to Wall Street and Capitol Hill. This is not a story about local corruption. It is a story about a government-run national criminal enterprise.

Before I begin, I want to recognize the fact that financial crimes are often difficult to understand. If you are not in the business, it can make your head spin. I would like to give you a few non-financial examples of what our government has been up to over the past decade. What occurs in these hypothetic instances is parallel to the financial crimes I'll detail over the course of the book. I hope this will pique your interest in reading more about this criminal empire.

Just for a moment, let's pretend that you had one million dollars and wanted to construct the best building possible. You hire the engineer to design the building and the construction company to put up the structure. One year after the building is in place, it collapses. It is a total loss. The headlines in the paper the next day may read "John Doe" loses one million dollars due to building collapse. All "John" can do is write off the one million dollars in losses on his taxes over the next few years. John lost everything. The building effort consumed all his savings.

But what if "John" found out that the engineering firm was working with or colluding with the construction company to maximize their profit? The engineer claims to have designed a sound building and provided you documents with false information. The real design was actually substandard. The construction company wanted to get in the on the act and constructs the building using those substandard designs but bills you for the more expensive, correct design work. The construction company also provides you with information and documents that are misleading and untrue. What if the building collapse was inevitable because of the substandard design and construction?

The new headline might read, "John" defrauded out of one million dollars by his engineering and construction company. If you were "John," was this a crime? Was your money actually stolen?

Here is the key question that you should ask yourself; would "John" have given the engineering firm and the construction company the one million dollars if "John" knew the building would likely collapse? If the answer is no, it is theft, clear and simple! John was tricked and defrauded out of his money.

This is exactly, at its core, what we will be covering in this book. In another example, "John" uses the one million dollars to buy government bonds. Instead of getting monthly rent payments from his tenants on a new building, "John" will get monthly interest payments on the bonds. The bonds were issued by a government agency that needed to borrow money. The bonds are expected to last thirty years. The paperwork claims they are a safe and conservative investment. Two years later, John loses all his money on the bonds. The true story is really much worse than either of these examples.

In this new analogy, "John's" house is robbed by a police officer. Since "John" did not know that the person who robbed his house was a police officer, he calls the police to report the robbery. Later that afternoon, "John" gets a visit from the very same police officer that robbed his house. The officer pretends to feel sorry for "John" and promises "John" that he will do his best to catch the person that robbed his house. He tells "John" they will run extra patrols in the area to deter any future robberies.

The police officer who robbed "John's" house also robbed many other homes in the area. He then took all the items he stole and sold them. The officer took the money he received from the sale of the stolen items and gave a share of that money to his supervisor and the police chief. The police chief would, in turn, give a share of his money to the local district attorney.

Two years later, another law enforcement agency raids a warehouse and finds a ton of stolen goods. They trace the goods to a series of home burglaries. A few weeks later, DNA tests and fingerprints lead them to the police officer who robbed "John's" house. During inter-rogations, the Police Officer cannot account for his time during which theses robberies were reported. The authorities also find money and assets at the police officer's home that are hard to account for on a po-lice officer's salary. In discussions with the police officer's friends, they find out that the police officer bragged to some of them about robbing people's homes.

When "John" reads this in the paper, his head feels like it will ex-plode. He is furious. This scumbag robbed his house and then looked him in the eye and promised to catch those responsible. "John" thought, *we pay this bastards salary, we give them the authority and power over us, we expect them to protect us and they just screw us over.*

"John" goes to the police chief and demands that this officer be arrested. The chief explains that these crimes are difficult to prosecute and there doesn't seem to be enough evidence to move forward. "John" can't believe what he is hearing. How about the DNA evidence, the fingerprints, the inability for the officer to account for his time and the confessions he made to his friends? The police chief doesn't respond.

John calls the District Attorney who disingenuously tells him that they can only prosecute crimes brought to them by the Police. The district attorney does nothing.

In these examples, the construction company and the engineer are like the credit rating agencies (engineer) and the banks (construction company). The policemen represent the senators, congressmen, FBI, U.S. Attorneys and the SEC officials that all betrayed us. They are no different than that local policemen. The evidence against the FBI, U.S Attorney's and our politicians is as strong as the evidence that we have against that local policemen.

This book, with the legal proof included within, can be the template for a criminal prosecutor. I believe there is enough evidence within this book to investigate and prosecute over one thousand high ranking government officials, politicians and wall street executives if our country has the will to do so.

CHAPTER TWO
OUR JOURNEY OF DISCOVERY NOW BEGINS.

Millions of victims were demanding answers, and we were determined to find those answers. We began by talking with employees of the Puerto Electric Power Authority (PREPA). One person after the other suggested that PREPA never intended to build any of the renewable power plants; they were simply trying to get the federal government off their back by issuing the contracts!

Further discussions disclosed a strong bias by the leadership at the utility and the Government of Puerto Rico to maintain its level of oil purchases at the utility: oil purchases that were not in the best interests of the utility or its customers. Finally, one employee suggested I should research the lawsuits being filed against PREPA.

As I did a search for lawsuits, I was both stunned and disturbed by what I found. Although all companies of PREPA's size will be subject to some amount of legal and regulatory activity, PREPA's list of lawsuits and regulatory violations was endless. One lawsuit in particular caught our attention.

It was a "RICO" lawsuit. RICO is an acronym for a piece of

legislation passed by Congress called the Racketeer Influenced and Corrupt Organizations Act. It was passed by Congress in 1970 to help Federal Law Enforcement Agencies combat activities by the mafia. Now a group of private individuals was using that law against the Government. PREPA is a government-owned utility company.

According to the Free Dictionary, **"Racketeering"** is defined traditionally as, obtaining or extorting money illegally or carrying on illegal business activities, usually by **organized crime**. A pattern of illegal activity carried out as part of an enterprise that is owned or controlled by those who are engaged in the illegal activity. Racketeering, as it is commonly understood, has always coexisted with business. In the United States, the term racketeer was synonymous with **members of organized-crime operations.**

Here is a reprint of a small section of the lawsuit:

Case 3:15-cv-01167-JAG   Document 1
Filed 02/24/15   Page 1 of 80
UNITED STATES DISTRICT COURT
DISTRICT OF PUERTO RICO

OVERVIEW

1. *"Plaintiffs and the Class complain of a scheme perpetrated by all Defendants to procure and provide the Puerto Rico Electric Power Authority ("PREPA") with millions of barrels of fuel oil for the combustion of electricity under the guise the fuel oil met the specifications of contracts between PREPA and certain of its Fuel Oil Suppliers, as well as specifications set by the Environmental Protections Agency ("EPA") in a 1999 Consent Decree, as amended in 2004 (collectively, "Compliant Fuel Oil"). In fact, Defendant Fuel Oil Suppliers supplied PREPA with fuel oil that did not meet contractual or EPA Specifications ("Non-Compliant Fuel Oil"),*

*but was nonetheless accepted by PREPA in exchange for, on in-
formation and belief, undisclosed kickbacks or commissions to the
PREPA Participants (defined below).*

*As a result of this scheme, PREPA overpaid its fuel suppliers for fuel
oil and passed through the entire cost of the Non-Compliant Fuel Oil to
Plaintiffs and the Class on their regular monthly electricity bills."*

PREPA, as is true with most other utilities, should have been purchasing high grade oil. The higher-grade oils burn more efficiently,
pollute less and are much better for the utilities' equipment. What
PREPA was doing was buying sludge oil, the lowest grade of oil available. Sludge oil is of such poor quality that it will not catch fire unless
preheated. The oil is heavily polluting and terrible for the environment.

Sure enough, a cursory look at PREPA's plants and you will find oil
preheaters -- equipment that is only necessary if you are trying to burn
sludge oil. If that evidence wasn't enough, PREPA has over twenty-five
pages of EPA violations. Violations that could only be explained by the
burning of the sludge oil.

Sludge oil is 54% less expensive than the higher-grade oil PREPA
was claiming to have purchased over the last decade. PREPA spends
approximately three billion dollars a year purchasing fuel oil. Some
simple math and you find yourself asking where the missing fifteen
billion dollars are? Fortunately, we know something about that fifteen
billion dollars.

The RICO lawsuit does an excellent job of explaining how PREPA
would bribe the lab officials that have to do the required tests on the
oil deliveries. The suit suggests that this criminal empire was run out of
PREPA's Fuel Procurement Office. The law suit stated the following:

*"William Rodney Clark is a resident of Puerto Rico and a citizen of the
United States. Clark was the Administrator of PREPA's Fuel Procurement*

*Office from July 1996 to May 2014 and worked in the office from 1988 to 2014. As Clark states on his own LinkedIn biography, from 1994 to 2014, he was responsible for all the activities associated with fuel procurement such as preparation of bid invitations, bid evaluation, management of contracts, scheduling, invoice processing and price assessment. Also, responsible for all administrative aspects of PREPA's Fuel Procurement Office including official representation of PREPA with the US Coast Guard, Puerto Rico Ports Authority, Harbor Pilots and Inspection companies serving as official gaugers for the importation of goods into US territory. These activities represent approximately ... 70% of all operating expenses for the company."
5 In fact, within PREPA, according to a former employee, Clark was referred to as the "Emperor" for his power in the Fuel Oil Cartel Enterprise."*

I reached out to Mr. Clark numerous times and he did not respond. I was however able to connect with one of his daughters through Facebook. She told me, "Do not judge my father; he did what he had to do." She asked me to leave their family alone.

I shared this information with PREPA. One of the directors at PREPA started pushing for a more thorough internal investigation. That director was removed from his position a short time later.

By this time, PREPA was in extreme financial distress. PREPA hired a consulting firm called AlexPartners. Their job was to assist in raising capital and present a positive "face" for PREPA under increasing claims of fraud and misconduct.

It was at this time that I first filed a criminal complaint with the FBI. I filed that FBI complaint in March of 2015. I went to their website and told them this story. The FBI did not respond, so in June of 2015 I wrote the Puerto Rico U.S. Attorney to make her aware of all this criminal activity.

June 2, 2015
US Attorney for Puerto Rico
Rosa Emilla Rodriguez-Velez
Torre Chardon, Suite 1201
350 Carlos Chardon Street
San Juan, PR 00918

RE: PREPA Oil for Money Kick-Backs

Dear Rosa,

I am forwarding this directly by return receipt mail for fear of it getting sidetracked. I have been working with PREPA since 2011, and I was shocked at the level of (alleged) corruption at the firm. I will continue to write articles regarding what we uncover and will continue to seek recourse for those that were damaged. In my next series of articles and editorials I will mention that a copy of the attached complaint we delivered to the US Attorney in Puerto Rico.

I hope, if you have not already seen this, that you find the complaint helpful. If you need more information and some actual documented activity, you can contact the Hagens Berman attorney by calling 708-628-4949 or by emailing PREPA@hbsslaw.com.

Sincerely,

Richard Lawless

Richard R. Lawless

As I was researching the criminal act's I noticed that there was a Securities and Exchange (SEC) Whistleblower Program. The SEC claims that their function as a government agency is the following:

"The mission of the U.S. Securities and Exchange Commission is to protect investors, maintain fair, orderly, and efficient markets, and facilitate capital formation.

As more and more first-time investors turn to the markets to help secure their futures, pay for homes, and send children to college, our investor protection mission is more compelling than ever.

As our nation's securities exchanges mature into global for-profit competitors, there is even greater need for sound market regulation.

And the common interest of all Americans in a growing economy that produces jobs, improves our standard of living, and protects the value of our savings means that all of the SEC's actions must be taken with an eye toward promoting the capital formation that is necessary to sustain economic growth.

The world of investing is fascinating and complex, and it can be very fruitful. But unlike the banking world, where deposits are guaranteed by the federal government, stocks, bonds and other securities can lose value. There are no guarantees. That's why investing is not a spectator sport. By far the best way for investors to protect the money they put into the securities markets is to do research and ask questions.

The laws and rules that govern the securities industry in the United States derive from a simple and straightforward concept: all investors, whether large institutions or private individuals, should have access to certain basic facts about an investment prior to buying it, and so long as they hold it. To achieve this, the SEC requires public companies to disclose meaningful financial and other information to the public. This provides a common pool of knowledge for all investors to use to judge for themselves whether to buy, sell, or hold a particular security. Only through the steady flow of timely, comprehensive, and accurate information can people make sound investment decisions."

The principals here are very simple. The seller must be honest and transparent about what he is selling you. If a realtor sells you a house and that house has a broken foundation, but the realtor does not tell you, the realtor committed fraud. "Would your decision to buy that house have been different if the realtor told you about the foundation? Of course, it would be! Realtors sell real estate, "brokers" sell stocks or bonds. A broker must disclose all information, so you can make a fully educated decision, no different than the realtor. The SEC's job is to make sure those disclosures happen.

I saw the whistleblower program as an opportunity to recover some of the funds lost by our company. I could pay the company's creditors, payback some of the employees who worked with no pay. I could even pay for my kids' college again. This was an opportunity to repay all those that trusted us to complete the project for the Puerto Rico Electric Power Authority. The SEC would share ten to thirty percent of the fines levied against companies with the Whistleblower Program. With theft in the tens of billions of dollars, there was a good chance the fines would be material. This was a ray of hope. I have to admit, I was excited. This was the first time I felt some level of hope since it all started. For a few weeks I was even able to sleep normally. Little did I know at the time, it was all just more government bullshit.

I continued to send the SEC new information as it became available. I did the same with the FBI and U.S. Attorney's Office. So many people were aware of all this criminal activity, surely an investigation by any of these agencies would yield more information and some great witnesses?

*According to WikipediA, "**Misprision of felony**" is still an offense under United States federal law after being codified in 1909 under 18 U.S.C. § 4:*

Whoever, having knowledge of the actual commission of a felony cognizable by a court of the United States, conceals and does not as soon as possible make known the same to some judge or other person in civil or military authority under the United States, shall be fined under this title or imprisoned not more than three years, or both.

This offense, however, **requires active concealment of a known felony** *rather than merely failing to report it.*[7]

The Federal misprision of felony statute is usually used only in prosecutions against defendants who have a special duty to report a crime, such as a government official's. . ." [bold and underlines by book author.]

Keep this law in mind as you progress through this book.

We contacted the "ad hoc group" of (PREPA) bondholders and shared our concerns about all this. The ad hoc group represented a significant number of bondholders. Their response was that any discussion about the corruption at PREPA would only hurt bond values, so they see no benefit in dealing with that. The committee will take a look at forcing alternative, lower cost energy sources but only if it does not interfere with a solution.

To understand the new bondholders' position, you have to better understand who they are. This group of bondholders purchased many of the original bonds from the original owners, who were senior citizens who wanted desperately to sell before the bonds were completely worthless. The bonds totaled about seventy-billion dollars. The bonds were down in value almost 50% and were no longer paying interest. The new bond holders (ad hoc group and others) bought most of them for a total of about thirty-six billion dollars. They purchased the bonds hoping the bonds would regain value or be paid off by tax payers' dollars sometime in the future -- a gamble, worth tens of billions in profit, depending on what happens in the next few years.

The people who run these companies and come up with these creative strategies are often called "investment bankers" and their companies are often referred to as "hedge funds" or less falteringly, "vulture funds." They do serve a purpose: assuming no criminal activity was involved, they provide an exit, a solution for someone who had a financial accident. Without them, there would be no place to turn. In this case, however, they appear to be part of the "Evil Empire," full-fledged Criminal Underground Members, "made men" so to speak.

I promised when I wrote this book, I would name names. The following article will tell you who they are, and I will tell you something you can't find in the press.

Who Owns Puerto Rico's Debt?

Information derived from a number of newspapers and websites indicated the following; An alliance called the Mutual Fund Group holds $7.1 billion in debt, the Ad Hoc Group holds $3.3. billion in debt, the Cofina Senior Bondholders Coalition holds $3.1 billion in debt, ERS Secured Creditors holds $1.4 billion and QTCB Noteholder Group holds $600 million in debt.

These groups are often called Vulture Funds and can hire powerful law firms to advocate for their respective positions. There are approximately thirty-five firms like this that various sources have identified. Of that, over seventy-five percent of them appear to be Vulture Funds.

Where do vulture funds get a lot of their cash to buy these bonds? You guessed it -- banks...

In a May 2017 *Wall Street Journal* article, I read that **Goldman Sachs Group, Inc**. came under fire after its asset management group bought Venezuela bonds at a deep discount.

According to HSBC's website, HSBC's bank offers **HSBC's hedge fund** client solutions, our hedge fund solutions have been developed to suit different client needs, as well as differing levels of client involvement.

As hard as it is to believe, banks first sell these alleged fraudulent bonds to their best customers. When the bonds begin to default, many of the banks invest in hedge funds and vulture funds that repurchased those bonds for fifty cents on the dollar. Now the Banks can indirectly profit a second time from their nefarious involvement.

My company and I spoke with the Puerto Rico "Ad Hoc" bondholders' group (vulture fund) a number of times and exchanged a few emails. We shared with them that the bonds were all fraudulent, and they responded by saying that public knowledge of that could hurt their holdings! They said they saw no reason to make the fraudulent bond issuance a "thing" because it could destroy the billions they invested in the bonds. With full knowledge of this, they intended to hold the bonds until they could sell them for a profit.

Shortly after, I wrote an article about this activity. I quickly received a blocked phone call from someone claiming to be associated with the "ad hoc" group of bond holders. The caller suggested that if I stop writing articles about the bond fraud, the "bond holders" could help with financing for my project. It made my skin crawl. I guess the caller assumed anyone could be bought off. I penned the following article shortly after this call.

Just once, I would like to see Wall Street held accountable

By Richard Lawless

Special to Historic City News

*This article was reprinted with permission from
The Historic City News, and is available at historiccity.com*

Let's face it, if you or I were to participate in a scheme that caused $30 billion dollars in losses, we would be sent away for the rest of our natural lives. Unfortunately, if you work for one of the big three Credit Rating Agencies (Moody's, Fitch or S&P) or a major Bank, like Chase, Citibank or Goldman Sachs, you have a get out of jail free card.

Starting back in 2007 and 2008 when the mortgage backed securities crisis brought our country to its knees, it became clear that Wall Street would have to find another vehicle to replace the huge fees they were earning from rating and selling junk mortgage bonds as safe investments. Before 2007 came to an end, Wall Street decided to transfer that very same business model to the municipal bond market -- the same strategies that caused the 2007-2008 financial meltdown.

Starting in 2007 the Municipal Bond market exploded, not by accident, but by design. In 2007 there was less than a trillion dollars in bonds in the market. Today that number is over 4 trillion dollars. This kind of reckless expansion takes cooperation between all parties, the issuing agencies, the ratings companies and Wall Street's biggest banks.

Everyone knows that the 2007-2008 financial crisis was a result of the big three credit rating agencies, knowingly and willingly, issuing high credit rating for packages of mortgages that everyone in the industry knew were unpayable. The banks then knowingly and willingly sold those mislabeled investments to innocent investors. The rating agencies and banks earned record fees and the American economy lost trillions of dollars. Only one poor banker was ever prosecuted. So, why not, do it again? So, they did.

We know that trillions in municipal bonds are now in the market place carrying ratings that indicate they are safe investments. A simple read of the bonds offering memorandum shows many of the issuing agencies to be technically bankrupt. These issuing agencies have huge, unmanageable pension obligations. Many of these agencies are also facing significant lawsuits, are in violation of critical bond agreements and reflect actions that indicate unsafe management by the Agencies leaders. Still, they receive investment grade credit ratings.

Like the mortgage bond crisis, the agencies could never pay for the debt they issued, so they are required to refinance this debt frequently to avoid the inevitable defaults non-payment would create. The ratings agencies and banks make record fee income as long as the refinancing continues. This is called a "Ponzi scheme" and Bernie Madoff went to jail for the same thing.

The house of cards collapsed in Puerto Rico this year, and all these facts have come to light. We know the personnel who signed off on the fraudulent credit ratings; we know the personnel who sold these junk bonds as safe investments. To my knowledge, none of these folks have been interviewed by the SEC or the FBI. These Wall Street firms appear to be in clear violation of the Dodd Frank legislation and any number of criminal codes.

Once again, the power of Wall Street and lack of "political will" only guarantees future defaults. Today it is $30 billion, next year, Chicago, Connecticut or California and maybe a few trillion in losses. All created intentionally by what one could only consider a criminal enterprise.

It is easy to forget how self-serving these folks are and the damage they have done and will continue to do. Most people think bond buyers must be rich, but that is far from the truth. The average bond holder is a senior citizen with retirement income of less than forty thousand a year; many make less than thirty thousand a year in income. They are you, your parents, your grandparents.

Let's pretend that one day a retired couple receives a solicitation to attend a seminar with someone like Merrill Lynch or Bank of America. The seminar is about using your retirement dollars more wisely. They attend the seminar and the representatives see that the retired couple have ten thousand dollars in the bank, almost all their life savings. The couple is earning only two percent interest and has to pay tax on that interest income. The seminar representative suggests they buy a safe and conservative Puerto Rico Government Bond that will pay five percent interest, tax free.

It is a no brainer for most. They buy the bond. Two years later the bond stops making the interest payments and drops in value by fifty percent. Desperate to save part of their ten thousand dollars in life savings, they sell the bond for five thousand dollars. Now the couple does not have enough income to make their mortgage payment and buy their prescription drugs.

Maybe that ten thousand dollars would have grown over the years if it were not stolen. Maybe they could have helped their kids with a small gift for their home down payment or had some left after they passed away for a start on their grandchild's college fund. Instead, these criminals, these crooks, intervened and changed the lives of everyone in their family tree.

Almost every day, I ask myself, what good did thirty years of hard work do for me? I now have nothing left to take care of myself, let alone help my kids or grandchildren. A decision that was made by these bad actors, changed my life and millions of others.

Financial Crisis Cost U.S. $12.8 Trillion Or More: Study
This article was reprinted with permission from The Huffington Post,
and is available at huffingtonpost.com

The crisis-cost estimate, generated by Better Markets, a non-profit group lobbying for financial reform, is only a measure of actual and potential lost economic growth due to the crisis. It does not include many other costs, including the costs of extraordinary government steps taken to avoid "a second Great Depression." It does not include unquantifiable costs like the "human suffering that accompanies unemployment, foreclosure, homelessness and related damage," the authors noted.

In April and May of 2015, the Puerto Rico Senate held Special Hearings regarding the alleged oil scam and other even more significant criminal activity. In the hearing, many participants, under oath, spoke about the Oil Scheme. You will be hearing much more about this Puerto Rico Senate Hearing in later chapters but for now, this is what the final Senate Report had to say.

TRANSLATION 7/15 MIP
COMMONWEALTH OF PUERTO RICO
17th Legislative 5th Ordinary Assembly Session
HOUSE OF REPRESENTATIVES
FINAL REPORT
H.R. 1049
(House of Representatives Resolution 1049)
JUNE 24, 2015
TO THE PUERTO RICO HOUSE OF REPRESENTATIVES:

SCOPE OF THE MEASURE

"House Resolution 1049 warrants Small and Medium Businesses, Commerce, Industry and Telecommunications Commission to carry out an investigation with regard to the operational energy expenses of several industries,

pymes and businesses located in the Island, taking into account recent decisions made by the Puerto Rico Electric Power Authority ("PREPA"); evaluate different alternatives in the current energy market and would portend to mitigate the economic impact they represent; and analyze the liquidity and financial claims of bondholders, and how decisions made thereof translated into energy rates/tariff increases."

During the Senate Hearings oil executives appeared with their attorneys. One oil company executive, feeling pressure from the direct questions on the oil scheme, walked out of the hearings. Witnesses made it clear that the Oil Purchase Program and the actions of the employees of the Oil Procurement Office were involved in purchasing the sludge oil. The Senate made the following recommendations:

RECOMMENDATIONS

"In order to prevent what we have described in this Report from happening again, and to keep Control of PREPA's treasury and its operations, we recommend:

1. *That this Report be forwarded to the Justice Department of the Commonwealth of Puerto Rico and the United States of America for their corresponding actions;*
2. *That this Report be forwarded to the United States Securities and Exchange Commission for its corresponding action;*
3. *The annulment of the current agreement with the consulting engineer's firm and initiation of a claim against its underwriters of the last 20 years and request restitution of the moneys paid to them;*
4. *An investigation of PREPA projects estimates department for possible judgement flaws in the past years;*
5. *An investigation of the purchasing costs of equipment, goods and other services from PREPA's suppliers, under a presumption of possible overbilling for construction works in the past years;*

6. *An investigation of costs incurred for construction projects work-force in past years;*

7. *Adoption of a rate adjustment process that no longer has the detrimental effect it has had until now for small and medium business owners in Puerto Rico; and*

8. *That the necessary guidelines and norms be defined by an audit so that events that led PREPA to its current economic situation are not allowed to happen again.......*

Now we had both the Government of Puerto Rico and me filing criminal complaints and reports with the FBI and the SEC. Still, nothing was being done by any law enforcement or any regulatory agency. I guess that fifteen billion dollars in stolen money isn't big enough to raise any red flags with the Department of Justice or the SEC. Out of a sense of outrage and frustration, I started to write newspaper articles about all this activity. Below is one of the earlier articles I wrote.

You will notice that the amount of money stolen or unaccounted for varies in these articles. As time went on, more and more evidence was uncovered. The amount of stolen money grew dramatically.

How can anyone trust yet another PREPA revitalization plan?

BY RICHARD LAWLESS — 10/23/15 03:00 PM EDT 2

THE VIEWS EXPRESSED BY CONTRIBUTORS ARE THEIR OWN AND NOT THE VIEW OF THE HILL

This article was reprinted with permission from The Hill, and is available at thehill.com

What is that saying? Fool me once, shame on you, fool me twice, shame on me. For over a decade the Puerto Rico Electric Power Authority (PREPA) has reached out to the bond market promising up-graded facilities, new cheaper electricity with natural gas, solar and wind. Time and time again, it didn't happen.

Yes, PREPA took the money: Nine billion dollars in bond and bank debt. The banks didn't hold them responsible for their lack of action nor did the bondholders, ever.

I went back and looked at S&P, Fitch and Moody's reports and almost without exception every bond offering over the last decade had "up-grades" as a critical component of the bond offering. Again, none of the reports looked back and said, hey wait a minute, we heard this before and they didn't do any of that!

The open secret is that politicians and company executives were using PREPA as their personal piggy bank and redirecting $100,000,000 a year or more for their own personal uses. Any upgrade to the facilities would put an end to this scheme. The Hagens Bermen RICO suit filed in February of 2015 claims this has been going on for over a decade and continuing today. That's nine billion dollars in bond fraud! They promised upgrades knowing those upgrades would never happen!

With Alixpartners on board will things be different? Let's look. Alixpartners has played the role of the ultimate insider since 2014 and has taken over $20,000,000 in public money for their assistance. Over that time, Alixpartners to the best of my knowledge, has not reported any of the numerous SEC violations, the falsified oil quality reports, the altered book-keeping or the alleged theft of $100,000,000 in public funds to anyone. Did the $20,000,000 in fees cause Alixpartners to look the other way?

Are there any honest people involved with this organization? Are there any honest people in the Puerto Rico government? What do you call someone who has been fooled four times?

Unfortunately, people are lining up and dropping their trousers for one more ride on the PREPA train. This time I am not buying a ticket for that train ride!

Lawless is CEO of California-based Commercial Solar Power, Inc.

Alixpartners were the ultimate insiders. The senior consultants with Alixpartners should have known about all the fraud at PREPA. Just in case, I wrote and emailed each member of the management board at Alixpartners and shared with them what I knew about all the alleged crimes at PREPA. I wanted to make it easy to prosecute Alixpartners in the future. Now they couldn't deny they knew.

To the best of my knowledge, no one from Alixpartners picked up the phone to speak with the FBI, U.S. Attorneys or the Securities and Exchange Commission. Did it have something to do with the twenty plus million dollars PREPA was paying Alixpartners?

We know with great certainty because of the letters I sent, that all the Senior Executives at Alixpartners knew about the fraudulent financials, oil scheme and much more. But Alixpartners continue to seek financing for PREPA, possibly using those misleading financials. Not only did they have full knowledge of the serious felonies; to the best of my knowledge, Alixpartners didn't disclose that information. It is possible, due to this lack of transparency, that Alixpartners may have participated in criminal acts. I shared this with the FBI and SEC: *no action was taken.*

I penned a brief follow-up article about the oil scheme that appeared in a number of Caribbean papers. At the time, I had no idea how much this article would change my life.

Wednesday, November 18, 2015

This article was reprinted with permission from The Puerto Rico Monitor, and is available at puertoricomonitor.blogspot.com

Who is William Rodney Clark? Mr. Clark was the former Administrator for the Fuel Oil Office at Puerto Rico's largest utility, PREPA. William

Clark is accused in a RICO Lawsuit filed earlier this year of setting up a decades long scheme to steal $100,000,000 a year in public funds. Mr. Clark is alleged to have put together a number of oil contracts for the utility that would overcharge the people of Puerto Rico for the fuel oil and then kickback the over payment to Mr. Clark for his own personal use. This has been going on for over 10 years and the kickbacks amount to over one billion dollars.

William Rodney Clark is not a household name yet, but I am willing to bet a billion dollars that over the next few months he will become pretty famous.

Unfortunately for Mr. Clark, he allegedly shared this windfall with Puerto Rico Government officials, oil testing companies, police officials and some say, Federal law enforcement officials. Luckily for the people of Puerto Rico, there is no honor among thieves. Once the lawsuit was filed, self-preservation kicks in and these same want-to-be "Goodfellas" will roll over for lighter sentencing and/or smaller civil penalties.

William Rodney Clark may be the lead actor in this made for TV movie, but the cast of characters is long and deep. Each day this week I will highlight a key supporting actor or actress in this drama to help our readers piece together one of the largest thefts of Public Funds in history and a likely $9,000,000,000 bond fraud.

Shortly after this article appeared, I received a number of phone calls from Mr. Clark's Associates and Attorneys suggesting I got it all wrong, Mr. Clark was basically a saint. I also received two calls from unidentified people who suggested that pursuing this may not be the healthiest endeavor. I was so pissed off about all of this that the threatening calls just made me more determined than ever to see those responsible punished.

I was angry; I still could not believe I was in the process of losing everything I had worked so hard for. I would pace back and forth in the house trying to blow off some steam and come up with a solution for all this. I was ready to explode and deliver some payback, but how? What didn't I know? How much more to this was there? *Why are the authorities blowing me off?*

During this period of time, it occurred to me that the stolen fifteen billion dollars was not likely the reason PREPA (the utility company) went bankrupt. They only had to buy slightly more fuel than would have been needed normally because sludge oil is not as efficient. The sludge oil is also much harder on the equipment, increasing maintenance needs dramatically. Even if you take into consideration an extra two hundred million dollars per year, it was not enough to drive the utility into bankruptcy. PREPA is huge; two hundred million a year is material but represents a small percentage of PREPA's annual expenses.

Based on this logic, I thought it was time to take a hard look at PREPA itself. Using many of the same skills I used as a banker, I grabbed the utilities' audited financial statements, operating statements, management agreements and operating budgets and started my deep dive. What was to come from this investigation would move this criminal enterprise from Puerto Rico to Wall Street to Washington D.C.

In the meantime, I received a call from a news editor who wanted to know if he could give my phone number to a government official who wanted to talk. I said he could.

I received a call from someone in Alexandra Virginia suggesting he worked for a government agency that was well aware of what was going on in Puerto Rico. Further discussion with the caller led me to believe he was with the CIA.

The caller claimed that the intelligence agency has been tracking large wire transfers off the island for the past decade. In the process of tracking these wire transfers, they began to tape record telephone conversations of the people involved in this alleged illegal activity.

The caller said they have been reading my articles and they were of great interest. This person went on to say that his organization shared their information with the Puerto Rico FBI, and that for years, nothing was done about it. He seemed very frustrated with the state of affairs at the Department of Justice.

The caller said that one of the recorded phone calls disclosed that the family members of the FBI Officials and family members of the U.S. Attorney Office in Puerto Rico were getting payoffs. The payoffs were made to make sure no investigation or prosecution would ever happen.

This helps explain how this criminal enterprise has gone on for well over a decade!

I couldn't be sure if what I was being told was true. I needed a second source, and I got that source within days from Barry Randall, Editor of *Caribbean NewsNow*. Mr. Randall was able to contact a completely separate source within the U.S. Intelligence Agencies and confirm almost word for word, what I had been told.

Holy cow! How did I get in the middle of a CIA Investigation? I was shocked, relived. I wasn't sure how to feel. This was all getting a bit scary for me now. Who could I trust? The Department of Justice is actually participating in this. I went a little numb, not sure what to do about all of this now.

According to multiple intelligence agencies, the money was being laundered in countries that were hostile to the United States. The ratings agencies, the banks and our politicians were funding anti-American activity against their own people and they couldn't care less.

I took a few days to get my bearing's and decided to move forward and raise public awareness. I thought writing articles would be a good way to protect myself. By shining a light on all of this, I could pass this information on to the public. If everyone knew, I would no longer be the single source of this information.

These revelations seemed surreal to me. I felt as if I were living life in a poorly written spy novel. I shared this information with a few friends. I got the feeling that they thought I was losing my grip on reality. Who could blame them? Who the hell am I? Nobody! How could I, Richard Lawless, be in the center of a real-life black-helicopter-type conspiracy?

I need to mow the lawn and go grocery shopping. Did I get the mail today? Now I could add, *did I talk to my CIA contacts today?* Honey, British Intelligence is on line one?

Puerto Rico Monitor
June 9th, 2016

American and British Intelligence Uncover Payoffs to the FBI & U.S. Attorney's Office

This article was reprinted with permission from The Puerto Rico Monitor, and is available at puertoricomonitor.blogspot.com

Based on this credible second source, I penned the following article. The article appeared in both *Caribbean* and *New York* newspapers and would be reprinted over the following month in numerous other periodicals. Based on the tracking I was able to do, well over one million people read the first printing of this article.

Wednesday June 20, 2018

CURACAO CHRONICLE

Breaking News >

Personal conflicts obstruct FBI investigation into Puerto Rico fraud

This article was reprinted with permission from the Curacao Chronicler, and is available at curacaochronicle.com

SAN JUAN - *The ongoing controversy over Puerto Rico's insolvency and efforts to enlist congressional support for legal bankruptcy protection for the US territory have resulted in fingers being pointed at the local Federal Bureau of Investigation (FBI) and the Puerto Rico US Attorney's office for an alleged failure to investigate and prevent a reportedly massive fraud that may have contributed to the island's financial crisis.*

According to Richard Lawless, the CEO of Commercial Solar Power, Inc., a company that was reportedly forced into bankruptcy by what he described as the "bizarre behavior" of the Puerto Rico Electric Power Authority (PREPA), the utility has been used to redirect as much as $100 million a year from the people of Puerto Rico to select government officials.

On February 24, 2015, a private law suit was filed using the Racketeer Influenced and Corrupt Organizations Act claiming that government officials at PREPA stole over one billion dollars in public money over ten years and committed one of the largest municipal bond frauds in US history.

Increasing municipal bond defaults have been a growing concern among investors and politicians over the past few years. With the pending defaults on almost $70 billion dollars in municipal debt issued by various Puerto Rico municipalities, the Securities and Exchange Commission (SEC) has reportedly increased its efforts to monitor this sector.

"Confidential sources have indicated that SEC audits have uncovered material irregularities relating to the issuance of unjustified credit ratings by Fitch Group, Inc. The confidential source has indicated that the initial probe will focus on bonds issued by Puerto Rico's largest utility company PREPA," Lawless said.

However, Daniel Noonan, global head of communications at Fitch Group, stated in an email, "We have no knowledge of any of the investigations alleged by Mr. Lawless."

It has also been alleged that law enforcement authorities in Puerto Rico stood by and did nothing for a number of years, which assertion was substantiated by a phone call originating in Alexandria, Virginia, that Lawless said he received some months ago from a man stating that he worked for the US government, which Lawless said he inferred was the Central Intelligence Agency (CIA).

Lawless was told that Puerto Rico came on the agency's radar years ago because the head of the PREPA fuel purchase office started making direct calls to the then president of Venezuela, Hugo Chavez. They listened in and found out that PREPA was buying sludge oil from Venezuela and billing the utility for high grade oil. The difference in value, hundreds of millions per year (today it would be $700 million a year and is said to be still going on) was allegedly kicked back to the fuel office manager and distributed to politicians and government officials on the island.

As the unnamed government agency continued to listen in on the calls, the caller claimed it became clear that family members of Puerto Rico FBI agents and family members in the Puerto Rico US Attorney's office were receiving payments based on these "kickbacks".

"He went on to tell me that the Puerto Rico FBI and US Attorney will do nothing about the oil kickback scheme and the bond rating scheme because they were participating in it. He went on to suggest that because of the

separation laws regarding CIA activities and US national law enforcement that there was not much he could do," Lawless said.

On Monday, a senior source in a related US government agency, speaking to Caribbean News Now on condition of anonymity, confirmed almost word for word what Lawless had apparently been told.

In the meantime, a voice message left for Lawless by someone said to be calling from the San Juan FBI office in response to complaints made by Lawless to members of congress, claimed that the matter was being "looked at" to determine whether or not the circumstances cross the boundary from civil fraud to a criminal offence.

However, on June 24, 2015, the government of Puerto Rico issued a 23-page legislative report, described by Lawless as "no less than a detailed confession," which outlines how government officials in Puerto Rico conspired with Wall Street firms to commit $11 billion dollars in financial fraud.

"After reviewing this document and other evidence for many months, the FBI is claiming that the best prosecutors in the DOJ have not yet found criminal grounds to move forward," Lawless pointed out.

According to the legislative report itself, PREPA paid previous bondholders with capital received from new investors, which is the classic hallmark of a Ponzi scheme.

"The abovementioned was done to benefit the financial community that issued the debt and who today is collecting same, without any moneys having been invested in improvements to infrastructure, all to the detriment of the best interest of the people of Puerto Rico. We believe that the actions and circumstances mentioned above caused the economic insolvency which has plagued PREPA in the past years," the report said.

The debt was sold at discount, a large quantity of it between .60 to *less than .50 cents to the dollar with the agreement to pay to the dollar in full upon its maturity. Plus, the annual return yield was agreed to set high interest rates, and the principal and return are three-fold exempt from payment of local and federal taxes, the report continued.*

The report claimed that the financial intermediaries and the institutional bondholders, despite being fully aware of PREPA's fiscal situation, had no qualms with unjustly enriching themselves and with having the consequences of their negligent acts be paid for by the people of Puerto Rico.

"Meanwhile, and fully aware that PREPA did not have the resources to repay the debt, investment firms, banks, credit houses, consulting engineers, and PREPA itself failed to bring out into public light the need to make adjustments to the rates charged by PREPA," the report said.

Investors allowed PREPA to issue bonds, then, PREPA borrowed from private banks to pay the bond's interests; then, borrowed from the Government Development Bank (GDB) to pay back the private bank loans, and the GDB, in turn, issued more bonds to refinance all. Afterwards, PREPA would issue a new debt to pay GDB's outstanding interests, pay principal and pre-pay the new bonds' interests for several years – a cycle that is repeated over and over – and in which the original debt is never paid, the report outlined.

"This practice could constitute a fraud scheme for which the federal agencies that regulate financial instruments and the Security Exchange Commission could take action against and/or pursue civil suits against these institutions," the report said.

It was also recommended that the report be forwarded to the US Justice Department and the SEC for corresponding action.

Lawless pointed out that the Puerto Rico Legislature itself was clearly suggesting that a criminal act had occurred and should be investigated.

As I have been doing all along, I shared this information with the Washington D.C. FBI Office, U.S. Attorney and the Securities and Exchange Commission. Once again, nothing was done.

I started to receive death threats. I received a number of blocked calls on my cell phone. In one call, the caller told me a story about a Puerto Rico bank official who also wanted to do the "right thing;" they found his body months later. In another call, the caller suggested everyone was involved and no matter how much noise I made, nothing would happen to them. He said the same can't be said for me.

With CIA involvement and alleged corruption at the Department of Justice, the death threats started to concern me. I have two daughters. What would become of them if I were to be killed? *I have stumbled on to a huge National Criminal Empire. What would it members do to keep it all a secret?* It was clear the callers thought I knew more about what was really going on than I did at the time._

It was time for me to catch up; I wanted to bury myself in this investigation going forward. *Before I do that, maybe I should call the FBI about the death threats. They can't all be involved?*

I live in California, so I called the headquarters for the FBI in Riverside County, CA. I told them that I was getting death threats because of my investigation. The Riverside FBI never responded to my phone calls.

CHAPTER THREE
THE DEEP DIVE

It was now time to take a deep dive into the inter-workings of the Puerto Rico Electric Power Authority (PREPA). As a career banker, I have been blessed with an education and training that is perfectly in tune with what has to be done now.

What follows is a lot of detail that some readers may find dry. It is critical that you understand how these alleged crimes are taking place. It is easy to lose interest when you hear terms like "bonds," "venture capital" or "vulture funds." But at its very basic level, it is really easy to understand. In later chapters, when I name names, I want you to see how this would have been impossible without those specific individuals' participation.

Why should you care? In the 2008 financial crisis, eight million people lost their homes, tens of million lost their jobs, and countless families were broken up by the resulting financial pressures. This is still going on and will only get worse. Criminals who know they will never be investigated, arrested or prosecuted will only get more emboldened.

As a banker, I know trust is everything. If people don't trust me, they will not part with their money. What will happen to this country when enough people realize that the government and the credit rating agencies cannot be trusted? How will towns, cities, states and even our federal government raise money to pay for services? Services we all rely on. Electricity, water, roads, schools, food stamps, and much more. All made possible only from borrowing money. What if no one wants to lend that money anymore?

"Borrow 50p? Sorry, I'm staying out of the sub-prime lending market."

Image has been provided by Cartoon Stock Dot Com
and is available at cartoonstock.com

I will be examining PREPA's books, looking for inconsistencies that might conflict with what PREPA is telling the public. Here are some examples of what I will be looking at:

- Is PREPA showing significant interest income? If so, do the bank balances match up with interest being claimed? If they are claiming one million dollars in interest income, and today's interest rates are 3%, the company should have balances approximating thirty-three million dollars ($1,000,000 divided by 3%). Where is the thirty-three million dollars?

- Is the company extending credit to its customers? If so, the company will have something called an account receivable (A/R). If they are in fact providing electricity today for money they will collect in the future, are those bills being paid? Are they being paid on time? Are the accounts receivable they are claiming, real?

- Does PREPA pay its bills on time? Accounts Payable is an account that should reflect all the short-term obligations of the company. Is PREPA showing all their short-term debt? How do their payments compare to other utility companies?

- Are PREPA's sales supported by their inventory and current expenses? Is their fuel expense in line with the electricity being generated?

- As a utility, PREPA will be equipment-heavy. Are the values that are stated for that equipment, consistent with industry norms? Does the equipment actually exist and where is it located? Is the equipment in good repair?

- Does PREPA have off-balance sheet obligations that could negatively impact the company's ability to perform in the future? Common off-balance sheet obligations might include items like unpaid pension expenses (very common today) or legal obligations, etc.

- Is the company well run? How do their profits compare to others in the industry? What is the character and experience of the leadership team? Does the company have an unusual number of lawsuits against it? Are there regulatory violations? What does the Better Business Bureau or other similar organizations say about it? What is their credit rating? Where is the industry going and is PREPA moving in that direction too?

You can see where I will be going with my investigation. This is identical to what most bankers do on loan requests. The larger the loan, the more due diligence (investigating) we do.

Before I discuss my findings, I feel I need to take a brief moment and review some financial, legal, industry terms and concepts. If you are not specifically in the financial and legal industry you are not likely to know much of this.

I hope this helps you better understand the scope of this criminal enterprise and the shocking disclosures that will follow.

The Three C's of Credit

Character:

Refers to how a person has handled past debt obligations, ranging from the credit history and personal background, honesty and reliability of the borrower to pay credit debts.

Capacity:

Refers to how much debt a borrower can comfortably handle. Income streams are analyzed, and any legal obligations looked into, which could interfere in repayment.

Capital:

Refers to current available assets of the borrower, such as real estate, savings or investments that could be used to repay debt if income should be unavailable.

These are critical financial concepts.

For smaller loans, character is often solely determined by a personal credit report from Transunion, Equifax or Experian. On larger loans, a company will often pay Moody's, Fitch or S&P to analyze their company and render an opinion.

Capacity in the simplest of terms refers to a person's <u>debt to income</u>. The lender will add up a borrower's debt payments. Let's say you have a mortgage of $2,000 per month and a car payment of $350 for a total of $2.350.00. You make $5,000 a month and after taxes you have $3,000 in income. The lender will take your net income and divide it by your debt payments. In this case, $3,000 divided by $2,350 will give you a debt to income ratio of 1.28 to 1. In other words, for every dollar in debt you have 28 cents to use as a reserve. The industry average suggests that a debt ratio of 1.2 or 1.25 to 1 is sufficient. For larger companies you go through a similar but more complex exercise, but the fundamentals are the same.

It is critical to maintain acceptable debt to income ratios, so the borrower has the ability to pay for the broken air conditioner or washing machine and still make his loan payments. Companies have the same issues, just on a larger scale.

Capital is simple. If the borrower cannot make his loan payment, what assets does he have that could be sold to repay the debt? The clearest example is a home. If you can't pay the mortgage payment, the lender can take the home back and sell it to pay off the loan. For a company -- What real estate do they have? Equipment, inventory, etc. could be sold?

Image has been provided by GLASBERGEN CARTOON
SERVICE and is available at glasbergen.com

Please keep in mind that when a bank makes a loan, the bankers are generally taking their customer's checking account balances and savings balances and lending it to another person or company. The interest rate on the loan is used to pay the interest rate on the customer's checking and savings account. The difference between the two is the lender's profit.

You can be sure that the bank's depositor will want his money back when he needs it. *Lending is a balancing* act, and a bad economy or large-scale fraud (2008 financial crisis) will throw everything out of balance.

We talked about how banks lend money. Banks and other types of lenders are good sources of capital for smaller loan amounts. When someone wants to borrow hundreds of millions or billions, he uses other ways to fund his loans. Below is a sample of just two of them.

Typically, when corporations need to raise large sums of capital, they issue stocks and bonds.

Instead of going to the bank and having their loan needs filled by one company, they go to the bond market and borrow a little bit of money from millions of individuals. The bond market is *much larger* than the stock market; most people don't know that.

According to Wikipedia, the bond market is part of the credit market, with bank loans forming the other main component. The global credit market in aggregate is about 3 times the size of the global stock market. Worldwide, the bond/credit market is $81 trillion-dollars.

To issue a bond, the corporation will typically go to a law firm and have them write the bond agreement; it will state how much they want to raise and how they will pay it back. Most investors don't have time to read these seventy to hundred-page documents and they rely on the credit rating given to the bond by Moody's, Fitch or S&P. For a healthy fee, either of these three companies will analyze the bond offering an assign a rating. You have seen them before: AAA, Aa, BBB, etc. These ratings give the investors a quick an easy way to determine if they want to buy an interest in this bond. The company then goes to a number of banks and brokerage firms to see if they would be the lead underwriter of the bonds. What that simply means is that the banks will use their customer base to sell the bonds to. The lead underwriter is simply the sales department that will sell (fund) the bonds.

Municipal Bonds are issued by a government entity. The advantage is that the interest paid is often Federal and State tax free. This allows the government to borrow money at lower rates than, say, corporate bonds, where the owners of those bonds pay normal taxes on their interest income. The process of issuing a municipal bond is almost identical to issuing a corporate bond.

Both a bond and a municipal bond, at their core, are simply loans. The three C's of lending and all other lending fundamentals apply to bonds.

As you will see shortly, the credit rating Agencies, Moody's, Fitch and S&P are the "hub" of this alleged criminal enterprise and the bond market is the place where most of the alleged fraud takes place.

Let's take a minute to discuss the big three credit rating agencies. For individuals, the companies that report on credit are typically Transunion, Equifax or Experian. Lenders sign up for their service and voluntarily report on their customers' payment history. The three credit rating agencies then consolidate that information and make it available to the public for a small fee. They also assign a "rating" that is reflected as a number. You have a 720 FICO Score. Most people pay attention to their "credit score" because they know it would have an impact on their ability to borrow.

Moody's, Fitch and S&P serve a very similar purpose but go about it in a very different way. There are few sources that report to the three agencies. Moody's, Fitch and S&P employ tens of thousands of individuals that investigate borrowings and companies and for a fee they will render an opinion. Often that opinion is in the form of a credit rating. "Buying" a rating from these agencies is very expensive and can at times even run into hundreds of thousands of dollars.

The following is a sample of S&P's (largest of the three) credit rating chart.

	Moody's	S&P	Fitch	Meaning
Investment Grade	Aaa	AAA	AAA	Prime
	Aa1	AA+	AA+	High Grade
	Aa2	AA	AA	
	Aa3	AA-	AA-	
	A1	A+	A+	Upper Medium Grade
	A2	A	A	
	A3	A-	A-	
	Baa1	BBB+	BBB+	Lower Medium Grade
	Baa2	BBB	BBB	
	Baa3	BBB-	BBB-	
Junk	Ba1	BB+	BB+	Non Investment Grade Speculative
	Ba2	BB	BB	
	Ba3	BB-	BB-	
	B1	B+	B+	Highly Speculative
	B2	B	B	
	B3	B-	B-	
	Caa1	CCC+	CCC+	Substantial Risks
	Caa2	CCC	CCC	Extremely Speculative
	Caa3	CCC-	CCC-	
	Ca	CC	CC+	In Default w/ Little Prospect for Recovery
		C	CC	In Default
			CC-	
	D	D	DDD	

Information and image structure provided by Wikipedia

With each rating, there is a description of the risk that rating agency perceives the lender or investor is taking by buying that bond offering for example:

Moody's	S&P	Meaning
Investment Grade Bonds		
Aaa	AAA	Bonds of the highest quality that offer the lowest degree of investment risk. Issuers are considered to be extremely stable and dependable.
Aa1, Aa2, Aa3	AA+, AA, AA-	Bonds are of high quality by all standards, but carry a slightly greater degree of long-term investment risk.
A1, A2, A3	A+, A, A-	Bonds with many positive investment qualities.
Baa1, Baa2, Baa3	BBB+, BBB, BBB-	Bonds of medium grade quality. Security currently appears sufficient, but may be unreliable over the long term.
Non Investment Grade Bonds (Junk Bonds)		
Ba1, Ba2, Ba3	BB+, BB, BB-	Bonds with speculative fundamentals. The security of future payments is only moderate.
B1, B2, B3	B+, B, B-	Bonds that are not considered to be attractive investments. Little assurance of long term payments.
Caa1, Caa2, Caa3	CCC+, CCC, CCC-	Bonds of poor quality. Issuers may be in default or are at risk of being in default.
Ca	CC	Bonds of highly speculative features. Often in default.
C	C	Lowest rated class of bonds.
--	D	In default.

Information and image structure provided by Wikipedia

If you are a conservative or careful investor/lender, you might only lend or buy from companies with a "AAA" rating. Because of that excellent rating, you will pay lower interest for the lower risk you are offering. In this case, let's say the company is paying 2.5% on its bonds.

Or you could buy a very high risk CCC bond and the company will pay you 7%, but you may not get your interest in a timely manner or at all. You could lose your money.

The bond "ratings" companies can get from these agencies are critically important for them. If S&P gives your company a CCC rating, when you try to borrow money you will have to pay a very high interest rate, similar to an individual with bad credit. A triple A rating is like hitting the lottery; you can borrow for almost nothing, and investors will be beating down your door to buy your bonds.

What if the big three agencies sold fabricated credit ratings? Let's say that lenders put together bonds that were secured by mortgages (collateral) and the people that owned those mortgages were not paying on time or at all (Capacity & Character). What if the homes' values were insufficient to repay the mortgage if the home was sold? Normally, if this were all true, the bond issuer could not get a credit rating from Moody's, Fitch or S&P. If they did manage to get a rating, it would be a very bad rating, making it unlikely they could sell the bonds anyway.

But let's pretend for a minute that the three big credit agencies are criminal enterprises and their board of directors and executives are criminals. If that were true, they could sell fabricated or fraudulent credit ratings for higher fees. Do this thousands of times and the credit rating agency makes a boat load of money. If the agencies were to do this, there would be a lack of confidence from the people that fund these loans, driving up mortgage costs and availability of loans.

Remember the 2008 financial crisis. Here are some headlines:

THE 2008 FINANCIAL CRISIS

We are in the worst financial crisis since Depression, says IMF
Quote from IMF press release, available at imf.org

Financial Crisis Cost Tops $22 Trillion, GAO Says
This article was reprinted with permission from the Huffington Post, and is available at huffingtonpost.com

Financial Crisis to Hit $7.6 Trillion by 2018
This article was reprinted with permission from MartketWatch, and is available at marketwatch.com

Remember all that? Well you guessed it, the three credit rating agencies allegedly sold fabricated credit ratings, and the whole house of cards collapsed.

Wall Street and the financial crisis:
The role of investment banks (Sen. Carl Levin)
This article was reprinted with permission from The Hill,
and is available at thehill.com

"Credit rating agencies, specifically case studies of Standard & Poor's and Moody's, the nation's two largest credit raters. While WaMu and other lenders dumped their bad loans into the river of commerce and regulators failed to stop their behavior, the credit rating agencies assured everyone that the poisoned water was safe to drink, slapping AAA ratings on bottles of high-risk financial products."

What is the credit rating agency's motivation to sell fabricated credit ratings? It is really quite simple. The agency can demand a higher than normal fee. Since the borrowers (in this case municipal agencies) can't really make long-term bond payments or pay the money back at all, they have to refinance every few years to keep people in the dark. The credit rating agencies then get another fee, sell another fabricated credit rating.

No FBI Investigations
No U.S. Attorney Investigations
and it took the Securities and Exchange Commission
8-10 years to fine the bad actors.

If you or I did this, we would be in prison for the rest of our lives -- unless of course we were members of this alleged criminal empire. In the meantime, things were getting really bad for my family and my company. We were both running on fumes. The kid's college expenses were coming in, and I had no resources to help. I have been draining my savings to meet our payroll and to pay for legal expenses. Our creditors were threatening to sue, the staff at work was losing confidence in the company and I had no idea how to fix things.

The company sold all its remaining projects for pennies on the dollar. The money was barely enough to keep up with our loan payments and legal fees for a few months. In a couple of weeks, I would start receiving attorney letters threatening lawsuits against me and my company. It is hard to explain the hopelessness that was starting to creep in. I felt like I was locked in some sort of box and could not find my way out.

It was becoming clear that the borrowers (government agencies) are probably running something called a Ponzi scheme.

How does a *Ponzi Scheme* work?

Blue wants to make a quick buck

Blue tells Red that if Red gives Blue $10, Blue will make it into $20 for $2 commission

Blue then goes to Orange and Green and offers them the same deal

With the money from Orange and Green, Blue pays back Red and makes his $2 commission

To pay back Orange and Green, Blue has to find 4 more people to take this deal

Eventually, Blue will run out of people willing to take this deal, and he won't be able to pay people back

Provided by Dreamtimes @ dreamstime.com

A Ponzi scheme is a fraudulent investment operation where the operator, an individual or organization, pays returns to its investors from new capital paid to the operators by new investors, rather than from profit earned through legitimate sources.

It is like making credit card payments with another credit card. It all works fine until you run out of credit cards.

As long as the municipal agencies can keep borrowing and you're not the last holder of a bond issued by them, you are safe and somewhat clueless that this is going on. In the case of Puerto Rico, things got so bad that it was impossible for the credit rating agencies to keep selling the alleged fraudulent ratings.

The whole house of cards collapsed and resulted in the largest public bankruptcy in this country's history.

Here are some other famous Ponzi schemes

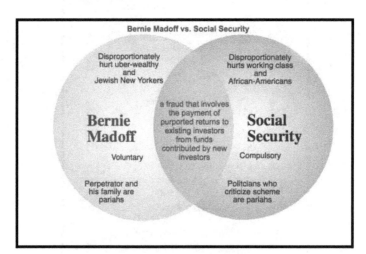

Provided by FreedomWoks .org

Everyone, well most people, understand that Social Security is a Ponzi scheme. Without the introduction of new tax payers in greater numbers, the government could not pay retired people their Social Security benefits. Your contributions over your working lifetime were used to pay someone else's benefits. Someone new must start contributing so you can be paid with their contributions. The last taxpayers who contribute to this scam will get nothing.

I believe that the Bernie Madoff Ponzi scheme helps better illustrate what I am up against here. Mr. Madoff provided falsified statements to his clients and potential clients about the investments he was selling. To keep his clients in the dark, he would take new clients' money and make interest and dividend payments to older clients, leading them to believe he was actually earning money for them. When he ran out of new clients, the whole house of cards collapsed.

How did Mr. Madoff keep everyone in the dark so long? *He didn't!* Many people, people with backgrounds similar to mine, would look at his documents and ask how these profits were possible. The documents they reviewed didn't really support Mr. Madoff's claims.

Dozens of people filed complaints with the SEC and FBI. Nothing happened? You see, Bernie was a powerful player in New York Politics. He made contributions (some call them payoffs) to all the major politicians in New York. Those politicians probably leaned on their political appointees in the Department of Justice and the Securities and Exchange Commission, to leave Mr. Madoff alone.

Even powerful politicians, like New York Senator Chuck Schumer (much more later on this) were not enough to protect Mr. Madoff when the news about his fraud became a "national event." Although Bernie contributed money to the New York Congressmen and Senators, he made relatively few contributions (payoffs) to national politicians. There are four hundred and thirty-five Congressmen and one hundred

Senators. Most of them did not get their fair share of the stolen money Mr. Madoff took. No contributions (payoffs), no political favors.

Finally, after a number of years, the FBI and SEC took action against Mr. Madoff. Below are excerpts from some newspaper articles that appeared in the papers at about that time.

New Book: Senator Schumer Was Regular Visitor to Madoff Offices
This article was reprinted with permission from Wall Street on Parade and is available at wallstreetonparade.com

"New York City has 8.4 million people living in its boroughs. But when it comes to defending those charged with financial crimes, it's a very small, clubby world of people who are either related to each other or have worked together in the past. And this clubby group has one more thing in common: most of its members seem to be lavishing huge campaign contributions on U.S. Senator Charles (Chuck) Schumer of New York – a man who is in a position to recommend Federal Judge appointments and the Justice Department's U.S. Attorney who will prosecute the financial crimes – or not."

SEC Didn't Act on Madoff Tips
This article was reprinted with permission from the Washington Post and is available at washingtonpost.com

By Binyamin Appelbaum and David S. Hilzenrath
Washington Post Staff Writers
Tuesday, December 16, 2008

"The Securities and Exchange Commission learned about what it describes as one of the largest securities frauds in history when Bernard L. Madoff volunteered his confession, raising questions about the agency's ability to police the financial marketplace.

The SEC had the authority to investigate Madoff's investment business, which managed billions of dollars for wealthy investors and philanthropies.

Financial analysts raised concerns about Madoff's practices repeatedly over the past decade, including a 1999 letter to the SEC that accused Madoff of running a Ponzi scheme. But the agency did not conduct even a routine examination of the investment business until last week".

Bernie Madoff
AMERICAN HEDGE-FUND INVESTOR

This article was reprinted with permission from Encyclopedia Britannica and is available at britannica.com

"Some skeptical individuals concluded that his promised investment returns (10 percent annually, in both up and down markets) were not credible and questioned why the firm's auditor was a small storefront operation with few employees. In 2001 Barron's financial magazine published an article that cast doubt on Madoff's integrity and financial analyst Harry Markopolos repeatedly presented the Securities and Exchange (SEC) with evidence, notably a detailed investigation, "The World's Largest Hedge Fund Is a Fraud," in 2005. Still, the SEC took no actions against Madoff." [Underlines added by author.]

We have very likely uncovered a national crime syndicate not unlike Mr. Madoff's New York based operation. The Ratings Agencies and Banks have all four hundred and thirty-five Congressmen and all one hundred Senators on their contributions list. They are all getting varying contributions (payoffs) in exchange for protection. There is no one in Washington D.C. who is likely to turn on his benefactors. The congressmen and senators need the Wall Street money to win re-election and they couldn't care less about the American people.

I read some recent articles on the web where credible newspaper reporters said that the Wall Street money contributed to our politicians in the 2014 elections was over one billion dollars. Assuming a material amount went to local and state elections, that leaves a vast some of money to be split between four hundred and thirty-five Congressmen and one hundred senators. What would you do for a piece of that action? We can already see what our elected officials were willing to do, and there is so much more to tell.

What is fraud? "The most authoritative treatise on federal jury instructions advises judges to instruct juries in securities fraud cases that fraud is "a general term which embraces all ingenious efforts and means that individuals devise to take advantage of others." Modern Federal Jury Instructions, Instruction 57-15."

If an investor or lender were not given transparent, true and honest information about his investment or loan, it is fraud. Pretty simple.

If you were fully informed and take a loss, you could consider that a market loss. Maybe you could write it off your taxes. If you take a loss and the underlying information you based your investment decision on was untrue or intentionally misleading, then you are a simple victim of theft. You can sue or try to get the Department of Justice to press criminal charges.

When the papers started to report on Puerto Rico's financial problems, the value of the island's debt (municipal bonds) started to decline. Panicked bond holders rushed to sell the $70 billion dollars in bonds and lost $34 billion dollars. Or was it really a theft? A crime?

What if I were to tell you that politicians fill the most powerful positions within the Department of Justice and the Securities and Exchange Commission with their political appointees? What if the politicians told the ratings agencies and the banks that as long as they get their fair share, their political appointees will insure there are no investigations and no prosecutions? Could that explain what took place in 2008 when trillions were stolen?

What if the alleged criminals, the banks, board of directors and executives, the ratings agencies' Board of Directors and executives and the Municipal Agency executives were so full of arrogance and disdain for the American people that they left a trail of evidence that was impossible to hide?

The politicians could use their political appointees in the FBI and SEC to prevent criminal action. But how do they prevent a flood of civil litigation? How do they keep tens of millions of potential victims from suing? They would have to do a few things.

First, they would try to roll back the Dodd Frank legislation that was passed right after the 2008 financial crisis. That legislation allows the criminal justice system and others to hold Wall Street Executives accountable for the actions of their companies (banks and credit rating agencies). Here are some recent headlines:

In June of 2018 an article on the Nasdaq website said Dodd Frank rollbacks are now behind us. The article explored what that might mean in the future.

In March of 2018, Forbes published an article suggesting the rollback of Dodd Frank Regulations means,
Dodd-Frank Is now officially A dud!

And here is the record from the Congressional Session

One Hundred fifteenth Congress
Of the
United States of America

AT THE SECOND SESSION
Begun and held at the City of Washington on Wednesday, the third day of January, two thousand and eighteen

An Act

To promote economic growth, provide tailored regulatory relief, and enhance consumer protections, and for other purposes.

Be it enacted by the Senate and House of Representatives of the United States of America in Congress assembled,

(Sec. 303) The bill extends immunity from liability to certain individuals employed at financial institutions who, in good faith and with reasonable care, disclose the suspected exploitation of a senior citizen to a regulatory or law-enforcement agency. Similarly, the employing financial institution shall not be liable with respect to disclosures made by such employees.

IMMUNITY FOR COVERED FINANCIAL INSTITUTIONS. —A covered financial institution shall not be liable, including in any civil or administrative proceeding, for a disclosure made by an individual described in subparagraph (A) if—

(Sec. 403) This bill amends the Federal Deposit Insurance Act to require certain municipal obligations to be treated as level 2B liquid assets if they are investment grade, liquid, and readily marketable. Under current law, corporate debt securities and publicly traded common-equity shares, but not municipal obligations, may be treated as level 2B liquid assets (which are considered to be high-quality assets).

(Sec. 504) The bill amends the Investment Company Act of 1940 to exempt from the definition of an "investment company," for purposes of specified limitations applicable to such a company under the Act, a qualifying venture capital fund that has no more than 250 investors. Specifically, the bill applies to a venture capital fund that has less than $10 million in aggregate capital contributions and uncalled committed capital. Under current law, a venture capital fund is considered to be an investment company if it has more than 100 investors.

Seriously, this happened! Next, how can our Politicians protect their alleged criminal contributors from a flood of civil lawsuits? You take away American's legal rights! That can't happen in the United States, can it? Here are some headlines:

The Promise of PROMESA

An article appeared on the Breitbart website in April of 2016 that did an excellent job of discussing how Speaker Paul Ryan used his position to force additional votes for the PROMESA legislation. Forcing legislation that would cause innocent bond holders to take massive losses while the rating agencies and banks walked away from this train wreck.

A wreck the banks and rating agencies arguably caused themselves.

Puerto Rico Oversight Law Puts Creditor's Lawsuits on Hold

This article was reprinted with permission from Bloomberg Company and is available at www.bna.com

"After three separate plaintiffs brought actions against the Commonwealth of Puerto Rico alleging that they were stripped of their contractual and property rights, the Commonwealth asked the court to stay the actions under Section 405(b)(1) of PROMESA."

You guessed it. Our politicians almost certainly knowing that the $70 billion-dollar Puerto Rico bond default was likely due to fraud, voted to take away the victims' legal rights. Our rights. And the money rolled into Capitol Hill. Good for our congressmen and senators, good for Wall Street, not so good for us.

You can't make this stuff up. Our public servants moved in large numbers against the American people. One could assume that money (contributions) had something to do with it. But don't worry, odds are they will all be reelected so they can do this kind of thing over and over again. Remember it's always the other guys politician that is the bad guy, not yours.

Richard Larkin, now with Stoever Glass and Company wrote in the article saying he felt the board members selected by our senators and congressman were heavily weighted for the benefit of the Commonwealth and not the bondholders.

An article appeared on the Breitbart website in April of 2016 that did an excellent job of discussing how Speaker Paul Ryan used his position to force additional votes for the PROMESA legislation. Forcing legislation that would cause innocent bond holders to take massive losses while the rating agencies and banks walked away from this train wreck.
A wreck the banks and rating agencies arguably caused themselves.

The Center for Individual Freedom posted an excellent article on their website that talked about the Congress's Role in Puerto Rico's financial mess. I remember the article talking about PROMESA legislation that did not respect the retirees (bond holders) legal rights and what that legislation cost the innocent bond holders. This was one of many articles that saw PROMESA for what it was.

Legislation that help protect Wall Street and punish elderly Americans!

"Monsters exist, but they are too few in number to be truly dangerous. More dangerous are the common men, the functionaries (government bureaucrats) ready to believe and to act without asking questions." — Primo Levi

Primo Michele Levi spent eleven months imprisoned at the Auschwitz concentration camp complex

Before you continue on to the next few chapters, I want to issue a warning. This explanatory chapter was meant to prepare you for what I am about to tell you. Once you move forward through the next few chapters, if you have trusted our government, you will never feel the same. Sometimes it is better not to know. Give yourself a minute before you turn the page.

CHAPTER FOUR

PUERTO RICO IS JUST THE TIP OF THE ICEBERG

As I said in earlier chapters, in March of 2015 I started to take a deep dive into PREPA's books. PREPA's audited financial statements and the companies bond offerings are available on their web site and are easy to get your hands on. Ernst & Young, the large national accounting firm, was PREPA's accountant of record and prepared their fully audited statements.

The first thing I noticed was that PREPA would expense hundreds of millions of dollars for projects in one year and those numbers (projects) would show up again in following years. The work never got done and the projects were never completed. I shared this with many Puerto Rico congressmen and senators. In a later Senate Hearing on the matter, the government of Puerto Rico admitted to the following:

The Puerto Rico Senate Report

"With regard to previous years, this Commission's President visited PREPA's headquarters, and despite requesting that same data (on construction projects) for the years between 2000 and 2012, it was never provided. However, with the evidence at hand, we detected that PREPA repeatedly

59

underestimated the costs of these improvements and capital investments for each project, which amount to 200% in excess from the budgeted amount, without reaching a 100% project completion. There are instances within the 12-month period evaluated, where PREPA incurred in costs exceeding the budget, construction was not finished, and the project was abandoned."

The report went on to say: *"This Commission also found that the consulting engineers were negligent and failed in the obligation imposed to them by the Trust Agreement Section (706) when they allowed PREPA's energy-generating stations and the whole system in general, to become obsolete (equipment value?); in violation of federal regulation established by the Mercury and Airborne Toxic Emissions Standards (MATS)."*

The report additionally claimed that in most cases, over a ten-year period, one person signed off on these projects without any oversight. How many companies have you worked for where one-person controls hundreds of millions of dollars without oversight? Let's take a minute and recap:

- I first went to the FBI and told them that $15 billion dollars over ten years was stolen from PREPA through their oil purchase program.

- I told them that, based on the EPA violations and the presence of the oil pre-heaters, they must be burning sludge oil.

- I made them aware of the RICO lawsuit that made the same claims and went on to tell them about the CIA tracking the large wire transfers from Puerto Rico to Venezuela where the money was being laundered.

The FBI and U.S Attorney Offices in Puerto Rico and now in Washington D.C. said it sounds like a civil matter. They could not find any criminal laws that were broken.

I then went back to the FBI and U.S. Attorney's and told them that the PREPA financial statements strongly indicate that hundreds of millions each year was and is being stolen from the utility for work that is never done. I went on to tell them that the Puerto Rico Government held special hearings and made the same claims.

The FBI and U.S Attorney Offices in Puerto Rico and now in Washington D.C. said it sounds like a civil matter. They could not find any criminal laws that were broken.

The FBI continues to claim this is a civil matter. Why not sue the rating agencies and the utility company? Normally when you get robbed or defrauded you file a police report. That is exactly what Commercial Solar Power did. Most law enforcement agencies would find our claims to have the makings of a very strong criminal case. Based on the behavior of the FBI and the Department of Justice, it is pretty clear to the victims that the FBI and DOJ are fully involved criminal co-conspirators in this massive, trillion-dollar, criminal enterprise. That behavior also helps explain why the FBI has gone to extremes to prevent any investigations or prosecutions.

To sue the ratings agencies the victims must have paid for the alleged fraudulent and misleading credit ratings. Although Commercial Solar Power was a direct victim of these credit ratings it did not contribute to the cost of paying for those ratings and hence, it cannot sue over the ratings. We did consider suing the utility company but the judge that was handpicked for the bankruptcy case has made it clear that evidence of wrongdoing (massive fraud) regarding the Utilities debt will not be considered by her court! Is that even legal? When it comes to trillions of dollars, it appears anything is possible. That is why I wrote this book.

As a twenty-five-year banker, I have had the pleasure of working with FBI field agents and U.S. Attorney's. When a bank is robbed and $5,000 is stolen, or when a fraudulent loan application appears with manufactured tax returns attempting to support non-existing income, we call the FBI. I have even been asked to give expert testimony. Testimony that was never used because in each case, the criminal defendant agreed to a plea deal. I would gage the FBI's interest in each of these cases as extremely strong.

Why so much interest in a $5,000 bank robbery or a $75,000 loan request and no interest in a $15 billion-dollar theft or the theft of hundreds of millions of dollars in equipment funds? I was starting to feel that the FBI and U.S. Attorneys were using the power we entrusted to them to protect the bad actors involved with this. As this book goes on, it will leave you with little question about the FBI and U.S. Attorney's motives here. They will be undeniable.

It was at about this time in our investigation that a feeling of complete hopelessness encased my life. We were out of money, I was served with a number of lawsuits, and feared that I would lose our home. I put the house on the market and sold it, using the proceeds to pay loan payments and legal fees. It bought us a few months. The FBI and SEC were completely unresponsive, my legal options were few, and I was now technically homeless. Luckily the kids were living near their college campus, so I only had to find a place for myself. I wasn't sure I could go on, I wasn't sure I wanted to go on, and soon things would get much worse.

As if the $15 billion dollars in oil money theft and the hundreds of millions per year in construction and maintenance theft were not enough, the financial statements reflected even more extreme criminal activity. Activity that will take all of us from Puerto Rico to Wall Street to Washington D.C

As I studied the financial statements, looking closely at PREPA's cash flow (income), I noticed that PREPA was claiming sizable accounts receivable as current income. As I looked to see who PREPA was extending credit to and if they were paying PREPA on time, the whole direction of this investigation changed.

PREPA included accounts receivable (a claim for payment for goods supplied and/or services rendered) in its revenues that should not have been included. In years 2009 through 2013, the utility had significant accounts receivable that were not collectable and by all accounting standards should have not be used in their revenue assumptions.

Many of these PREPA customers haven't paid their bills in over a decade. The accounting standards say the following:

GAAP Accounting Rules

GAAP stands for Generally Acceptable Accounting Principles

Accounts receivable are expected income for services performed or goods sold that are unpaid. Report receivables on your books as current assets, <u>anticipated to turn into cash within the year</u>. When you perform services or deliver goods before payment, you're usually an unsecured creditor unless your services come under a lien statute in your state. A mechanic's lien, for example, may make you a secured creditor. An unsecured creditor has no security interest in the assets of the debtor, and <u>you'll probably receive nothing</u> if the debtor (customer) declares bankruptcy. A small-business owner must expect some write-offs for uncollected debts GAAP uses the less optimistic view when two possibilities exist. When using GAAP rules, a business owner uses a conservative estimate of the number of accounts receivable that won't be paid, relying on the principle of conservatism.

The government also has its own accounting standards and it says the following:

Government Accounting Standards

The revenue-generating activities of an agency will frequently result in receivables on the agency's accounting records. If the agency arrives at the conclusion that any of the amounts so established cannot be collected using the criteria in the Collectible or Uncollectable? section of this fiscal policy and procedure (FPP), reduce the amount of the receivable. The USAS transaction entry to specifically write off a revenue receivable bad debt, regardless of appropriation year.

If we were to remove the uncollectable accounts receivable from PREPA's income, they have a debt to income of less than 1 to 1. In other words, for every dollar in debt payments, PREPA has less than a dollar to pay it. Add in all the phantom construction expenses (theft) and the extra oil they have to buy to make up for the poor quality of the sludge (more theft), they have far less than one dollar to pay each one dollar in expenses.

If you remember the three C's of Credit, PREPA just failed the first C, "capacity." They don't have the ability to pay their bills.

Now I am looking at the second "C" of Credit: Capital. If PREPA cannot pay its bills, does it have enough assets to sell to repay all of their obligations? PREPA has a negative net worth and 1.7 billion dollars in unfunded pension obligations.

PREPA just failed the second C: Capital. They don't have enough assets to sell.

Lastly, we take a look at the third C: character. PREPA has over twenty-five pages of serious EPA violations and numerous very serious law suits, including RICO lawsuits. A RICO lawsuit on the surface is suggesting this is a criminal organization.

PREPA just failed the third C: Character. Their legal and regulatory history points to very bad management.

In almost all cases, when you can't pass the three C's of Credit, you are <u>technically bankrupt</u>. Let's look at what the special Puerto Rico Senate Hearings had to say about this:

"PREPA's current economic insolvency was the product of, among other factors, negligent acts on the part of its creditors, who in spite of knowing that PREPA's financial and competitive situation was weak, and knowing that its infrastructure was obsolete, they negligently granted PREPA a good credit rating; <u>disregarding that by 2010, PREPA was technically bankrupt</u>. This fact was corroborated by Arturo Ondina, CPA and consulting partner of Ernst & Young, firm who has audited PREPA for This occurred while the financial consultants and consulting engineers indicated in their reports that the PREPA financial condition allowed it to issue more bonds, when the fiscal reality was that PREPA was not generating sufficient income to repay the debt."

Okay, there is a lot of nonsense here, so let me help you sort through it for what it is. The government of Puerto Rico is claiming "Wall Street" forced them to issue bond debt they knew they couldn't repay. They are also claiming that Moody's, Fitch and S&P somehow forced the Puerto Rican Government to buy fraudulent "good ratings" from them. Give me a break!

In my opinion, the politicians in Puerto Rico knew all along what was going on and were willing to break any laws to keep this Ponzi scheme going. Did I even need to say that? This report was written by those politicians who in many cases, participated in this.

But the report does say some very important things. First, the lead Ernst & Young auditor -- you know, the guy who prepared the audited financial statements -- claimed under oath that he knew that PREPA has been bankrupt since 2010 but happily provided fraudulent financial statements.

The government leaders in Puerto Rico and the senior managers at PREPA claim that the three big credit rating agencies all knew them to be bankrupt but were willing to sell them fabricated (fraudulent) credit ratings. The report goes to say that the major banks, Like Citibank, Wells Fargo and B of A, to name a few, all knew the bonds were no good but were willing to sell them to their clients. According to published reports, twenty-four million American's bought Puerto Rico bonds.

Does this sound like a criminal organization to you? It does to me, and the evidence for all of this criminal activity is overwhelming.

As I pondered all this information, I thought I would take a look at other municipal agencies in Puerto Rico. PREPA only represents about $9 billion out the $70 billion in bonds Puerto Rico defaulted on.

The Center for Individual Freedom posted an article on its website back in February of 2016. I remember reading the article a few months ago. It suggested most American's don't realize that Puerto Rico has a strong culture of corruption. I wish I saw that article five years ago.

You guessed it! Much of the same thing. Phantom income, alleged theft on a grand scale, movement of money in and out of The Puerto Rico Government Development Bank to try and hide this from everyone. It would be reasonable to assume we are looking at a $70 billion-dollar fraud here.

Keep in mind that Puerto Rico municipal bonds are tax-free in all fifty states. The bonds are bought mostly by retired American's to supplement their Social Security income. Florida residents lost almost $3 billion dollars, New York residents a little over $2 billion dollars, and Californians a little under $2 billion dollars. Even the smallest States had residents losing hundreds of millions.

It is almost the perfect crime. Most retired American's owned five thousand dollars or ten thousand dollars' worth of these bonds and have no idea how the financial markets work. Even if they found out, how are they going to spend millions in legal costs to recover their five to ten thousand dollars? The total theft relating to these bonds topped $34 billion-dollars. The $34 billion represents what the original bond holders lost when they sold their bonds.

At about this time I hit rock bottom. The lawsuits were progressing against me, and I had no money to defend them. What would be my defense anyway? I owed them the money; this wasn't their fault. At the same time, I failed to make my agreed-upon payments to the IRS for past due taxes, and they were about to seize my small checking accounts. I barely kept a few thousand in the accounts to pay for gas and groceries. Soon I feared, I wouldn't be able to do even the basic things.

The whistleblower award from the SEC was a pipedream. The SEC appeared more concerned about the alleged criminals then the victims. The FBI was useless. We have been defrauded, robbed and there was nothing I could do about it.

I seriously thought about ending it at this point. I was an embarrassment to my family, to my company and to my friends. If I could muster the courage, the kids would at least get my life insurance proceeds. I could leave them something. Strangely, that thought gave me strength to go on another day. I could always end it tomorrow. I was in control of something! Maybe it was that feeling of control that let me move forward?

As I absorbed all of this new information, I wondered if this fraud was just taking place in Puerto Rico. I pulled up a list of the states with the most municipal debt and began to take a look at their bond offerings.

United States Census Bureau 2015

California	$151,715,007,000
New York	$137,369,089,000
Massachusetts	$75,307,661,000
New Jersey	$66,923,327,000
Illinois	$64,221,381,000
U.S. Total State Debt	**$1,149,926,081,000**

I informally looked at about_forty bond offerings_ from these States. I could not find any bonds rated, AAA, AA or single A where there were any indications of fraud. That all changed when I moved to the more common bond ratings, bonds that carried BBB, BB or B ratings. In about 40% of the cases there were strong indications of fraud. Given the size of the bond market, we are talking about 40% of trillions of dollars.

As you could imagine, at this point, I took all this new information on PREPA and Puerto Rico to the FBI, U.S. Attorney and the Securities and Exchange Commission. This is getting sadly comical because this was their response:

The FBI and U.S Attorney Offices in Puerto Rico and now in Washington D.C. said it sounds like a civil matter. They could not find any criminal laws that were broken.

The Securities and Exchange Commission, where I am trying to win a Whistleblower Award to repay my company debts, didn't respond at all, nor have they taken any action. The SEC opened a case based on my complaint and assigned the case to a Senior Attorney. Over time that Senior Attorney simply stopped communicating with me. Her favorite line was, do you have any new information for me! As if this is not enough!

If you were to follow the evidence, you would have a diagram that looks something like this:

The politician fills the key positions in the FBI, U.S. Attorney Offices and the SEC with his political appointees. The politician can now provide protection in exchange for political contributions, family jobs and God knows what else. By doing this, they no longer have to spend as much time raising money to keep their jobs. The FBI appointees make sure no investigations are undertaken. The U.S. Attorney appointees make sure there are no prosecutions. The Securities and Exchange Commission appointees delay all possible action until the criminal and civil "Statue of Limitations" expire, then they negotiate favorable fines for the companies and sometimes, their executives.

Because of the 2008 related fines, the congress quietly passed legislation allowing the fined firms to use their tax write-offs to pay the fines. Shhhh, you are not supposed to know this!

The Statue of Limitation states how many years a victim has to sue or press criminal charges. Once those time limits expire, there is nothing they can do.

The evidence indicates there is a government-run "protection racket" going on. It has gotten to the point when the politicians' control over the DOJ or SEC isn't enough; the politicians break or change the laws to protect these folks. It is really unbelievable! And the sums of money being stolen add up to trillions.

The political appointees at the SEC have likely been told by their political benefactors that any payment of fines could be argued as an admission of guilt in a criminal prosecution or civil lawsuit. The SEC appears to almost always postpone their actions against the large Wall Street firms until the "Statue of Limitations" has run out. If you are a little guy, you are shit out of luck. They will throw the book at you. The same is true with our courageous FBI agents; as long as there is no risk to their career or pensions, they will pursue you.

The Municipal Bond Issuers are often part of local government organizations that employ many local voters. The agencies are packed with high-paying, normally unqualified, political appointees as rewards from the local politicians for their support. There is usually bad management, theft and corruption throughout these agencies. Keeping them afloat to hide all this and continue providing public services seems to be the number one concern of most politicians.

The credit rating agencies (Moody's, S&P and Fitch) appear to sell fabricated and fraudulent credit ratings, allowing the municipal agency to raise capital by issuing bonds. The ratings agencies share their income with the politicians (contributions) likely as payment for protection. Sound like the mafia, anyone?

The major banks appear to knowingly sell these fraudulent bonds to their best customers for healthy fees, knowing that most of those bonds will refinance before they become worthless (Ponzi Scheme). Bond refinancing is the issuing of new bonds to replace outstanding bonds at or prior to the bond's maturity or repayment date. The banks share their income with the politicians (contributions) likely in exchange for "protection".

Let's talk specifically now about the role the big three credit agencies play (Moodys, Fitch and S&P). In my mind, they are hub in the wheel of this alleged criminal organization. Without the rating agencies, none of this works. The three firms issue ratings on somewhere between 85% and 90% of all rated bonds sold today. If the bonds that are issued were all held to maturity, twenty to thirty years for most bonds, the three agencies would not make much money. It does, however, make sense for companies to refinance their bonds when interest rates go down. With interest rates at 2009 to 2018 levels, most of these bonds will not be refinanced in the future. Rates have been really low. This leaves the agencies in a predicament.

How can the agencies insure a steady flow of business in an environment that does not encourage bond refinancing? Historically, bond refinancing is much larger than the issuance of new bonds, similar to home mortgages. Home mortgage refinancing is a much larger market then the market for new home mortgage loans.

What if the agencies knowingly sold good ratings to bad companies? The companies could not pay off the debt or even make payments for very long, forcing them to refinance every few years. No one would be the wiser as long as the refinancing continued. It is like making credit card payments by getting new credit cards every few years. Your credit stays good and no one is the wiser. This is the essence of a Ponzi scheme: the last one holding the bond is the only one who takes the loss.

Most politicians know that they can't stay in office very long if they are cutting back on services, food stamps, welfare etc. They will do almost anything to avoid being put in that position. They appoint the heads of these municipal agencies and make it clear to those appointees they need to keep delivering the services (Local, State & Federal).

The needs of the troubled municipal agencies align perfectly with the needs of the three big rating agencies.

How would it be possible for the three big ratings agencies to accidently issue hundreds, probably thousands, of incorrect ratings? If you are familiar with their internal policies, you know it is not possible. If you remember the sworn testimony in the Puerto Rico Senate Hearings, many people testified that both the banks and the rating agencies knew PREPA (Puerto Rico as a whole) was technically bankrupt.

As a banker, I can add some value here. Within a bank, when we have borrowers looking for a $2,500 loan or a $5,000 loan, the request will normally be handled by a young employee with a bachelor's degree and three to six months of bank training. If the borrower needs $50,000 to say $500,000, the request will go to a more senior employee with an advanced college degree and five to ten years of experience. You get my point, the more dollars that are involved, the more experience the lender or lenders need to have.

When you are talking about bond debt, you are normally looking at hundreds of millions, possibly billions. The folks in the three big credit agencies that handle this normally have a Master's Degree or PhD, fifteen to twenty years' experience and a team of junior lenders that support them. Even when the senior employee makes a decision, the rating decision would go on for legal review with attorneys and up the ladder to a credit committee of some sort. If the dollars involved were big enough, the board of directors would have final approval authority.

There is no reasonable argument that the FBI or U.S. Attorney could make that would suggest this alleged fraud is anything other than a corporate decision made at the highest levels of these companies. Add the fact that I have disclosed all this fraud to the leadership of Moody's, S&P and Fitch, making it more difficult to claim it is anything other than their corporate policy to defraud people.

This appears to be an organized criminal effort to defraud the bond holders. To make sure the authorities could charge the board members and executives at Moody's, Fitch and S&P, three years ago, I Federal Expressed all of the board members and executives a document outlining what their companies were doing. Because of Board Member changes, I re-sent those letters out to them again in April of 2018.

April 4, 2018

S&P Global Ratings
55 Water Street
New York, New York 10041
Attention: Monique F. Leroux – Board Director

RE: Municipal Bond Ratings Fraud – S&P Global, Moody's & Fitch

Dear Ms. Leroux,

Commercial Solar Power, Inc. (CSP) reached out to S&P Global Ratings almost three years ago. We notified the S&P Global Board Members and executives that the Puerto Rico Municipal Bond Ratings were not consistent with the actual financial condition of the bond issuing municipalities. A forensic investigation by CSP uncovered overwhelming and publicly available evidence that the municipalities were technically bankrupt when they received the BBB and BBB+, S&P Ratings.

CSP asked S&P to reimburse us for our losses and to put in place policies and procedures to avoid this happening again in the future. S&P declined our request and stated they did nothing wrong.

Since that time, almost three years ago, we have been in contact with all your Board Members and Executives. It is legally inconceivable that the Board and executives didn't participated in this $70 billion-dollar fraud and they all failed to report it to the SEC, DOJ or their shareholders, when told about it.

Since it appears that S&P is content in participating in a criminal enterprise that steals money from America's senior citizens and has no intention of righting their ship, we are moving forward to educate your shareholders, inform the FBI, inform the U.S. Attorney General's and inform all the State Attorney Generals. Hopefully public pressure and the threat of criminal indictments will accomplish what I was unable to do.

Below is a sample of the communications that are going out:

Sincerely,
Richard Lawless

April 4, 2018
United States Attorney's Office
100 Middle Street, East Tower, 6th Floor
Portland, ME 04101
Attention: Halsey B. Frank - United States Attorney

Dear Mr. Frank,

It appears that there is a small group within the Department of Justice who have taken it upon themselves to determine who will be investigated *and prosecuted and who will not. I am writing you in the hopes that you are not one of those bad actors.*

When our company lost everything in the 70 billion-dollar Puerto Rico bond default, we initiated a forensic investigation to find out the causes, to avoid it happening in the future. The investigation turned up massive corruption at the big three credit rating agencies: Moody's, S&P Global and Fitch. It appears that the three big credit agencies simply fabricated good credit ratings for "a fee," allowing the Puerto Rico Municipalities to borrow the 70 billion-dollars they defaulted on. It is also clear that the Board of Directors and executives at each of the companies had full knowledge of this.

Puerto Rico Bonds are triple tax free and were mainly purchased by retired Americans' throughout all fifty States. States like Florida and NY had resident losses of over 2 billion-dollars while smaller states experienced losses in the tens of millions.

Below is a list of links that will allow you to quickly understand this and review the overwhelming amounts of evidence available.

I hope you will act on this criminal complaint.

Sincerely,
Richard R. Lawless
Commercial Solar Power, Inc. – CEO

To my knowledge, none of the following board members or executives reported this to the FBI, U.S. Attorney, the Securities and Exchange Commission or their shareholders, likely breaking dozens of laws in the process.

I had sent some e-mail messages to the agencies in-house legal counsels. I communicated with David Goldberg at S&P, John Goggins at Moody's and Charles Brown at Fitch. Based on my emails I am confident that the three General Counsels were fully aware of what was going on. It may be possible that they are openly supporting and participating in these alleged felonies, and they appear fully prepared to protect their companies. My personal opinion only. Everyone deserves their day in court. Remember the FBI insists no crimes were committed and everyone is innocent until proven guilty.

I often wonder: Do executives at these large corporations go home and tell their wife and kids, *hey, I helped our company steal billions from senior citizens and now we can get that vacation home in the Hamptons?* Or do they pretend to be good people and let everyone believe they are decent human beings? What kind of a piece of work do you have to be to do this once, let alone over a decade?

I am pissed, I can't retire, I can't help my kids any more, I can't pay my bills, but many of the participants in these organizations can go out every year and get the newest BMW 7 series for themselves. If people go to jail for many years for stealing ten thousand dollars, how long should someone go to jail for stealing trillions of dollars?

Below is a list of the leadership at these firms. The public should know who they are.

S&P Global Ratings **55 Water Street** **New York, New York** **10041** **212-438-2000** **212-438-1000**	**Moody's Investors** **Service, Inc.** **7 World Trade Center** **at 250 Greenwich** **Street** **New York, NY 10007** **212-553-1653**	**Fitch Ratings** **33 Whitehall Street** **New York, NY 10004** **212-908-0500**
John Berisford - President	Raymond W. McDaniel, Jr. - President	Paul Taylor – President

David Goldenberg – Executive Managing Director	Mark E. Almeida - President	Charles D. Brown - General Counsel
Christopher J. Heusler -Executive Managing Director	Richard Cantor – Chief Risk Officer	Jon Ewing - Chief Marketing Officer
Holly Kulka – Executive Managing Director	Robert Fauber - President	Eileen Fahey - Chief Risk Officer
Yann Le Pallec – Executive Managing Director	John J. Goggins - EVP	Robert Harpel - Chief Technology Officer
Elizabeth O'Melia - Senior Vice President	Linda S. Huber - EVP	Andy Jackson - Head of Human Resources
Soon Marie Rabb – Vice President	Melanie Hughes - SVP	Theodore E. Niedermayer - Chief Financial Officer
Kelly Shen – Executive Managing Director	Scott Kenney - SVP	Daniel Noonan - Head of Communications
Charles E. Haldeman, Jr. – Chairman of the Board	Michel Madelain – Vice Chairman	David Samuel - Chief Accounting Officer
Marco Alverà – Chief Executive Officer	David B. Platt – Managing Director	Ian Linnell – President
William D. Green – Former CEO	Blair L. Worrall - SVP	Karen Skinner - Chief Operating Officer
Stephanie C. Hill - Director	Henry A. McKinnell Jr., Ph.D. - Chairman	Jeremy Carter - Chief Credit Officer
Rebecca Jacoby - Director	Basil L. Anderson - Director	Brett Hemsley - Global Analytical Head
Monique F. Leroux- Director	Jorge A. Bermudez - Director	Mark Oline - Head of Business
Maria R. Morris- Director	Darrell Duffie, Ph.D. - Director	Peter Patrino - Chief Criteria Officer

Douglas L. Peterson- President	Kathryn M. Hill - Director	
Sir Michael Rake - Director	Ewald Kist - Director	
Edward B. Rust, Jr. - Director	Raymond. W. McDaniel Jr - Director	
Kurt L. Schmoke – Director	Leslie F. Seidman – Director	
Richard E. Thornburgh - Director	Bruce Van Saun - Director	

The FBI's most common excuse is that they can't prove the executives knew anything about this. They can't say that anymore! Every executive on this list received a letter.

To further cover my bases, I sent tracked letters out to all the stock analysis covering the stock for Moody's and S&P. Fitch is owned by the Hearst Corporation, a company in New York that owns many businesses including TV networks, magazines, newspapers, Buzzfeed and Vice, and letters went out to their leadership. I believe the analysis have a legal obligation to report this information and share it with their clients.

March 28, 2018
Morgan Stanley
1585 Broadway Street
New York, NY 10036
Attention: Eric F. Grossman – General Counsel

RE: Municipal Bond Ratings Fraud – S&P Global, Moody's & Fitch

Dear Mr. Grossman,

Morgan Stanley provides one of the most followed Analysts of S&P Global Stock. We feel it is critical that we notify you of the allegations that

S&P knowingly and willfully fabricated good credit ratings for numerous municipalities in Puerto Rico. These fraudulent ratings resulted in a $70 billion-dollar bond default.

Complicating the massive financial jeopardy these three ratings firms have exposed their Shareholders to, the Board of Directors and Executives had full knowledge of this activity and withheld this information from the Securities and Exchange Commission, the Department of Justice and their Shareholders.

The SEC, The FBI and the U.S. Attorney's office found these claims to be credible enough to open a number of on-going investigations.

I am providing Morgan Stanley with sufficient information (attachments and links) so they can determine for themselves the validity of the Rating Agency's actions in regards to the Puerto Rico Bond Default.

We feel that Morgan Stanley and its Affiliates have an affirmative regulatory and legal obligation to disclose this risk to their customers. A copy of this transmission will be sent to the appropriate personnel at the Securities and Exchange Commission, the FBI and the U.S. Attorney's Office. It is also likely that this notification to Morgan Stanley will become known in the public arena, possibly exposing Morgan Stanley to an unknown amount of civil liabilities.

If you should have any questions, feel free to contact me at the number listed below.

Sincerely,
Richard Lawless

To my knowledge, none of the analysis did what they were required to do by law once they had knowledge of this activity. No one was investigated or prosecuted for their respective roles in this massive alleged fraud.

According to FindLaw a Thomson Reuters Company; The various federal statutes and regulations that make up the Federal Securities Laws contain specific rules regarding truth and fair dealing in the issuance and sale of covered securities. In addition, most states have their own laws addressing some aspect of securities sales that allow the state's securities commissions to conduct investigations and bring securities fraud actions. Remedies for losses associated with securities also exist under various state and federal common law doctrines."

Those issuing securities face clear rules about disclosures of information affecting the value of the investment. Securities issuers must file multiple documents with the SEC regarding the value of their company and assets and they must follow Generally Accepted Accounting Principles (GAAP). Individuals within a company may not use knowledge gained from their position to get an unfair advantage over less knowledgeable investors. Failure to follow these and other rules support the following securities litigation claims.

Misrepresentation and omission occur when a securities firm or individual broker purposefully gives out wrong information or conceals true information. A securities fraud is a type of serious white-collar crime in which a person or company, such as a stockbroker, brokerage firm, corporation or investment bank, misrepresents information that investors use to make decisions. Securities Fraud can also be committed by independent individuals (such as by engaging in insider trading).

Department of Justice

Securities And Financial Fraud Unit

An Overview

According to the FBI's website; The Securities and Financial Fraud Unit ("SFF") focuses on the prosecution of complex and sophisticated securities, commodities, and other financial fraud cases. Working closely with regulatory partners at the SEC, CFTC, and other agencies, SFF has tackled some of the largest frauds in the financial services industry and a wide mix of market manipulation and insider trading cases. The SFF Unit also focuses on a broader array of financial fraud, including mortgage fraud, bank fraud, and government procurement fraud.

Fraud Section, Criminal Division
U.S. Department of Justice
ATTN: Chief, Securities and Financial Fraud Unit
950 Constitution Ave., NW
Washington, DC 20530

Trillions of dollars allegedly stolen and this department within the Department of Justice, to the best of my knowledge, did nothing! Is it possible the SEC and FBI employees and leadership are just stupid? Maybe I should dumb this down and send them something they can easily follow?

Based on all these findings, I prepared a formal forensic audit document to help the Securities and Exchange Commission and others better understand what was taking place in Puerto Rico and elsewhere. I also faxed a copy of this audit to all 435 congressmen and 100 senators prior to the PROMESA vote. I wanted them to know that the Puerto Rico bankruptcy was likely caused by fraud. Below is a sampling of the audit's findings.

The Audit (Selective Excepts)

The bond documents claim:

"The Power Revenue Bonds are payable solely from the Revenues of the System after payment of Current Expenses of the Authority and any reserve therefor." [sic]

The Authority went on to state that based on their revenues, the bonds will have debt service coverage of 1.38:1. More specifically, that the Authority will have $1.38 in revenue for each dollar needed for the bonds' repayment. 1.38 debt service coverage is considered moderate to good debt service coverage (DSC).

Neither statement was true. The only way to pay the bonds was to frequently refinance them, because the utility often had less than one-to-one debt service coverage. In other words, they had less than one dollar for each dollar in payments due.

Unbelievably, the rating agencies gave the bonds a good rating. These ratings were incomprehensible! In addition to inadequate DSC (Under 1 to 1), PREPA has a negative net worth and 1.7 billion dollars in unfunded pension obligations. By PREPA's own admission they were meeting their bond payments through the use of short- term debt, not revenues. Yet, this was all ignored by the credit rating agencies.

The report also stated;

What I have seen in these financials has all the makings of a Ponzi scheme.

The audit summary: It is clear to me from my experience that I have reviewed the financials of a criminal enterprise. The company made misleading and false statements that resulted in the sale of $673,000,000 in non-performing bonds to the general public. It would be my conclusion that this bond issuance not be supported and that the utility should be put under receivership.

What I have seen indicates the probable commission of a series of felonies, and I would normally have been required to report what I have found to the appropriate authorities for further investigation.

The audit could not be any clearer. I felt that once the congressmen and senators saw this, they would do something. Even the SEC could not deny the fraud. They must act right? But just the opposite happened.

The legislation in congress to amend the Dodd Frank Act picked up steam and moved very quickly. The relationship with my SEC contact, the Senior Attorney in charge of this investigation, changed. All of a sudden, I felt as if her job was to manage me and not help me. It was a noticeable change and left me with the impression she was probably part of the problem and not a possible solution. Another career government employee more interested in her career then the American people. It was at this point I started to realize there was no one in the SEC with the character and courage to make a difference. The SEC would protect the status quo.

SAMPLE BOND ISSUE

NEW ISSUE - BOOK-ENTRY ONLY

**RATINGS
(see RATINGS herein):
S&P: BBB
Moodys Baa3
Fitch BBB-**

$673,145,000

PUERTO RICO ELECTRIC
POWER AUTHORITY

Power Revenue Bonds, Series 2013A

The Power Revenue Bonds, Series 2013A (the "Bonds") of Puerto Rico Electric Power Authority (the " Authority") are being issued pursuant to a Trust Agreement, dated as of January 1, 1974, as amended, between the Authority and U.S. Bank National Association,

New York, New York, successor trustee (the "Trust Agreement"). The Bonds, the outstanding bonds previously issued under the Trust Agreement, and any additional bonds that the Authority may from time to time issue under the Trust Agreement, are payable solely from the Net Revenues (as described herein) of the Authority's electric generation, transmission and distribution system.

The Bonds will have the following characteristics:

- The Bonds will be dated their date of delivery.

- The Bonds will be registered under the book-entry only system of The Depository Trust Company ("DTC"). Purchasers of the Bonds will not receive definitive Bonds.

- Interest on the Bonds will be payable on January 1, 2014 and on each January 1 and July 1 thereafter.

- The Bonds will be subject to redemption, commencing on July 1, 2023, as described herein. See *Mandatory Redemption* and *Optional Redemption* under DESCRIPTION OF THE BONDS for more information.

- The inside cover page contains the maturity schedule, interest rates and prices or yields of the Bonds.

- In the opinion of Bond Counsel, under the provisions of the Acts of Congress now in force, (i) subject to continuing compliance with certain tax covenants, interest on the Bonds will not be ineluctable in gross income for federal income tax purposes and (ii) the Bonds and interest thereon will be exempt from state, Commonwealth of Puerto Rico and local income taxation under existing law. However, see TAX MATTERS herein for a description of alternative minimum tax consequences with respect to interest on the Bonds and other tax considerations.

• The Authority expects that the Bonds will be available for delivery through DTC on or about August 21, 2013.

• The issuance of the Bonds and the purchase of the Bonds by the Underwriters are subject to the approval of legality by Sidley Austin LLP, New York, New York, Bond Counsel, and certain other conditions. Fiddler Gonzalez & Rodriguez, P.S.C., San Juan, Puerto Rico, will pass upon certain legal matters for the Underwriters.

The Bonds are not a debt or obligation of the Commonwealth of Puerto Rico or any of its municipalities or political subdivisions, other than the Authority, and neither the Commonwealth of Puerto Rico nor any of its municipalities or political subdivisions, other than the Authority, shall be liable for the payment of the principal of or interest on the Bonds.

Morgan Stanley, Wells Fargo Securities, Citigroup JP Morgan, B of A Merrill Lynch, Barclays Mesirow, Firstbank PR Services, Goldman Sachs & Company, Jeffries Financial Inc., Oriental Financial Services, Popular Securities, Ramirez & Co, Inc., RBC Capital Markets, Santander Securities, Scotia MSD, UBS FS Puerto Rico

On this specific bond offering, Morgan Stanley, Wells Fargo Securities, Citigroup and J.P. Morgan are the "big dogs." The other banks listed played a lesser role. What is most shocking: according to testimony, they all knowingly participated in Securities Fraud.

Do you recall the Puerto Rico Senate Hearings? Here is some of the testimony given:

"This goes to show that the financial intermediaries (banks) and the institutional holders (also banks), despite being fully aware of PREPA's fiscal situation, had no qualms with unjustly enriching themselves and with having the consequences of their negligent acts be paid for by the people of Puerto Rico.

Meanwhile, and fully aware that PREPA did not have the resources to repay the debt, investment firms, banks, credit houses, consulting engineers, and PREPA itself failed to bring out into public light the need to make adjustments to the rates charged by PREPA."

This sounds like a confession to me. The FBI told me that the Puerto Rico Senate was not credible and therefore this confession wasn't useful. Really?

Best of all was the testimony that all participants (Rating Agencies and the Banks) knew this was one big "Ponzi scheme".

The Senate Report said; "Investors allowed PREPA to issue bonds, then PREPA borrowed from private banks to pay the bond's interest; then, borrowed from the Government Development Bank (from herein "GBD") to pay back the private bank loans, and the GDB, in turn, issued more bonds to refinance all. Afterwards, PREPA would issue a new debt to pay GBD's outstanding interests, pay principal and prepay the new bonds' interests for several years – a cycle that is repeated over and over-and in which the original debt is never paid. This practice could constitute a fraud scheme for which the federal agencies that regulate financial instruments and the

Security Exchange Commission could take action against and/or pursue civil suits against These institutions."

We now have the government of Puerto Rico and PREPA executives admitting they ran a Ponzi scheme and that the Securities and Exchange Commission should get involved.

I reported this to the Securities and Exchange Commission and to the best of my knowledge, no action was taken.

I reported this to the FBI, and they said no criminal acts have been committed!

The FBI Anti-Trust Division claims the following:

"The mission of the Antitrust Division is to promote economic competition through enforcing and providing guidance on antitrust laws and principals. The goal of antitrust laws is to protect economic freedom and opportunity by promoting free and fair competition in the marketplace.

Competition in a free market, benefits American consumers through lower prices, better quality and greater choice. Competition provides businesses the opportunity to compete on price and quality, in an open market and on a level playing field, unhampered by anticompetitive restraints. Competition also tests and hardens American companies at home, the better to succeed abroad.

Federal antitrust laws apply to virtually all industries and to every level of business, including manufacturing, transportation, distribution, and marketing. They prohibit a variety of practices that restrain trade, such as price-fixing conspiracies, corporate mergers likely to reduce the competitive vigor of a particular markets, and predatory acts designed to achieve or maintain monopoly power."

When the three credit rating agencies all assigned the "same ratings" allegedly fraudulently, did they or did they not provide a price fixing strategy to these bonds? Was it a predatory act? According the FBI's anti-trust division, it was neither!

Let's talk about the banks. Unfortunately for them, I am an "insider." I worked for Wells Fargo Bank for fifteen years and other banks for another ten years. How could these experts miss the fact that these bonds had insufficient income to make bond payments, insufficient collateral to repay the loans and that PREPA and many others had a terrible management history? How could the experts miss that the banks had a terrible reputation if you were to look at their regulatory and legal history? They can't! It would be impossible to miss any of that, let alone all of that. There are numerous checklists, individual bank officers who approve the offering, additional bank officers that check the work of the approving officer and committees and auditors that review it all. It is self-evident that all these banks knowingly committed alleged fraud.

Did the banks collude with each other to make this all happen? Did the credit rating agencies do the same? What are the odds that there was no collusion?

The Puerto Rico Senate Report stated clearly that all three credit rating agencies -- Moodys, Fitch and S&P -- knew they were bankrupt. But all three credit rating agencies offered to sell Puerto Rico fraudulent bond ratings. Were they working together? What are the odds that all three credit rating agencies and dozens of banks, independently and accidently came to all the same wrong conclusions? How could the agencies and banks that require analyses to look at literally hundreds of individual items, all get the same hundreds of items wrong?

If you were to break this down to a mathematical calculation (a probability formula) you would have to take hundreds of items times dozens of banks and credit rating agencies and you would likely get a result that looks like 10 squared by 10 squared almost to infinity. You get my point! Even if you were to get hit by lighting and win the lottery on the same day, you would not come close. They colluded. Yet the SEC, FBI and U.S Attorneys think otherwise!

The three rating agencies control eighty-five to ninety percent of their markets. They are all apparently issuing these alleged fraudulent ratings on the same trillions in bonds. Coincidence? The major Wall Street banks all decided to sell these alleged fraudulent bonds to people like you. Another coincidence?

Below are some newspaper articles commenting on just this;

Bankers from America's largest Banks still haven't been held responsible for financial crash

This article was reprinted with permission from The Center for Public Integrity. and is available at publicintegrity.org.

"In the seven years since the financial crisis, none of the top executives at the giant Wall Street banks that fueled and profited from the housing bubble have been personally held to account. These bankers, who were the architects and major traders in mortgage-backed securities, have been largely immune to criminal charges and personal liability even as their institutions have admitted wrongdoing and paid billions in fines and restitution."

"A review by the Center for Public Integrity of the enforcement actions and civil lawsuits filed by the Justice Department, Federal Deposit Insurance Corp. and Securities and Exchange Commission reveals that these agencies have been far more likely to charge or sue individuals who work at small and medium sized banks, and foreign financial firms, than those that work at domestic banking giants such as J.P. Morgan Chase & Co. or Citigroup".

A Frontline investigation and follow-up article claimed a UBS Insider said it was the Banks that fueled the financial crisis in Puerto Rico

The report went on to say that If the banks would have been more diligent, if they limited Puerto Rico to only borrowings they could afford, we would not be in this position today.

According to an article in the International Business Times, Puerto Rico's Bond Debt Risk was passed on to the Bond Owners!

The article suggested that the banks enabled Puerto Rico's borrowing to collect billions in fees.

I filed multiple complaints with the FBI's Anti-Trust Division. On the first three complaints, they claimed no laws were broken. On the fourth complaint, they said this belongs in their criminal division and I should contact that group. Our tax dollars at work folks... Our great protectors?

Earlier, I said I purposely sent United States Postal Service trackable letters to the board of directors and executives at the big three credit rating agencies. I did that so the board members and executives could not deny knowing about all of this and so they could be criminally charged. I did something similar with Wells Fargo, Citibank and B of A. Here is one of their responses:

Wealth Brokerage Services
MAC H0005-087
One North Jefferson Avenue
St. Louis, MO 63103

May 3, 2018

Richard R. Lawless
30279 Redding Avenue
Murrieta, CA 92563

Subject: Wells Fargo Advisors ("WFA") – Brokerage

Dear Richard Lawless:

I am writing in response to your recent correspondence dated April 12, 2018 and addressed to Elizabeth A. Duke, Chairman, Wells Fargo & Company.

Mr. Lawless, while you write in your letter of serious concerns involving Wells' involvement in the underwriting of debt securities issued by the Commonwealth of Puerto Rico, and you suggest that credit-rating agency Moody's Investors Service failed in its role in the issuance of these municipal bonds, this letter also confirms certain additional facts which you shared with me during our telephone conversation of April 26, 2018.

This note also confirms your verbal representation to me that you neither expect nor seek to receive back any form of response and that you shared with me that your purpose for writing the letter was simply to share the information and resources provided for the general benefit of Wells Fargo.

Mr. Lawless, we appreciate you sharing the information you have offered and, in consideration of your request, will be limiting our written communications to you with this reply.

Nevertheless, should you have any further questions, please contact me at 415-947-1356, Monday through Friday, 8:00 a.m. to 4:00 p.m. Central Time.

Thank you.

Sincerely,

Douglas Neubrand
Case Manager
Complaint Resolutions Group

Together we'll go far

91

As a banker, I realized that every wire transfer sent through our banking system relating to fraudulent bonds would constitute "wire fraud." I believe that the participants could be charged with crimes for each wire transfer sent.

I contacted the Controller of the Currency, one of the many regulators charged with overseeing our banking system. This is what he/she responded with:

Office of the Comptroller of the Currency
February 20,201

Richard Robert Lawless

RE; Case #03122363

Dear Mr. Lawless:

Thank you for your correspondence and bringing this matter to our attention. Your comments and concerns have been forwarded to the appropriate divisions within the OCC.

This information that you provided helps the OCC to ensure that the national banks and federal savings associations operate in a safe and sound manner, provide fair access to financial services, treat customers fairly, and comply with applicable laws and regulations.

No further action is needed on your part at this time. This concludes the process at this time. Thank you for your assistance.

Sincerely,
Customer Assistance Group

The Customer Assistance Group' s consumer complaint process is a service that is provided to customers of national banks and federal savings associations (thrifts). Information provided within this letter is specifically related to an individual consumer complaint and should not be construed as either a legal opinion of the OCC or a supervisory action. If you are not satisfied with the resolution of your complaint, you may wish to consult legal counsel so as to preserve your rights.

Customer Assistance Group, 1301 McKinney Street, Suite 3450, Houston, Texas 77010-9050
Phone: (800) 613-6743, FAX: (713) 336-4301
Internet Address: www.helpwithmybank.gov

Out of a sense of great frustration I sent a letter to every FBI Office in the country. I directed the letter to the 'Special Agent in Charge." In the letter (below) I provided each "Special Agent" with all the evidence discussed in this book. This action would make it possible to identify the leadership with the FBI that knew about this and didn't act.

March 30th, 2018

FBI Offices
26 Federal Plaza, 23rd Floor
New York, NY 10278-0004
Attention: William F. Sweeney, Jr.- Special Agent in Charge

Dear Mr. Sweeney,

It appears that there is a small group within the Department of Justice who have taken it upon themselves to determine who will be investigated and who will not. I am writing you in the hopes that you are not one of those bad actors.

When our company lost everything in the 70 billion-dollar Puerto Rico bond default, we initiated a forensic investigation to find out the causes, to avoid it happening in the future. The investigation turned up massive corruption at the big three, credit rating agencies, Moody's, S&P Global and Fitch. It appears that the three big credit agencies simply fabricated good credit ratings for "a fee" allowing the Puerto Rico Municipalities to borrow the 70 billion-dollars they defaulted on. It is also clear that the Board of Directors and Executives at each of the companies had full knowledge of this.

Puerto Rico Bonds are triple tax free and were mainly purchased by retired American's throughout all 50 States. States like Florida and NY had resident losses of over 2 billion-dollars while smaller States experienced losses in the tens of millions.

Below is a list of links that will allow you to quickly understand this and review the overwhelming amounts of evidence available.

I hope you will act on this criminal complaint.

Sincerely,

Richard R. Lawless

Richard R. Lawless

Commercial Solar Power, Inc. – CEO

Like the credit rating agencies and the banks, we can put names to those responsible within the FBI and hold them accountable. The following FBI employees received this information and to the best of my knowledge, did nothing:

FBI Offices 200 McCarty Avenue Albany, NY 12209 Attention: Vadim Thomas – Special Agent in Charge	

FBI Offices 101 East Sixth Avenue Anchorage, AK 99501 Attention: Marlin L. Ritzman – Special Agent in Charge	FBI Offices 4200 Luecking Park Avenue NE Albuquerque, NM 87107 Attention: Terry Wade – Special Agent in Charge
FBI Offices 3000 Flowers Road S Atlanta, GA 30341 Attention: David J. LeValley – Special Agent in Charge	FBI Offices 2600 Lord Baltimore Drive Baltimore, MD 21244 Attention: Gordon B. Johnson – Special Agent in Charge
FBI Offices 1000 18th Street North Birmingham, AL 35203 Attention: Johnnie Sharp, Jr. – Special Agent in Charge	FBI Offices 1000 18th Street North Birmingham, AL 35203 Attention: Johnnie Sharp, Jr. – Special Agent in Charge
FBI Offices 201 Maple Street Chelsea, MA 02150 Attention: Harold H. Shaw – Special Agent in Charge	FBI Offices One FBI Plaza Buffalo, NY 14202 Attention: Adam S. Cohen – Special Agent in Charge
FBI Offices 7915 Microsoft Way Charlotte, NC 28273 Attention: John A. Strong – Special Agent in Charge	FBI Offices 2111 W. Roosevelt Road Chicago, IL 60608 Attention: Jeffrey S. Sallet – Special Agent in Charge
FBI Offices 2012 Ronald Reagan Drive Cincinnati, OH 45236 Attention: Angela L. Byers - Special Agent in Charge	FBI Offices 1501 Lakeside Avenue Cleveland, OH 44114 Attention: Stephen D. Anthony - Special Agent in Charge

FBI Offices 151 Westpark Boulevard Columbia, SC 29210-3857 Attention: Alphonso Jody Norris - Special Agent in Charge	FBI Offices One Justice Way Dallas, TX 75220 Attention: Eric Jackson - Special Agent in Charge
FBI Offices 8000 East 36th Avenue Denver, CO 80238 Attention: Calvin A. Shivers - Special Agent in Charge	FBI Offices El Paso Federal Justice Center 660 South Mesa Hills Drive El Paso, TX 79912 Attention: Emmerson Buie, Jr. - Special Agent in Charge
FBI Offices 91-1300 Enterprise Street Kapolei, HI 96707 Attention: Sean Kaul - Special Agent in Charge FBI Offices 8825 Nelson B Klein Pkwy Indianapolis, IN 46250 Attention: Grant Mendenhall - Special Agent in Charge	FBI Offices 1 Justice Park Drive Houston, TX 77092 Attention: Perrye K. Turner - Special Agent in Charge FBI Offices 1220 Echelon Parkway Jackson, MS 39213 Attention: Christopher Freeze - Special Agent in Charge
FBI Offices 1300 Summit Street Kansas City, MO 64105 Attention: Darrin E. Jones - Special Agent in Charge	FBI Offices 1501 Dowell Springs Boulevard Knoxville, TN 37909 Attention: Renae M. McDermott - Special Agent in Charge
FBI Offices 1787 West Lake Mead Boulevard Las Vegas, NV 89106-2135 Attention: Aaron C. Rouse - Special Agent in Charge	FBI Offices 24 Shackleford West Boulevard Little Rock, AR 72211-3755 Attention: Diane Upchurch - Special Agent in Charge

FBI Offices 11000 Wilshire Boulevard Suite 1700 Los Angeles, CA 90024 Attention: Paul D. Delacourt - Special Agent in Charge	FBI Offices 12401 Sycamore Station Place Louisville, KY 40299-6198 Attention: Amy S. Hess - Special Agent in Charge
FBI Offices 225 North Humphreys Boulevard Suite 3000 Memphis, TN 38120 Attention: Michael Gavin - Special Agent in Charge	FBI Offices 2030 SW 145th Avenue Miramar, FL 33027 Attention: Robert Lasky - Special Agent in Charge
FBI Offices 3600 S. Lake Drive St. Francis, WI 53235 Attention: R. Justin Tolomeo - Special Agent in Charge	FBI Offices 1501 Freeway Boulevard Brooklyn Center, MN 55430 Attention: Robert C. Bone, II - Special Agent in Charge
FBI Offices 200 North Royal Street Mobile, AL 36602 Attention: James E. Jewell - Special Agent in Charge	FBI Offices 600 State Street New Haven, CT 06511 Attention: Patricia M. Ferrick - Special Agent in Charge
FBI Offices 2901 Leon C. Simon Boulevard New Orleans, LA 70126 Attention: Eric J. Rommal - Special Agent in Charge	FBI Offices 26 Federal Plaza, 23rd Floor New York, NY 10278-0004 Attention: William F. Sweeney, Jr. - Special Agent in Charge

FBI Offices Claremont Tower 11 Centre Place Newark, NJ 07102 Attention: Bradley W. Cohen - Special Agent in Charge	FBI Offices 509 Resource Row Chesapeake, VA 23320 Attention: Martin Culbreth - Special Agent in Charge
FBI Offices 3301 West Memorial Road Oklahoma City, OK 73134-7098 Attention: Kathryn Peterson - Special Agent in Charge	FBI Offices 4411 South 121st Court Omaha, NE 68137-2112 Attention: Randall C. Thysse - Special Agent in Charge
FBI Offices William J. Green, Jr. Building 600 Arch Street, 8th Floor Philadelphia, PA 19106 Attention: Michael Harpster - Special Agent in Charge	FBI Offices 21711 N. 7th Street Phoenix, AZ 85024 Attention: Michael DeLeon - Special Agent in Charge
FBI Offices 3311 East Carson Street Pittsburgh, PA 15203 Attention: Robert Johnson - Special Agent in Charge	FBI Offices 9109 NE Cascades Parkway Portland, OR 97220 Attention: Loren 'Renn' Cannon - Special Agent in Charge
FBI Offices 1970 East Parham Road Richmond, VA 23228 Attention: Adam S. Lee - Special Agent in Charge	FBI Offices 2001 Freedom Way Roseville, CA 95678 Attention: Sean Ragan - Special Agent in Charge

FBI Offices 5425 West Amelia Earhart Drive Salt Lake City, UT 84116 Attention: Eric Barnhart - Special Agent in Charge	FBI Offices 5740 University Heights Blvd. San Antonio, TX 78249 Attention: Christopher Combs - Special Agent in Charge
FBI Offices 10385 Vista Sorrento Parkway San Diego, CA 92121 Attention: John A. Brown - Special Agent in Charge	FBI Offices 450 Golden Gate Avenue, 13th Floor San Francisco, CA 94102-9523 Attention: John F. Bennett - Special Agent in Charge
FBI Offices 1110 3rd Avenue Seattle, WA 98101-2904 Attention: Jay S. Tabb, Jr.- Special Agent in Charge	FBI Offices 900 East Linton Avenue Springfield, IL 62703 Attention: Sean Cox - Special Agent in Charge
FBI Offices 2222 Market Street St. Louis, MO 63103 Attention: Richard Quinn - Special Agent in Charge	FBI Offices 5525 West Gray Street Tampa, FL 33609 Attention: Eric Sporre - Special Agent in Charge
FBI Offices 601 4th Street NW Washington, DC 20535 Attention: Andrew Vale - Special Agent in Charge	

I received no responses from any of the FBI offices. No action was taken that I was aware of. It really is an indication, a commentary, on how broke The Department of Justice is. Everyone in charge appears to have been appointed with the understanding that certain criminal activities are to be overlooked. Tens of billions of dollars, tens of millions of victims. It really is amazing how the leaders of this criminal enterprise were able to usurp the mission of the FBI and U.S Attorney Offices to accommodate their alleged criminal activity. If you had any questions about the character and motives of the Department of Justice, this final communication with the Department of Justice, Inspector General, should settle all of that.

Inspector General (IG) Michael Horowitz's works for the Department of Justice. One of his jobs is to address possible corruption and maleficence within the FBI. During Michael Horowitz's tenor, there appears to have been significant corruption within the Department of Justice and little to no meaningful action by his office.

I forwarded the Inspector General all the evidence on the fraudulent bonds and information relating to the alleged payoffs of the FBI and U.S. Attorney's in Puerto Rico and elsewhere. You have read much about what has taken place. Even if you are the world's biggest skeptic, it would be worthy of further investigation. Take a look at his response:

U.S. Department of Justice
Office of Inspector General
Investigations Division

April 30, 2018

Richard Lawless
Commercial Solar Power, Inc.

Dear Mr. Lawless:

Thank you for your correspondence dated March 23, 2018. The U.S. Department of Justice (DOJ), Office of the Inspector General, investigates allegations of misconduct by employees and contractors of DOJ, as well as waste, fraud and abuse affecting DOJ programs or operations.

We have thoroughly reviewed the material and concluded that the issues raised do not warrant an investigation by our Office. Accordingly, we will take no further action regarding your correspondence and consider the matter closed.

Of course, if you have new information that involves other allegations or issues regarding DOJ employees, contractors, programs or operations, please feel free to submit that information to us.

Thank you for giving us the opportunity to review your concerns.

Sincerely,
Office of the Inspector General Investigations Division

I was so frustrated by this letter, I penned another article regarding this response, and it appeared in a number of papers.

In the face of overwhelming evidence, the U.S. Attorney's Office was somehow able to clear itself!

This article was reprinted with permission from Caribbean News Now and is available at caribbeannewsnow.com

This is a story about the largest, longest running, government created, government protected, organized criminal enterprise in American history and if it were not for the financial collapse of Puerto Rico, no one would ever know.

When Puerto Rico started to experience financial difficulties in 2012, people started to ask questions. The criminality of it all wasn't fully clear until the island defaulted on its $70 billion dollars in municipal bonds, the largest default in American history.

This journey started for me simply enough. I was asking myself how the largest government owned public utility in North American, the Puerto

Rico Electric Power Authority (PREPA), could have a BBB+ credit rating one day and be bankrupt the next day.

As I started to investigate PREPA, it became clear that the Utility has been billing its customers for high grade crude oil but purchasing the lowest grades of heavily polluting crude oil. As the largest utility in North America that burns oil for electricity, PREPA spends about $3 billion dollars a year in oil purchases.

The lower quality oil is 54% cheaper than what PREPA has been billing their customers for. 54% of $3 billion dollars each year is unaccounted for, and this has been going on for over a decade. Some very simple math has you asking where the $15 billion dollars has gone?

Well, we know the answers with great certainty. The money has been laundered in countries like Venezuela and Honduras. Wire transfers are then sent back to our favorite politicians and law enforcement personnel within the Department of Justice to make sure this can continue unabated.

Believe it or not, this is only the tip of the iceberg in criminal activities that have been taking place in Puerto Rico for over a decade.

Further investigation shows that PREPA and most other Puerto Rico Municipalities have all been technically bankrupt since 2010. PREPA and others however have been able to purchase fabricated credit ratings from Moody's, Fitch and S&P Global, allowing them to float worthless municipal bonds to America's senior citizens, the primary buyers of tax-free bonds.

When Puerto Rico defaulted on $70 billion dollars in bonds these senior citizens rushed to sell the bonds before they were completely worthless and lost $34 billion dollars. The impact was felt across the Country, $3 billion in Florida, over $2 billion in New York and California etc. I could go on and talk about the missing billions in bond proceeds, fabricated equipment and maintenance expenses, all adding up to tens of billions of dollars.

Over the past three to four years, dozens of Puerto Rico politicians, utility customers, municipal employees, government vendors, bond holders and U.S. intelligence officials have logged complaints with the Department of Justice, more specially, with the FBI, including myself.

Before I share the FBI's response, let me share just <u>some</u> of the evidence that has been given to the FBI.

Out of a sense of frustration with the Department of Justice's inaction, a private RICO lawsuit was filed on 2-24-15. If you are unfamiliar with RICO it stands for Racketeer Influenced and Corrupt Organizations Act. It is a piece of legislation designed by the Government to break up Mafia (organized Crime) activities. It is very rare that the courts will allow private individuals to use it, especially against the government.

Case 3:15 – cv-01167-JAG Document 1 Filed 2-24-15 Page 1 of 80

UNITED STATES DISTRICT COURT
DISTRICT OF PUERTO RICO

The lawsuit spells out many of the participants in the oil fraud and how they did it. The filed documents even include offshore bank account numbers used for the money laundering. Many government officials have challenged the lawsuit, but it has repeatedly been upheld by the courts.

In April of 2016 various newspapers reported that a court upheld a RICO lawsuit against PREPA

On June 24, 2015, the government of Puerto Rico issued a 23-page legislative report, no less than a detailed confession, which outlines how government officials in Puerto Rico conspired with Wall Street firms to commit $70 billion dollars in financial fraud. This report was given to the FBI by the Puerto Rico Senate Committee along with tons of supporting evidence.

COMMONWEATH OF PUERTO RICO
17th Legislative Assembly   5th Ordinary Session
HOUSE OF REPRESENATIVES
FINAL REPORT
H.R 1049

The above report recapped testimony where the KPMG Lead Auditor for PREPA stated that the three rating agencies, Moodys, Fitch and S&P Global along with Citibank, Wells Fargo and B of A all knew that PREPA has been technically bankrupt since 2010 but for the right fee's these institutions could get the bonds issued and sold. The Senate Committee also interviewed Government Employees involved with the oil fraud and money laundering.

In March of 2016 I penned an article about our preliminary findings regarding the corruption and theft being uncovered in Puerto Rico. I then received a call from someone claiming to be an intelligence official working the Caribbean Basin. This (likely CIA) official explained to me that they have been tracking large wire transfers off the island for over a decade.

Interest from our intelligence agencies peaked when they started tracking calls from Puerto Rico government officials to Hugo Chavez in Venezuela. At that point, the Intelligence officials started recording phone conversations. It didn't take long to understand that large sums of money for oil purchases were being laundered and wired back to politician's family members and other government officials. This source went on to say that they shared this information with the Puerto Rico FBI Office, but the FBI never acted on it. It was not until sometime later that it was disclosed on one of the recorded phone conversations that DOJ officials and/or their family members were getting payoffs.

I wrote about this conversation in an April article.

Wed, Apr 6th, 2016
Personal conflicts obstruct FBI investigation into Puerto Rico fraud
This article was reprinted with permission from Caribbean News
Now and is available at caribbeannewsnow.com

*"It has also been alleged that law enforcement authorities in Puerto
Rico stood by and did nothing for a number of years, which assertion was
substantiated by a phone call originating in Alexandria, Virginia, that
Lawless said he received some months ago from a man stating that he
worked for the US government, which Lawless said he inferred was the
Central Intelligence Agency (CIA).*

*Lawless was told that Puerto Rico came on the agency's radar years ago
because the head of the PREPA fuel purchase office started making direct
calls to the then president of Venezuela, Hugo Chavez. They listened in and
found out that PREPA was buying sludge oil from Venezuela and billing
the utility for high grade oil. The difference in value, hundreds of millions
per year (today it would be $700 million a year and is said to be still going
on) was allegedly kicked back to the fuel office manager and distributed to
politicians and government officials on the island.*

*As the unnamed government agency continued to listen in on the calls,
the caller claimed it became clear that family members of Puerto Rico FBI
agents and family members in the Puerto Rico US Attorney's office were
receiving payments based on these "kickbacks."*

*"He went on to tell me that the Puerto Rico FBI and US Attorney will
do nothing about the oil kickback scheme and the bond rating scheme because they were participating in it. He went on to suggest that because of the
separation laws regarding CIA activities and US national law enforcement
that there was not much he could do," Lawless said."*

Shortly after that article appears, the editor at the Caribbean News
Now, News Agency used his resources to speak with a completely

unrelated Intelligence official within the United States Intelligence Community and wrote the following:

Caribbean News Now!
April 2016
This article was reprinted with permission from Caribbean News Now and is available at caribbeannewsnow.com

"On Monday, a senior source in a related US government agency, speaking to Caribbean News Now on condition of anonymity, confirmed almost word for word what Lawless had apparently been told.

In the meantime, a voice message left for Lawless by someone said to be calling from the San Juan FBI office in response to complaints made by Lawless to members of congress, claimed that the matter was being "looked at" to determine whether or not the circumstances cross the boundary from civil fraud to a criminal offence."

Let's recap just the small amount of evidence that I have shared with you in this article.

A very rare private RICO lawsuit was filed and repeatedly upheld by the courts. The lawsuits spell out a massive conspiracy in which billions were stolen.

The Puerto Rico Senate held special hearings in which the Government itself admitted to floating completely fraudulent Municipal Bonds which they later defaulted on. This was done with the cooperation and participation of the three largest Wall Street credit rating agencies along with Citibank, Wells Fargo and B of A. The Committee also reported on the oil scam that was skimming billions. We have two independent sources that have confirmed that massive wire transfers have been leaving the island of Puerto Rico. Wire transfers that are later redistributed to well know politicians, DOJ employees and their family members.

I reported all this to the Inspector General at the Department of Justice and received the following response.

April 30, 2018

"We have thoroughly reviewed the material and concluded that the issues raised do not warrant an investigation by our Office. Accordingly, we will take no further action regarding your correspondence and consider this matter closed."

The article below is shocking! Rod Rosenstein, the Deputy Attorney General not only apparently refuses to prosecute big Wall Street firms and others, but he is promoting policies to reduce fines for those who commit these financial felonies! A DOJ employee speaking at a banker's conference promoting legislative changes to help Wall Street? You can't make this up!

Rod Rosenstein signals era of big corporate penalties is ending
This article was reprinted with permission from Bloomberg News and is available at bloomberg.com

Deputy Attorney General Rod Rosenstein thinks some companies are overpaying for their crimes, and he wants that to stop.

Rosenstein, in a speech Wednesday in New York, said companies in highly regulated industries such as banking were too often assessed multiple fines by various agencies and governments for the same misconduct. While large fines are sometimes warranted, Rosenstein said, they shouldn't be the result of "piling on" by several enforcement authorities.

Such an approach "can deprive a company of the benefits of certainty and finality ordinarily available through a full and final settlement," Rosenstein told a roomful of white-collar lawyers and prosecutors attending a New York City Bar Association conference.

"We need to consider the impact on innocent employees, customers and investors who seek to resolve problems and move on," he said. "We need to think about whether devoting resources to additional enforcement against an old scheme is more valuable than fighting a new one."

Financial penalties

Rosenstein, whose oversight of the special counsel's investigation of possible ties between the Trump presidential campaign and Russia has drawn public rebukes from the president, announced a new policy that urges federal prosecutors to work more closely with their counterparts in other enforcement agencies when determining financial penalties. Under the policy, fines and forfeitures paid to other agencies may be considered when deciding Justice Department penalties.

In the speech, Rosenstein questioned whether large corporate fines actually prevent individuals at other firms from committing crimes.

"Corporate settlements do not necessarily directly deter individual wrongdoers," Rosenstein said. "They may do so indirectly, by incentivizing companies to develop and enforce internal compliance programs. But at the level of each individual decision-maker, the deterrent effect of a potential corporate penalty is muted and diffused."

Former federal prosecutors said much of what Rosenstein announced on Wednesday was already being practiced at the department. In recent years, companies that resolved investigations for violations of the Foreign Corrupt Practices Act, for example, received credit from the Justice Department and the Securities and Exchange Commission for penalties paid to other jurisdictions.

In phone conversations with numerous FBI Officials I was told that the FBI officials stated they do not believe any laws were broken and I would be better served if I and others treated this as a civil matter. In other words, we could take these folks to court, but the FBI will not investigate or prosecute anyone. According to the FBI none of these laws were broken:

Securities Act of 1933
Securities Exchange Act of 1934
Trust Indenture Act of 1939
Investment Company Act of 1940
Investment Advisers Act of 1940
Sarbanes-Oxley Act of 2002
Dodd-Frank Wall Street Reform and Consumer Protection Act of 2010
Bank Fraud (18 U.S.C. § 1344[2])
Bankruptcy Fraud (18 U.S.C. § 157[3])
Computer Fraud (18 U.S.C. § 1030[5])
Mail and Wire Fraud (18 U.S.C. § 1343[8])
Mass Marketing Fraud
Securities Fraud (18 U.S.C. § 1348[9])
Tax Fraud (26 U.S.C. § 7201[10], et seq.)

Our politicians hold Americans in such low regard and with such disdain that little effort was made to hide much of the criminal activity coming out of Washington. And why not? These politicians control all levers of power, including our Justice System.

Unfortunately, there is so much available evidence that it was impossible to be certain that our leading politicians would get away with this again. To prevent anyone from taking action against those responsible, our politicians did the following:

The Puerto Rico Financial Crisis Management was handed off to former Treasury Secretary Lew, who by the way, was the Chief Operating Officer at Citibank while Citibank was knowingly selling Puerto Rico's fraudulent bonds. Secretary Lew initially lobbied Congress for a full taxpayer bailout ("let's make this problem go away" was the mantra). The Secretary was unsuccessful in his efforts. Working with other well-known politicians who are likely participating in this criminal enterprise, the new team came up with legislation that would reverse decades of case law (legal protections for the victims), delay or prevent lawsuits from victims and hand over control to a small group of government-appointed individuals, Individuals who openly participated in the original crimes. I kid you not!

House of Representative's Bill - H.R 4900 – April 12ᵗʰ, 2016

The new legislation known as "<u>PROMESA</u>" says the following:

The Oversight Board shall consist of 7 members appointed by the President who meet the qualifications described in subsection (e), except that the Oversight Board may take any action under this Act (or any amendments made by this Act) at any time after the President has appointed 3 of its members.

The Oversight Board, its members, and its employees may not be liable for any obligation of or claim against the Oversight Board or its members or employees or the territorial government resulting from actions taken to carry out this Act.

There shall be no jurisdiction in any United States district court to review challenges to the Oversight Board's certification determinations under this Act.

AUTOMATIC STAY UPON ENACTMENT. (No civil Lawsuits) For a Time to be Specified by the appointed Board.

Even before this Bill was passed politician's like Chuck Schumer, Elizabeth Warren, Richard Blumenthal and Harry Reed moved quickly to cash in. They were among the first to propose a ban on civil lawsuits relating to the Puerto Rico financial meltdown. If you follow the money, it paid off terrifically for all four of them but not so well for millions of honest Americans.

Yes, it is the same Chuck Schumer who went to great lengths to have his man, Preet Bharara, appointed as the New York U.S. Attorney General. During the 2008 financial crisis Preet Bharara appeared to make sure all the criminal complaints filed during the financial crisis were deemed "dead on arrival" and great sums of money flowed to Mr. Schumer and others for their efforts. See a trend here?

The most stunning action among many politicians was committed by Paul Ryan. Paul Ryan made it known that he was against revoking the legal rights of the victims who were impacted by the financial fraud taking place in Puerto Rico. It was however an election year for Mr. Ryan and after meeting with Secretary Lew and receiving sudden but material financial support from Wall Street, Paul Ryan changed his position and pushed the bill through. Now at least he can afford to retire. Unfortunately, retirement is not possible for the victims he threw under the bus with this legislation.

The corruption is so pervasive and so common a second-year law student could seek and win convictions against dozens of politicians, dozens of Wall Street Executives and dozens of DOJ employees.

Unfortunately, the system is rigged, and the likelihood of any prosecutions is minimal.

Over the past three years I have had an opportunity to speak with a number of FBI field agents. As a group, they all seem to pretty well aware of this criminal activity. When I push them on it, I almost always heard the same things. "This will never be allowed to go forward! Even if the FBI were to investigate (throwing their jobs and pensions at risk), the U.S. Attorney's Office will present a million disingenuous reasons why they will never prosecute the case."

As before, I wanted to make sure the leadership in the U.S. Attorney's Office could be held accountable at a later date. I sent the following letter to the entire leadership team via tracked mail.

April 2, 2018

United States Attorney's Office
555 4th Street, NW
Washington, DC 20530
Attention: Jessie K. Liu - United States Attorney

Dear Ms. Liu,

It appears that there is a small group within the Department of Justice who have taken it upon themselves to determine who will be investigated and prosecuted and who will not. I am writing you in the hopes that you are not one of those bad actors.

When our company lost everything in the 70 billion-dollar Puerto Rico bond default, we initiated a forensic investigation to find out the causes, to avoid it happening in the future. The investigation turned up massive corruption at the big three, credit rating agencies, Moody's, S&P Global and Fitch. It appears that the three big credit agencies simply fabricated good credit ratings for a fee allowing the Puerto Rico Municipalities to borrow the 70 billion-dollars they defaulted on. It is also clear that the Board of Directors and Executives at each of the companies had full knowledge of this.

Puerto Rico Bonds are triple tax free and were mainly purchased by retired American's throughout all 50 states. States like Florida and NY had resident losses of over 2 billion-dollars while smaller states experienced losses in the tens of millions. Below is a list of links that will allow you to quickly understand this and review the overwhelming amounts of evidence available.

I hope you will act on this criminal complaint.

Sincerely,

Richard R. Lawless

Richard R. Lawless

Commercial Solar Power, Inc.

I received about a dozen form letter responses. They all claimed the U.S. Attorney prosecutes and does not investigate. If the FBI were to bring them something, they would look at it.

> *Although most criminal complaints relating to the 2008 financial crisis, the Detroit Bankruptcy and the Puerto Rico bankruptcy were killed by the FBI, some investigations did move forward. The U.S. Attorney's offices, to the best of my knowledge, declined to prosecute most of them.*

Here is a list of the U.S. Attorney Offices Leadership. They were all given this evidence and to the best of my knowledge, failed to take any action:

United States Attorney's Office Central District of California 312 North Spring Street Suite 1200 Los Angeles, California 90012 Attention: Nicola T. Hanna - United States Attorney	United States Attorney's Office Robert T. Matsui United States Courthouse 501 I Street, Suite 10-100 Sacramento, CA. 95814 Attention: McGregor Greg Scott - United States Attorney
United States Attorney's Office Federal Courthouse 450 Golden Gate Avenue San Francisco, CA 94102 Attention: Alex G. Tse - United States Attorney	United States Attorney's Office 400 North Tampa Street Suite 3200 Tampa, Fl. 33602 Attention: Maria Chapa Lopez - United States Attorney
United States Attorney's Office New Haven Office Connecticut Financial Center 157 Church Street, Floor 25 New Haven, CT 06510 Attention: John H. Durham - United States Attorney	United States Attorney's Office 1007 Orange Street Suite 700 Wilmington, DE 19801 Attention: David C. Weiss - United States Attorney
United States Attorney's Office 1801 California Street Suite 1600 Denver, CO 80202 Attention: Bob Troyer - United States Attorney	United States Attorney's Office 400 North Tampa Street Suite 3200 Tampa, Fl. 33602 Attention: Maria Chapa Lopez - United States Attorney
United States Attorney's Office 111 North Adams Street 4th Floor U.S. Courthouse Tallahassee, FL 32301 Attention: Christopher P. Canova - United States Attorney	United States Attorney's Office 99 N.E. 4th Street Miami, Fl. 33132 Attention: Benjamin G. Greenberg - United States Attorney

United States Attorney's Office C.B. King United States Courthouse 201 W. Broad Avenue, 2nd Floor Albany, Georgia 31701 Attention: Charles E. Peeler - United States Attorney	United States Attorney's Office Richard B. Russell Federal Building 75 Ted Turner Dr. SW, Suite 600 Atlanta, GA 30303-3309 Attention: Byung J. Bjay Pak – United States Attorney
United States Attorney's Office 22 Barnard Street, Suite 300 Savannah, Georgia 31401 Attention: Bobby L. Christine – United States Attorney	United States Attorney's Office 300 Ala Moana Blvd., #6-100 Honolulu, HI 96850 Attention: Kenji M. Price - United States Attorney
United States Attorney's Office 800 Park Blvd., Suite 600 Boise, ID 83712 Attention: Bart M. Davis - United States Attorney	United States Attorney's Office 318 S. Sixth Street Springfield, IL 62701 Attention: John E. Childress - United States Attorney United States Attorney's Office 219 S. Dearborn St., 5th Floor Chicago, IL 60604 Attention: John R. Lausch, Jr - United States Attorney
United States Attorney's Office 9 Executive Drive Fairview Heights, IL 62208 Attention: Donald S. Boyce - United States Attorney	United States Attorney's Office 5400 Federal Plaza, Suite 1500 Hammond, IN 46320 Attention: Thomas L. Kirsch II - United States Attorney

United States Attorney's Office 10 W Market St, Suite 2100 Indianapolis, IN 46204 Attention: Josh Minkler - United States Attorney	United States Attorney's Office 111 7th Ave, SE Box #1 Cedar Rapids, IA 52401 Attention: Peter E. Deegan, Jr. - United States Attorney
United States Attorney's Office 110 East Court Avenue, Suite # 286 Des Moines, Iowa 50309-2053 Attention: Marc Krickbaum – United States Attorney	United States Attorney's Office 500 State Avenue, Suite 360 Kansas City, Kansas 66101 Attention: Stephen R. McAllister – United States Attorney
United States Attorney's Office 260 W. Vine Street, Suite 300 Lexington, KY 40507-1612 Attention: Robert M. Duncan, Jr. – United States Attorney	United States Attorney's Office 717 West Broadway Louisville, KY 40202 Attention: Russell M. Coleman – United States Attorney
United States Attorney's Office 501 Las Vegas Boulevard South Suite 1100 Las Vegas, NV 89101 Attention: Dayle Elieson – United States Attorney	United States Attorney's Office 650 Poydras Street, Suite 1600 New Orleans, Louisiana 70130 Attention: Duane A. Evans – United States Attorney
United States Attorney's Office 777 Florida Street, Suite 208 Baton Rouge, LA 70801 Attention: Brandon J. Fremin – United States Attorney	United States Attorney's Office 300 Fannin Street, Suite 3201 Shreveport, LA 71101 Attention: David C. Joseph – United States Attorney

United States Attorney's Office 100 Middle Street, East Tower, 6th Floor Portland, ME 04101 Attention: Halsey B. Frank - United States Attorney	United States Attorney's Office 36 S. Charles Street 4th Fl. Baltimore, MD 21201 Attention: Stephen M. Schenning - United States Attorney
United States Attorney's Office 1 Courthouse Way, Suite 9200 Boston, MA 02210 Attention: Andrew Lelling - United States Attorney	United States Attorney's Office 211 W. Fort Street, Suite 2001 Detroit, MI 48226 Attention: Matthew Schneider - United States Attorney
United States Attorney's Office 315 W. Allegan Room 209 Lansing, Michigan 48933 Attention: Andrew Byerly Birge - United States Attorney	
United States Attorney's Office 900 Jefferson Ave Oxford, MS 38655 Attention: William C. Lamar - United States Attorney	United States Attorney's Office 300 S 4th Street Suite 600 Minneapolis, MN 55415 Attention: Gregory G. Brooker - United States Attorney
United States Attorney's Office 501 East Court Street Suite 4.430 Jackson, Mississippi 39201 Attention: Mike Hurst - United States Attorney	United States Attorney's Office 111 S. 10th Street, 20th Floor St. Louis, MO 63102 Attention: Jeffrey B. Jensen - United States Attorney

United States Attorney's Office 400 East 9th Street, room 5510 Kansas City, MO 64106 Attention: Timothy A. Garrison - United States Attorney	United States Attorney's Office 2601 2nd Ave N. Suite 3200 Billings, MT 59101 Attention: Kurt G. Alme - United States Attorney
United States Attorney's Office 1620 Dodge St, Suite 1400 Omaha NE 68102 Attention: Joseph P. Kelly – United States Attorney **Patrick McGee, Assistant U.S.** **Attorney Did Respond**	United States Attorney's Office 53 Pleasant Street, 4th Floor Concord, NH 03301 Attention: Scott W. Murray – United States Attorney
United States Attorney's Office 970 Broad Street, 7th Floor Newark, NJ 07102 Attention: Craig Carpenito – United States Attorney	United States Attorney's Office P.O. Box 607 Albuquerque, New Mexico 87103 Attention: John C. Anderson – United States Attorney
United States Attorney's Office 271 Cadman Plaza East Brooklyn NY 11201 Attention: Richard P. Donoghue – United States Attorney	United States Attorney's Office P.O. Box 7198 100 South Clinton Street Syracuse, NY 13261-7198 Attention: Grant C. Jaquith - United States Attorney
United States Attorney's Office 1 St. Andrew's Plaza New York City, NY 10007 Attention: Geoffrey S. Berman - United States Attorney	United States Attorney's Office 138 Delaware Avenue Buffalo, NY 14202 Attention: James P. Kennedy, Jr.- United States Attorney

United States Attorney's Office 310 New Bern Avenue Federal Building, Suite 800 Raleigh, North Carolina 27601-1461 Attention: Robert J. Hidgon - United States Attorney	United States Attorney's Office 101 South Edgeworth Street, 4th Floor Greensboro, NC 27401 Attention: Matthew G.T. Martin - United States Attorney United States Attorney's Office 227 West Trade St. Suite 1650 Charlotte, NC 28202 Attention: R. Andrew Murray - United States Attorney
United States Attorney's Office 655 First Avenue North, Suite 250 Fargo, ND 58102-4932 Attention: Christopher C. Myers - United States Attorney	United States Attorney's Office Middle District of Alabama 131 Clayton Street Montgomery, AL 36104 Attention: Louis V. Franklin, Sr. - United States Attorney
United States Attorney's Office 222 West 7th Avenue, Room 253, #9, Anchorage, Alaska 99513 Attention: Bryan Schroder - United States Attorney	United States Attorney's Office Two Renaissance Square 40 N. Central Avenue, Suite 1800 Phoenix, AZ 85004-4408 Attention: Elizabeth A. Strange - United States Attorney
United States Attorney's Office 425 West Capitol Avenue Suite 500 Little Rock, AR 72201 Attention: Cody Hiland - United States Attorney	United States Attorney's Office 414 Parker Avenue Fort Smith, AR 72901 Attention: Duane (DAK) Kees - United States Attorney

United States Attorney's Office Birmingham Office 1801 4th Avenue North Birmingham, Alabama 35203 Attention: Jay E. Town - United States Attorney	United States Attorney's Office 63 South Royal Street, Suite 600 Mobile, AL 36602 Attention: Richard W. Moore - United States Attorney
United States Attorney's Office 801 West Superior Avenue; Suite 400 Cleveland, Ohio 44113-1852 Attention: Justin E. Herdman - United States Attorney	United States Attorney's Office 303 Marconi Boulevard, Suite 200 Columbus, OH 43215 Attention: Benjamin C. Glassman - United States Attorney
United States Attorney's Office 520 Denison Ave Muskogee OK 74401 Attention: Brian J. Kuester - United States Attorney	United States Attorney's Office 110 W. 7th Street Suite 300 Tulsa, OK 74119 Attention: R. Trent Shores - United States Attorney
United States Attorney's Office 210 West Park Avenue, Suite 400 Oklahoma City, Oklahoma 73102 Attention: Robert J. Troester - United States Attorney	United States Attorney's Office 1000 SW Third Ave Suite 600 Portland, Oregon 97204 Attention: Billy J. Williams - United States Attorney
United States Attorney's Office 615 Chestnut Street, Suite1250 Philadelphia, PA 19106 Attention: William M. McSwain - United States Attorney United States Attorney's Office 700 Grant Street, Suite 4000 Pittsburgh, PA 15219 Attention: Scott W. Brady - United States Attorney	United States Attorney's Office 235 N. Washington Avenue, Suite 311 Scranton, PA 18503 Attention: David J. Freed - United States Attorney United States Attorney's Office 50 Kennedy Plaza, 8th Floor Providence, RI 02903 Attention: Stephen G. Dambruch - United States Attorney

United States Attorney's Office 1441 Main Street Suite 500 Columbia, SC 29201 Attention: Beth Drake - United States Attorney	United States Attorney's Office PO Box 2638 Sioux Falls, SD 57101- 2638 *Attention:* Ronald A. Parsons, Jr - *United States Attorney*
United States Attorney's Office 800 Market Street, Suite 211 Knoxville, Tennessee 37902 *Attention:* J. Douglas Overbey - *United States Attorney*	United States Attorney's Office 110 9th Avenue South, Suite A-961 Nashville, Tennessee 37203 *Attention:* Donald Q. Cochran - *United States Attorney*
United States Attorney's Office 167 North Main Street, Suite 800 Memphis, TN 38103 *Attention:* D. Michael Dunavant - *United States Attorney*	United States Attorney's Office 350 Magnolia Ave., Suite 150 Beaumont, Texas 77701 *Attention:* Joseph D. Brown - *United States Attorney*
United States Attorney's Office 801 Cherry Street, Unit #4 Fort Worth, Texas 76102-6882 *Attention:* Erin Nealy Cox - *United States Attorney*	United States Attorney's Office *1000 Louisiana, Ste. 2300* *Houston, TX 77002* *Attention:* Ryan K. Patrick - *United States Attorney*
United States Attorney's Office 2500 N. Highway 118, Suite 200 Alpine Texas, 79830 *Attention:* John F. Bash - *United* *States Attorney*	United States Attorney's Office 111 South Main Street, Suite 1800 Salt Lake City, Utah 84111-2176 *Attention:* John W. Huber - *United States Attorney*
United States Attorney's Office Post Office Box 570 11 Elmwood Avenue, 3rd Floor Burlington, VT 05402-0570 Attention: Christina E. Nolan - *United States Attorney*	United States Attorney's Office 2100 Jamieson Ave Alexandria, VA 22314 *Attention:* Tracy Doherty- McCormick - *United States* *Attorney*

United States Attorney's Office 310 1st Street, S.W., Room 906 Roanoke, Virginia 24011 *Attention:* Thomas T. Cullen - *United States Attorney*	United States Attorney's Office P.O. Box 1494 Spokane, WA 99210-1494 *Attention:* Joseph H. Harrington *- United States Attorney*
United States Attorney's Office 700 Stewart Street, Suite 5220 Seattle, WA 98101-1271 *Attention:* Annette L. Hayes - *United States Attorney*	United States Attorney's Office 1125 Chapline Street, Suite 3000 Wheeling, WV 26003 *Attention:* Randolph J. Bernard - *United States Attorney*
United States Attorney's Office 300 Virginia Street, Suite 4000 Charleston, WV 25301 *Attention:* Michael B. Stuart - *United States Attorney*	United States Attorney's Office 2120 Capitol Avenue, Suite 4000 Cheyenne, WY 82001 *Attention:* Mark A. Klaassen - *United States Attorney*
United States Attorney's Office 222 West Washington Avenue, Suite 700 Madison, WI 53703 Attention: Scott C. Blader - *United States Attorney*	United States Attorney's Office *517 E. Wisconsin Ave, Ste 530* *Milwaukee WI 53202* *Attention:* Matthew D. Krueger - *United States Attorney*

The Department of Justice overseas numerous government agencies such as the FBI and U.S Attorney Offices. The United States Attorney General overseas the Department of Justice.

Here is a brief listing of the current and historic leadership:

Eric Holder, U.S. Attorney   2009-2015   Trillion's Stolen – No Prosecutions

Loretta Lynch, U.S. Attorney   2015 – 2017   Billions Stolen – No Prosecutions

Jeff Session, U.S. Attorney	2017 –	Amount Stolen Unknown – No Prosecutions
Robert Muller – FBI Director	2001- 2013	Trillion's Stolen – No Prosecutions
James Comey – FBI Director	2013 – 2017	Billions Stolen – No Prosecutions
Christopher Wray – FBI Director	2017 -	Amount Stolen Unknown – No Prosecutions

These were and are the people entrusted with protecting us. Most of the U.S. Attorneys are political appointees, all appear to have made sure that there are no prosecutions that would upset this alleged criminal empire. If you were to look and see what these former government officials are up to today, almost all of them went on to various firms that protect and serve Wall Street. These firms advise the credit rating agencies and banks how to best engage in this activity and defend against any claims made against them. They are almost all earning ten times what they made working for the government. Was this their payoff, their reward? Common sense would suggest it was.

The Securities and Exchange Commission is also led by political appointees. The following list reflects the names of the senior managers running the SEC. Almost all of these individuals were fully informed and to the best of my knowledge, did nothing to slow or stop all this alleged criminal activity.

The SEC even released a report claiming the rating agencies were doing a better job in recent years issuing ratings. Can you *believe* the SEC's arrogance and their disdain for the American people?

Chairman Jay Clayton	Commissioner Kara M. Stein
Commissioner Michael S. Piwowar	Commissioner Robert J. Jackson Jr.
Commissioner Hester M. Peirce	Mark Ambrose EDGAR Business Office
Stephanie Avakian Division of Enforcement	Dalia Blass Division of Investment Management
Wesley Bricker Office of the Chief Accountant	Vance Cathell Office of Acquisitions
Lacey Dingman Office of Human Resources	Peter Driscoll Office of Compliance Inspections and Examinations
Pamela C. Dyson Office of Information Technology	Rick A. Fleming Office of the Investor Advocate
Brent J. Fields Office of the Secretary	Pamela A. Gibbs Office of Minority and Women Inclusion
Peter Henry Office of Equal Employment Opportunity	William Hinman Division of Corporation Finance
Carl W. Hoecker Office of Inspector General	Kenneth Johnson Office of the Chief Operating Officer
Jessica Kane Office of Credit Ratings	Caryn Kauffman Office of Financial Management
Paul Leder Office of International Affairs	John Nester Office of Public Affairs

Rebecca Olsen Office of Municipal Securities	Steven Peikin Division of Enforcement
Brett Redfearn Division of Trading and Markets	Lori Schock Office of Investor Education and Advocacy
Robert Stebbins Office of General Counsel	Barry Walters Office of Support Operations
Bryan Wood Office of Legislative and Intergovernmental Affairs	

When people talk about the government and corruption, they are referring to many of these government employees, not just the politicians. Most of these individuals I named made a conscious decision to protect or enhance their own careers by throwing the American people under the pervertible bus. The SEC, The FBI and The U.S. Attorney's Office not only failed to protect us, but they appeared to use their power and authority to protect all those responsible for the theft of trillions of dollars! It is bad enough to be a crook but worse to hide under the cover of a government job. All these people have the gall to do this while being paid by the victims (taxpayers)! Many of these government officials took some sort of oath as a requirement for their position and appear to have broken that oath as soon as they got there.

If the Federal Government is this corrupt and broken, maybe I would have better luck going to the state governments? Each state has a similar structure. They all have an Attorney General that prosecutes crimes committed on its state's residents.

Many of the state's senior citizens and investors lost billions of dollars; even the smallest states had resident losses in the tens of millions. I can show the citizens that the bond issuers never had the cash to make payments on the bonds, they never had the assets to sell to repay the bonds, and the bond issuers reflected terrible management skills based on the abundance of law suits and regulatory violations. I will even tell them that our intelligence agencies have been tracking the major theft out of these municipal agencies and recording the phone conversations claiming payoffs were being made to the DOJ and politicians. *The State Attorney Generals will do something to protect their residents, won't they?*

With that thought in mind, I sent the following letters out to all the State Attorney General's across the Country:

April 12, 2018

United States Attorney's Office
300 Virginia Street, Suite 4000
Charleston, WV 25301
Attention: Michael B. Stuart - United States Attorney

Dear Mr. Stuart,

It appears that there is a small group within the Department of Justice who have taken it upon themselves to determine who will be investigated and prosecuted and who will not. I am writing you in the hopes that you are not one of those bad actors.

When our company lost everything in the 70 billion-dollar Puerto Rico bond default, we initiated a forensic investigation to find out the causes and to avoid it happening in the future. The investigation turned up massive corruption at the big three credit rating agencies: Moody's, S&P Global and Fitch. It appears that the three big credit agencies simply fabricated good credit ratings for "a fee" allowing the Puerto Rico Municipalities to borrow the 70 billion-dollars they defaulted on. It is also clear that the Board of Directors and executives at each of the companies had full knowledge of this.

Puerto Rico Bonds are triple tax free and were mainly purchased by retired American's throughout all 50 States. States like Florida and NY had resident losses of over 2 billion-dollars while smaller states experienced losses in the tens of millions.

Below is a list of links that will allow you to quickly understand this and review the overwhelming amounts of evidence available.

I hope you will act on this criminal complaint.

Sincerely,

Richard R. Lawless

Richard R. Lawless

Commercial Solar Power, Inc. — CEO

Florida residents (mostly senior citizens) lost almost three billion-dollars. Let's look at the response from Pam Bondi, Florida's State Attorney General.

From: attorney.general@myfloridalegal.com
Sent: Monday, May 14, 2018 5:02 AM
To: RICHARDRLAWLESS@GMAIL.COM
Subject: From Florida Attorney General Pam Bondi

Dear Mr. Lawless,

The Florida Attorney General's Office received your follow up correspondence regarding municipal bonds issued by Puerto Rico.

We appreciate that you consider our office as a source of assistance, and I am sorry for your ongoing difficulties. I note that you have been in contact with multiple agencies regarding your difficulties, including the U.S.

Department of Justice (DOJ), the Federal Bureau of Investigation (FBI), and multiple U.S. Attorneys. I encourage you to continue to work with these agencies for any assistance they may be able to provide.

You may also wish to reach out to the Financial Industry Regulatory Authority (FINRA), the federal agency dedicated to investor protection and regulation of the securities industry:

Financial Industry Regulatory Authority
FINRA Investor Complaint Center
9509 Key West Avenue
Rockville, Maryland 20850
Telephone: (301) 590-6500

Another resource may be the Consumer Financial Protection Bureau (CFPB), a federal consumer agency which reviews complaints about consumer financial products and services. You may contact the CFPB at:

Consumer Financial Protection Bureau
Toll-free: (855) 411-2372
Website: www.consumerfinance.gov

If you need legal guidance, please consult a private attorney. An attorney can provide the legal advice and opinions which our office is not at liberty to give to private individuals. The Florida Bar offers a Lawyer Referral Service toll-free at (800) 342-8011 or visit https://www.floridabar.org/public/lrs/.

Thank you for contacting Attorney General Bondi's office. We wish you the best outcome.

Sincerely,
Anna Rissinger
Office of Citizen Services
Florida Attorney General's Office
PL-01, The Capitol

Tallahassee, Florida 32399-1050
Telephone: (850) 414-3990
Toll-free within Florida: (866) 966-7226
Website: www.myfloridalegal.com

Our tax dollars at work again! They would like me to continue to work with the FBI and SEC even though I told her they were unresponsive. The Attorney General in Florida, the state with the biggest losses (billions) took no action that I am aware of to protect her residents.

I could fill this book with all the form letter responses that I was sent from the different state attorney generals. To the best of my knowledge, none of the States have taken any action on behalf of their residents.

As much as I would like to believe that the leadership within the Securities and Exchange Commission, the FBI and the U.S. Attorney's office all independently decided not to investigate, prosecute or fine the companies who issued or sold the alleged fraudulent bonds, it is likely there are Puppet Masters, pulling the strings elsewhere. The next chapter will help identify the "Godfathers" of this alleged criminal organization.

CHAPTER FIVE
OUR POLITICAL GODFATHERS

In the book preface, I spoke briefly about the increasing tenure of our congressmen and senators. I also dwelled on the common perception that each voter thinks their politician is the good guy and it is all the other politician's that are the bad apples. I hope this chapter changes a lot of peoples thinking about "their" politician.

I like to think I am not totally naïve. I do have sense enough to know that going to my politicians for help may be a wasted exercise. Most people probably realize that, as constituents, we all would be considered invisible and unimportant to our politicians unless we shower them with money or support. The longer they hold office, the truer that seems to be.

At the time this was all unfolding I lived in Temecula, California. My congressman was **Duncan Hunter**. Congressman Duncan D. Hunter represents California's 50th Congressional District consisting of East and Northern County San Diego. In 2008, Hunter was elected to his first term in the House of Representatives, succeeding his father, Duncan L. Hunter, who retired after serving fourteen consecutive terms in Congress. Duncan Hunter has been a congressman for nine years.

At the time I contacted him, I did not know that the congressman was under both a criminal and ethics investigation.

I was watching cable news today and they announced that Congressman Hunter and his wife were criminally indicted.

I wrote Congressman Hunter and told him that I had a successful business in Temecula, California that was ruined because of all the financial (Wall Street) fraud that had taken place in Puerto Rico and elsewhere. I asked if he could follow-up with the FBI on my criminal complaint. I also asked to speak to and/or meet with Duncan Hunter numerous times.

Congressman Hunter's staff did send in a "standard" follow-up form to the FBI for me. Several weeks later, the FBI called me to tell me they don't think any laws were broken. I explained to Mr. Hunter's office staff that our company lost three hundred high-paying jobs, and there was overwhelming evidence of criminal wrongdoing. Repeated efforts to speak or meet with him were unsuccessful.

Even though his office was fully informed about the fraudulent bond ratings, he later voted for the PROMESA legislation that revoked the legal rights of all the bond holders (innocent victims).

I can't help but to say this, what a piece of work this man is! These politicians appear willing to do anything to get their piece of the action. Let's face it, most of the people the FBI investigate, and the U.S. Attorney's prosecute are probably more trustworthy and of better character than the corrupt FBI, SEC, U.S Attorney and politicians that are putting them in jail.

If history is to be a guide, when the populace can no longer tolerate the corruption and cruelty of their government, there is a revolution. I hope we can change course before this happens.

Washington, DC 20535-0001

The Honorable Duncan Hunter Member of Congress
1611 N. Magnolia Avenue, Suite 310
El Cajon, CA 92020

Dear Congressman Hunter:

I am writing in response to our letter to the Department of Justice, which was forwarded to the FBI on behalf of your constituent, Mr. Richard Lawless, who wrote to you requesting an investigative update.

The FBI San Juan Field Office received Mr. Lawless' complaint and it has been brought to the attention of the appropriate personnel. In order to protect the integrity of all investigations, the FBI does not generally comment on the status or existence of any potential investigative matter. The San Juan Field Office will contact Mr. Lawless for additional information as necessary.

If Mr. Lawless has additional information he would like to provide, he may contact the FBI's San Juan Field Office, located at Federal Office Building, Suite 526, 150 Carlos Chardon Ave., Hato Rey, Puerto Rico 0918, telephone number (787) 754-6000.

I appreciate your bringing this letter to our attention, and I hope this information will be helpful to you in responding.

> *Sincerely,*
> *Timothy J. Delaney*
> *Deputy Assistant Director*
> *Criminal Investigative Division*

Not to beat a dead horse, but Mr. Delaney sent the complaint to the FBI Office that was accused by our intelligence agencies of taking kickbacks and bribes. Of *course,* they found no wrong doing. Does the FBI normally allow agents accused of such things to investigate themselves?

My full sixty-minute testimony to the SEC and FBI was videotaped and is available on the book's website for viewing.

I wrote to my States two Senators, **Dianne Feinstein** and **Barbara Boxer**. They were both likely informed about the bond fraud. My repeated requests for assistance were completely ignored and they both voted for PROMESA, knowing all about all the fraud and criminal activity.

These are the kind of people we put into office! A former senior executive of my company, so frustrated by the obvious role our government was playing in this alleged criminal enterprise, wrote a detailed letter to the House Oversight Committee on our company's behalf. Here is a small excerpt of the comprehensive document.

April 28th, 2016

The Honorable Jason Chaffetz, Chairman
Committee on Oversight and Reform
2157 Rayburn House Office Building
Washington, DC 20515

Re: Widespread Government-Enabled Fraud and Abuse in the $4T U.S. Municipal Bond Market. Environmental Protection Agency and Department of Energy Failure to Regulate. Federal Bureau of Investigation and Department of Justice Failure to Investigate. Treasury Department Conflicts of Interest and Ethical Violations.

Dear Mr. Chairman:

I am reaching out to your committee to make all committee members aware of the widespread fraud and abuse in the $4T United States municipal bond market that we discovered during our investigation into the *circumstances surrounding losses my former employer, Commercial Solar Power, Inc., suffered in Puerto Rico.*

This extensive document was completely ignored by the House Oversight Committee. Did the leaders of the House Committee just violate their own rules? Did they commit a chargeable crime by protecting their peers? What do you think? I penned the following article to help deal with my frustration:

Does Congressman Janson Chaffetz have the personal integrity and courage to Chair the Congressional House Oversight Committee?
This article was reprinted with permission from Sentinel News and is available at sentinelnews.net

Approximately 60 days ago, WWW.WallStFraud.Com made a detailed referral to Congressman Jason Chaffetz and the Oversight Committee regarding a $70 billion-dollar Wall Street Bond Fraud and strong evidence of an associated "pay to play" enterprise involving many members of the Congress and the Senate.

The Boston office of the Securities and Exchange told us that they found these allegations "very disturbing and concerning." The SEC is currently investigating this matter. The Anti-Trust Division of the FBI said they are, "taking this matter seriously" and the Criminal and Securities Fraud Divisions of the FBI are also investigating. In the allegations and criminal reports, it is claimed that bankrupt municipal agencies issued new bond debt they knew they couldn't repay. The agencies purchased fraudulent bond ratings from Moody's, Fitch and S&P and then the major Wall Street Banks knowingly sold this junk debt to innocent bond buyers.

When the $70 billion dollars in bonds defaulted, Wall Street showered money on our congressmen and senators to prevent prosecution and secure favorable legislation.

We all know politicians such as Paul Ryan, Chuck Schumer and Elizabeth Warren are at the center of this criminal conspiracy and Mr. Chaffetz does not have the stomach to investigate this matter.

Unbelievable, when Congressman Chaffetz was presented with a copy of the victims 60 sec TV commercial which does a fair job of explaining the basis of this complaint, thousands of pages of documentary evidence, which is also available to the public at and a 60 minute video of a press conference that summarizes the detailed SEC and FBI testimony, they were told to forward it to the Civilian office of Congressional Ethics (OCE). There is only one problem, the OCE refers cases to the Congressional Oversight Committee, not the other way around. It was the old "Washington Two Step," defer, delay, oviscape and cover it up.

It was clear from speaking to the staff at Congressman Chaffetz's office that they were concerned and frightened. They wanted nothing to do with this. It would blacklist Congressman Chaffetz or worse, if he were to submit this case to the Oversight Committee.

We need men and woman of good conscious and strong moral and ethically fiber. Congressman Chaffetz has proven he has neither.

Let us discuss the role of the Puppet Masters. What I am about to share with you is so outrageous, you will think it has to be fiction. I promise you, it is very real.

When Puerto Rico was in the midst of a complete financial meltdown and on the verge of declaring the largest municipal bond default in American history, President Obama reached out to **Treasury Secretary, Jack Lew.**

Jack Lew was the Chief Operating Officer at Citigroup at a time when the Bank was among the first to knowingly sell their clients the fraudulent Puerto Rico Municipal bonds. Here is an article that appeared in the papers at that time.

Jack Lew had major role at Citigroup when it nearly imploded

This article was reprinted with permission from the Washington Post and is available at washingtonpost.com

"Treasury secretary nominee Jack Lew has spent most of his career in government, but during the financial crisis, he was embedded inside one of the country's biggest banks as it nearly imploded.

From 2006 to 2008, he worked at Citigroup in two major roles, a notable line in his résumé given that as Treasury secretary, he would be charged with implementing new rules regulating Wall Street. But Lew did not have just any position at the bank.

In early 2008, he became a top executive in the Citigroup unit that housed many of the bank's riskiest operations, including its hedge funds and private equity investments. Massive losses in that unit helped drive Citigroup into the arms of the federal government, which bailed out the bank with $45 billion in taxpayer money that year.

The group had been under pressure to compete with similar units at other big Wall Street firms and, some analysts say, took on too many risks as it played catch-up.

"The mismanagement of risk was comprehensive at that organization," said Simon Johnson, an economist at the Massachusetts Institute of Technology.

Details about Lew's exact responsibilities at Citigroup, where he worked from 2006 to 2008, are scant. He declined to comment for this article.

Lew's first job at the bank was chief operating officer of Citigroup's wealth management unit, which flourished under his watch.

By the fall of 2007, the wealth management group handled $1.8 billion in client assets, up 34 percent from the year before, according to

financial statements. More than 15,000 financial advisers and bankers worked under Lew.

In January 2008, he switched to Citigroup's alternative investments unit. A press release announcing his new position as chief operating officer of the group said he would "oversee coordination between the operations, technology, human resources, legal, financial and regional departments."

The memo stated that Lew also would be a member of Citigroup's management committee, a group of senior executives who met regularly to discuss different parts of the bank's business.

During his 2010 confirmation hearings for chairing the Office of Management and Budget, Lew said his Wall Street experience was "as a manager, not as an investment adviser."

"Senator, I don't consider myself an expert in some of these aspects of the financial industry," Lew said in response to a question from Sen. Bernard Sanders (I-Vt.) about causes of the financial crisis.

Sanders said in a statement Wednesday that although he applauds Lew's public service, he worries about the number of economic advisers in the White House who have spent time on Wall Street. Michael Froman, deputy national security adviser for international economic affairs, also came from Citigroup's hedge fund and private equity shop, known as the alternative investments unit.

"In my view, we need a treasury secretary who is prepared to stand up to corporate America and their powerful lobbyists and fight for policies that protect the working families in our country," Sanders said. "I do not believe Mr. Lew is that person."

The beginning of 2008 was a brutal time to be working at the bank and certainly at Citigroup's alternative investments unit, which managed more than $54 billion.

The group was hemorrhaging money just as Lew joined. In the first three months alone, it lost $509 million, according to SEC filings. By contrast, just a year earlier during that quarter, the unit made $222 million.

"He stepped into the hedge-fund buzz saw," said Mark Williams, a lecturer in finance at Boston University and a former bank examiner for the Federal Reserve. "His timing wasn't the best."

Things continued to deteriorate the rest of the year. More than 50,000 employees, or one-seventh of Citigroup's global workforce, were laid off in November. That year, the stock price dropped about 75 percent. Lew, meanwhile, was paid at least $1.1 million in 2008, according to financial disclosure statements.

By the end of December 2008, Lew had lined up a new job: away from Wall Street and back in Washington as a deputy secretary of state under Secretary Hillary Rodham Clinton.

Meanwhile, Citigroup's alternative investments unit had become such a stain on the bank's record that it was relaunched three years ago with a new name. It's now known as Citi Capital Advisors."

Treasury Secretary Lew's first effort was to petition Congress for a full tax payer bailout of the Puerto Rico crisis. His mantra was "let's make this problem go away." His efforts at a full taxpayer bailout failed. During this time, Treasury Secretary Lew reached out to **Antonio Weiss** from Lazard Freres. Mr. Weiss could not be confirmed by the Congress because of his questionable activities on Wall Street. Secretary Lew hired him anyway. Both Lew and Weiss moved forward with a scheme that appears to help cover everyone's tracks while impeding or destroying the legal rights of the victims. Here is a series of timely articles that I found during my research.

ANTONIO WEISS, LAZARD FRÈRES
AND THE PUERTO RICO CRISIS

This article was reprinted with permission from the Hedge Clippers
web blog, it can be found at s3.amazonaws.com

The Hedge Clippers are working to expose the mechanisms
hedge funds and billionaires use to influence government and politics in order to expand their wealth, influence and power. We're
exposing the collateral damage billionaire-driven politics inflicts on
our communities, our climate, our economy and our democracy.
We're calling out the politicians that do the dirty work billionaires demand, and we're calling on all Americans to stand up for a
government and an economy that works for all of us, not just the
wealthy and well-connected.

*"Antonio Weiss must be recused from decisions on the Puerto Rico
crisis. Treasury official Antonio Weiss is currently leading the Treasury
Department's response to the Puerto Rico debt crisis. But Weiss received
a $21,200,000 golden parachute from his previous employer, Lazard
Frères, an investment bank with numerous ties to the Puerto Rico debt
crisis.*

*Lazard traded in Puerto Rican debt. Former Lazard partners incentiv-
ized Puerto Rico to underwrite more debt with Lazard. Lazard has reportedly invested in Puerto Rican debt.*

*And Lazard partners have come under scrutiny from law enforcement
officials for unethical and/or illegal business practices related to debt underwriting, including in Puerto Rico, for bribery, kickbacks and conflicts
of interest."*

Wall Street Pays Bankers to Work in Government and It Doesn't Want Anyone to Know

This article was reprinted with permission from the New Republic, it can be found at newrepublic.com

By **David Dayen**
February 4, 2015

"Citigroup is one of three Wall Street banks attempting to keep hidden their practice of paying executives multimillion-dollar awards for entering government service. In letters delivered to the Securities and Exchange Commission (SEC) over the last month, Citi, Goldman Sachs and Morgan Stanley seek exemption from a shareholder proposal, filed by the AFL-CIO labor coalition, which would force them to identify all executives eligible for these financial rewards, and the specific dollar amounts at stake. Critics argue these "golden parachutes" ensure more financial insiders in policy positions and favorable treatment toward Wall Street."

As far as I know, Mr. Lew and Mr. Weiss never disclosed their conflict of interest to any of the congressmen or senators they spoke with. Secretary Lew (Citibank) knowingly sold these fraudulent bonds to innocent investors, and Mr. Weiss likely knew of or directly participated in bribing the Government of Puerto Rico, while he or his company possibly received kick-backs relating to all this bond activity. But why mention it?

I wrote to the Treasury Department's Inspector General and complained about these obvious conflicts of interest. I was completely ignored.

February 13, 2016

U.S. Treasury Department
Office of The Inspector General
Attention: Eric Thorson

RE: Treasury Secretary Jack Lew - Conflict of Interest

Dear Eric,

I e-mailed your office a number of weeks ago expressing my concern about a conflict of interest. I have not received any response and it appears Secretary Lew continues to openly advocate a position that benefits his previous employer and damages tens of thousands of retired Americans.

Just to recap, approximately 7 months ago I filed a complaint with the SEC, FBI and Treasury Department regarding financial fraud and theft taking place at the Puerto Rico Electric Power Authority (PREP A). The SEC responded and expressed great concern about what I uncovered. The SEC has an open investigation and is currently auditing the bond issues coming out of Puerto Rico. The FBI has also responded. The FBI has told me they are taking these claims very seriously and their best prosecutors are currently working through the possible criminal changes that may follow. The FBI did express that although civil liability is obvious criminal charges regarding financial crimes are more difficult to prosecute. Not surprisingly, the Treasury Department responded to me and saw no reason to pursue an investigation. Both I and my attorneys are baffled.

Secretary Lew was the COO of Citibank from 2006-2008 when Citibank and other major Wall Street firms started marketing billions in municipal bonds for PREPA when the company was technically bankrupt. Now Secretary Lew is aggressively seeking bankruptcy authority and financial aid for the very same entities. I have attached what is essentially a 27-page confession from the Government of Puerto Rico claiming that

$11 billion dollars was fraudulently issued by PREPA (Citibank) and that Citibank and others conspired with them to sell these defunct bonds.

It could not be any clearer. For those that believe a confession is not enough (only in Washington) I have also attached an audit showing that the financials were intentionally misleading and fraudulent.

Both Mr. Lew and his direct reports should be excluded from taking a position that would benefit his former employer and the offending entities. We look forward to your response.

Working with Congressional Leadership and the Obama Administration, Treasury Secretary Lew concocted a complex piece of legislation referred to as "PROMESA." PROMESA is the "PUERTO RICO OVERSIGHT, MANAGEMENT, AND ECONOMIC STABILITY ACT".

This law will allow the Government of the United States to revoke the legal rights of the victims, delay or prevent lawsuits and hand control of this whole mess back to many of the people that participated at some level in the original criminal acts. This was what one billion dollars or more in political contributions, PAC contributions and lobbyists buys the three major credit rating agencies and the banks. This appeared to be payback from our politicians to Wall Street for their financial support. Here are some more timely articles from that time period.

"Obama announces 7 members of P.R. fiscal control board"
This article was reprinted with permission from News Is My Business the, it can be found at newsismybusiness.com

Conflict of Interest Shadows Members of the FOB
This article was reprinted with permission from the Center for Puerto Rican Studies, it can be found at entropr.hunter.cuny.edu/ events-news

"In an article by Centro de Periodismo Investigativo, concerns are raised about the conflict of interest that board members Carlos M. García and José R. González could have in the debt restructuring. Specifically, as noted in the appendix to this brief, both worked for Santander Bank, which played an important role in the issuing of the debt. During the Fortuño administration, Santander Securities played the role of an underwriter in the issuing of bonds, mostly the ones from COFINA. This means that the government of Puerto Rico paid millions of dollars in fees and commissions to Santander Securities, who helped to issue millions of dollars in bonds. According to reports, there could be a link between the role that García and González played in Santander Bank and in the GDB.

The case against García is more alarming because he was the president of the GDB under the Fortuño administration when a substantive portion of the debt was issued, and where he appointed several executives of Santander Bank to important position in the GDB.

The historical connections of García and González to the Santander Bank and the GDB raise question about their impartiality when making decisions. Are they serving the best interest of the people or the best interest of the banks for which they have worked? In a recent interview, González says that these accusations, primarily raised by the Hedge Clippers are irresponsible and that it evidences a lack of knowledge about the topic. Also, Gonzalez claims that the bonds that were issued during his time in the GDB should have expired or refinance, and that he worked at Santander Bank only until 2008. As for García, he has been silent about the Hedge Clippers' accusations.

In addition, there is some concern about the role that the law firm O'Neill and Borges have played in previous years, both as tax counsel for the government of Puerto Rico and representing Santander Bank, Banco Popular, and UBS Financial Services in various legal disputes. Here again, questions are raised about what interest this firm will look for if a restructuring process begins."

There are 435 members of congress and 100 senators. All likely knew that the Puerto Rico Municipal Bond bankruptcy was the probable result of Wall Street fraud. I know they all knew about the fraud because each of them was faxed a full copy of the audit document. I have the fax confirmations as proof. Regardless, 297 congressmen and 68 senators, voted for the bill.

Did those congressman and senators just participate in a criminal act with their votes? They knew the bonds were likely fraudulent but used the power and authority of their government positions to aid the criminals while ensuring they still get contributions (payoffs) from Wall Street.

Here are a few more notable examples of politicians who were likely fully aware that all this money was stolen from the American people but went on to tell us the following:

Representative Raul Grijalva of Arizona, *"Everything needs to be suspended, there needs to be loan forgiveness including and or suspension of any repayment."*

Statement on Representative Grijalva's website regarding Puerto Rico crisis

Republican Senator Marco Rubio: "We were already in a position where we need to do more to help Puerto Rico overcome its financial challenges."

Comment from Marco Rubio during presidential election campaigning

Let's shine a bright light on the government and explore how individual politicians' actions contributed to the existence and success of this on-going alleged criminal empire.

<u>Paul Ryan – Speaker of the House</u>

What Does It Cost to Buy a Paul Ryan Vote?
This article was reprinted with permission from the Daily Caller
website, it can be found at dailycaller.com

*Over the last decade he Government of Puerto Rico took on increasing
amounts of municipal bond debt. Debt that could not be supported by the
island's shrinking economy. By 2015, government officials in Puerto Rico
were reaching out to our Congress for a solution.*

*Many Democrats supported a taxpayer bailout or a wholesale bond de-
fault that would give Puerto Rico an opportunity to restructure its finances.
Republicans pushed for a market solution that would include a government
austerity program along with tax and regulatory changes that would promote economic growth.*

*It was clear that the Republicans as a group, did not want a solution
that utilized tax payer dollars or violated the bondholders' rights. There was
a growing concern amongst the Republicans that any such solution would
set up states and other municipalities for future defaults of their own.*

*Among the most ardent of those Republicans was Paul Ryan, the
Speaker of the House. Mr. Ryan was very concerned about safeguarding
core Republican principals that protected the bond holders, protected decades of case law regarding debtor's rights and prevented the use of tax payer
dollars as any part of the solution.*

*It was not widely known that Secretary Lew, while COO of Citibank
oversaw the issuance/sale of much of Puerto Rico's troubled debt from 2006-
2008 and Counsels Weiss and Campbell worked for Lazard who resold much
of this troubled Puerto Rico debt before joining the Treasury Department.*

*A few months ago, Secretary Lew met with Speaker of the House,
Paul Ryan. After that meeting, Speaker Ryan abandoned his position on a*

Republican Puerto Rico solution and began publicly supporting the administration's position. A solution that violated every core Conservative and Republican principal his party stood for.

Some say that Secretary Lew acknowledged Speaker Ryan's bright career prospects and how supporting his Puerto Rico solution would not be forgotten by Wall Street and go a long way in winning the financial support he would need to seek higher office one day. All of this is speculation and unprovable. However, after the meeting, the following contributions rolled into Paul Ryan's accounts. It should be noted that most were new contributors for Paul Ryan.

Some of Paul Ryan Contributions flowing in from his surprising support of the Puerto Rico Legislation

Blackstone Group Restructuring Advisor for Puerto Rico $72,900

Blackrock	*Troubled Debt Purchaser*	*$39,100*
Cerberus Capital	*Distressed Debt Specialist*	*$32,900*
Citadel	*Hedge Fund (Banco Popular)*	*$27,200*
Carlyle Group	*Hedge Fund - Distressed Debt*	*$20,800*
Bank of America	*Underwrote the Bonds*	*$21,050*
		$213,950

This <u>limited list</u> reflects $213,950 in contributions following the meeting of Treasury Secretary Lew and Paul Ryan. A real bargain for these Wall Street firms who are positioned to earn hundreds of millions, at the cost of American citizens.

Thanks to Secretary Lew's efforts and Speaker Ryan's support, the credit rating agencies and Wall Street's biggest Banks are now much less likely to be held accountable for any role they played in this $70 billion-dollar mess.

About twenty-four million Americans owned the Puerto Rico debt.

Now they have no legal rights and Ryan has a $7,000,000 surplus in his reelection war chest. Good for Ryan, good for Wall Street.

Paul Ryan likely knew about all the fraud. By using his office to benefit the criminals, did Paul Ryan commit a crime? What would a jury think?

Senator Chuck Schumer

I don't throw praise around lightly but Senator Schumer's apparent contributions to this alleged criminal organization make me think of him as the **Godfather** of this Mafia type organization.

For our politicians to earn the financial support of Wall Street, this alleged criminal empire must be able to control the actions of the Justice System (FBI-U.S. Attorneys) and the leadership at the Securities and Exchange Commission. After all, this is a "Protection Racket" and if the politicians can't offer protection, they would be out of business.

In my opinion, no one politician has done more to destroy our Justice System and Regulatory Agencies then Senator Schumer, that is also likely why he gets a larger share of the contributions (payoffs) from Wall Street.

Do you remember the U.S. Attorney, **Preet Bharara**? He was a political appointee of Senator Schumer. In fact, I believe he was the Senator's legal assistant before he became the third or fourth most powerful person within the Department of Justice. FBI Director Mueller and Attorney General Holder funneled most of the criminal cases related to the 2008 financial crisis to Preet Bharara -- cases involving fabricated credit ratings and banks that knowingly sold fraudulent bonds. U.S. Attorney Bharara appeared to make sure they were considered "dead upon arrival." Eight trillion dollars in stolen wealth and to the best of my knowledge, no one was investigated or charged at an American Financial Institution.

Here is an article where U.S. Attorney Bharara tries to explain why that was the case:

Schumer Aide Is Confirmed as United States Attorney
This article was reprinted with permission from the New York Times, it can be found at nytimes.com

Preet Bharara, the chief counsel to Senator Charles E. Schumer, was confirmed Friday as United States attorney for the Southern District of New York, the senator's office said.

How Wall Street's Bankers Stayed Out of Jail
This article was reprinted with permission from The Atlantic Monthly Group, it can be found at theatlantic.com

"The more meaningful number is how many Wall Street executives have gone to jail for playing a part in the crisis. That number is one. (Kareem Serageldin, a senior trader at Credit Suisse, is serving a 30-month sentence for inflating the value of mortgage bonds in his trading portfolio, allowing them to appear more valuable than they really were.) By way of contrast, following the savings-and-loan crisis of the 1980s, more than 1,000 bankers of all stripes were jailed for their transgressions.

*At an event at the National Press Club last February, Holder said the virtual absence of convictions (or even prosecutions) this time around did not result from a want of trying. "These are the kinds of cases that people come to the Justice Department to make," he said. "The inability to make them, at least to this point, has not been as a result of a lack of effort." **Preet Bharara**, the U.S. attorney for the Southern District of New York, made a similar argument to me. The evidence, he said, does not show clear misconduct by individuals. It's possible that Bharara is correct about that: Wall Street bankers make it their daily business to figure out ways to abide by the letter of the law while violating its spirit. And to be sure, much of the behavior that led to the crisis involved recklessness and poor judgment, not* *fraud. But even so, in light of various whistle-blower allegations—and the size of the settlements agreed to by the banks themselves—this explanation strains credulity. <u>The Justice Department's ethos regarding Wall Street, and the way the department went about its business, appear to be a large part of the story.</u>" <u>This brings up an important point which is how much of what you're pointing to as illegal is would get off legally as recklessness and poor judgement. [Bold and underline by author.]</u>*

"Preet Bharara on "Too Big to Prosecute"
This article was reprinted with permission from Sense on Cents, it can be found at senseoncents.com

"Let's listen to the U.S attorney for the southern district of New York, Preet Bharara, address this topic. You do not need to listen too hard to understand what Bharara is saying on this topic. While Bharara provides the standard party line that no institution is "too big to prosecute," he qualifies his answer in such a fashion that we should NEVER expect to see major indictments on Wall Street. I have no doubt that this question was planted by Bharara so he could buy cover from the barrage of criticism that has poured down upon him and his office."

By putting Preet Bharara in this key position, Senator Schumer was able to deliver for his Wall Street friends. I guess it is possible that Preet Bharara and the dozens of other political appointees that Senator Schumer recommended and supported, all independently decided that Wall Street executives should not be investigated or prosecuted? Or, were they following the instructions of their political benefactor, Senator Schumer?

Given the political contributions Senator Schumer received, it appears that Wall Street was supporting Senator Schumer with large sums of money. Did the bankers just like him or were they getting something in return?

Senator Schumer was among the first to try and pass legislation that would prevent the victims of this Wall Street fraud from suing. I believe he initially supported a full taxpayer bailout and later voted to revoke the victim's legal rights with the passage of PROMESA. I am sure this is all just a coincidence? What would a jury think? What do you think? Here is another timely article from that period.

Senators Warren, Blumenthal, Reid, Schumer Introduce Puerto Rico Emergency Financial Stability Act

Senator Elizabeth Warren's web site and it can be found at warren.senate.gov

"Washington, DC - *Today, United States Senator Elizabeth Warren (D-Mass.), Senator Richard Blumenthal (D-Conn.), Senate Democratic Leader Harry Reid (D-Nev.) and Senator Charles E. Schumer (D-NY) introduced the Puerto Rico Emergency Financial Stability Act.* This legislation would establish a short-term stay on creditor litigation *until Congress takes action to allow Puerto Rico to restructure its debts."*

For all the actions Senator Schumer appears to have taken to support this alleged Criminal Organization, an Organization that targets senior citizens in an effort to move massive amounts of wealth from tens of millions of innocent Americans to a few thousand bad actors; A public servant paid by us who pretends he cares while helping others steal our savings and retirement funds, Senator Schumer earns the title of "Godfather." If this is true, I have to believe there is a special place in hell for Senator Schumer.

Sen. Charles Schumer (D-N .Y.)
Terms: 2 (9 in House)
Total raised: $62.2 million
Top donors: A major defender of
Wall Street interests before the crash,
Schumer has netted more big-bank
money than any member of Congress
who hasn't run for President.

Over <u>one-hundred-million dollars</u> was given to Chuck Schumer over the past decade!

Here are some articles that appear to support these assumptions.

Charles Schumer's Wall Street Dance
This article was reprinted with permission from CBS News, it can be found at bsnews.com

Over the course of his career, Schumer has raised half a million dollars from Goldman Sachs - and nearly as much from Citigroup, Morgan Stanley and JPMorgan Chase. Between 1989 and 2010, according to the nonpartisan Center for Responsive Politics, Schumer took in nearly $9 million from the entire securities and investment industry, a haul that helped him become one of the most powerful politicians in America, a deep-pocketed kingmaker with unrivalled connections among the wealthiest players on Wall Street.

The seeming contradiction between Schumer's public posture and his closed-door fundraising efforts had gone little-noticed by the general public before the financial crisis. But when the securities and investment industry was thrust into chaos - and the spotlight - in 2008, Schumer's Wall Street ties suddenly became a political liability.

After all, Schumer's biggest donors were the very folks who President Obama would later, in response to public anger, deem "fat cat bankers." In the years leading up to the crisis, Schumer had been pushed hard to deregulate the financial industry; as the New York Times documented in the wake of the crisis, he had repeatedly protected the industry from oversight and helped companies avoid billions of dollars in taxes and fees.

A Champion of Wall Street Reaps Benefits
This article was reprinted with permission from the New York Times,
it can be found at nytimes.com

"An exceptional fund raiser — a "jackhammer," someone who knows him says, for whom "'no' is the first step to 'yes,'" — Mr. Schumer led the Democratic Senatorial Campaign Committee for the last four years, raising a record $240 million while increasing donations from Wall Street by 50 percent. That money helped the Democrats gain power in Congress, elevated Mr. Schumer's standing in his party and increased the industry's clout in the capital.

But in building support, he has embraced the industry's free-market, deregulatory agenda more than almost any other Democrat in Congress, even backing some measures now blamed for contributing to the financial crisis.

But Mr. Schumer, a member of the Banking and Finance Committees, repeatedly took other steps to protect industry players from government oversight and tougher rules, a review of his record shows. Over the years, he has also helped save financial institutions billions of dollars in higher taxes or fees.

He is serving the parochial interest of a very small group of financial people, bankers, investment bankers, fund managers, private equity firms, rather than serving the general public," said John C. Bogle, the founder and former chairman of the Vanguard Group, the giant mutual fund house. "It has hurt the American investor first and the average American taxpayer."

Mr. Schumer became a magnet for campaign donations from wealthy industry executives, including Jamie Dimon, now the chief executive of JPMorgan Chase; John J. Mack, the chief executive at Morgan Stanley; and Charles O. Prince III, the former chief executive of Citigroup. And he was not at all reluctant to ask them for more.

*The SEC has grown deeply concerned about lack of oversight of the nation's largest credit-rating agencies, like **Standard & Poor's** and **Moody's** Investors Service. Linchpins of the financial system, their ratings are vital to safeguarding investors by evaluating the risks of bonds and other debt."*

*They knew Schumer would support them," said one former Moody's executive, who asked not to be named because he still works in the industry. **"He was their go-to guy,"** the executive said.*

While the Manhattan-based agencies were not significant campaign donors to Mr. Schumer or the Senate campaign committee, their lobbyists and many of their clients were. [Bold added by author.]

Here is a clear and direct link between the trillions stolen through fraudulent credit ratings and Senator Schumer. And if you follow the money, Mr. Schumer received massive contributions (payoffs) for his role.

The SEC promoted legislation for better oversite of the rating agencies. Newspaper articles stated Chuck Schumer *killed the widely supported legislation by adding amendments* that he knew couldn't pass.

The credit rating agencies had to abandon their fraudulent ratings on mortgage bonds because no one would buy them anymore. Shortly after that, Moody's Fitch and S&P allegedly started to issue massive amounts of fraudulent ratings on municipal bonds. This appears to have been made possible by Mr. Schumer's political actions. Actions that generated huge contributions (payoffs) from Wall Street.

Here is another newspaper quote:

"These executives had more than his words at the fundraiser to go by. Schumer had in the past "succeeded in limiting efforts to regulate credit-rating agencies"

This article was reprinted with permission from Alternet; it can be found at alternet.org

I feel like I need to take a shower to rub off all the sleaziness with steel wool every time I discuss the deceptive practices of these politicians. Schumer must have known what he was doing was wrong otherwise he would have just spoken up against the legislation. This is one of the many deceitful tricks politicians uses to mislead their constituents. The senator's deceit is evident everywhere I look. When he knows his vote is meaningless, when a bill will pass or fail regardless of what vote he makes, the senator will often intentionally cast a meaningless vote to trick his constituents into thinking he supports a certain issue.

I created and ran a TV Commercial stating that the Congress knew about all the bond fraud but passed PROMESA anyway. I ran the commercials for a limited time in Washington DC. during the *Morning Joe* show. I read that the politicians work out in the morning in the Congressional Gym with *Morning Joe* on the TV. Our commercial ran, and the very next day Chuck Schumer sent out a press release. He wrote the SEC asking them to look into the Puerto Rico mess. The man is a cool operator. It appeared he wanted to cover his bases with the public in case our commercial had any impact. The commercial is available for viewing on the book's website.

"Leadership by deception isn't leadership. It's fraud."
— **DaShanne Stokes**
This quote can be found at Goodreads @ goodreads.com

Letter to the Hon. Mary Jo White, Chair, Securities and Exchange Commission - SEC Investigation into Potential Illegal Activity Leading to Puerto Rico Debt Crisis Letter

By: Kirsten Gillibrand Bob Menendez Jeff Merkley Richard Blumenthal Bernie Sanders Chuck Schumer Elizabeth Warren

Date: *June 14, 2016*
Location: *Washington, DC*

Dear Chair White:

Puerto Rico is in the midst of a dire debt crisis, with approximately $71 billion in debt and an estimated pension liability of $46 billion. Faced with debt service payments that consume more than one-third of its revenues, the government of Puerto Rico has undertaken significant cuts to essential services. The 3.5 million American citizens who reside in Puerto Rico are in immediate need of a solution that will allow the island to restructure its debts, protect public employees and pension holders, and provide essential services. However, beyond these common-sense solutions, Puerto Ricans deserve to know whether illegal activity contributed to the current debt burden. Therefore, the residents of Puerto Rico and its municipal entities merit the full attention of the Securities and Exchange Commission (SEC) to investigate any possible misconduct by financial advisors to municipal entities in Puerto Rico in the years leading to the current crisis.

As you know, the Dodd-Frank Wall Street Reform and Consumer Protection Act of 2010 (Dodd-Frank Act) included important provisions to reform the regulation of the municipal bond markets and specifically mandated that municipal entities be protected from fraud and abuse. In light of Puerto Rico's municipal debt crisis, we write to ask that you investigate possible market manipulation, conflicts of interest, trading practices, and fraud in the underwriting, sale, distribution, and trading of municipal securities of and relating to Puerto Rico, as well as any other fraudulent, illegal or wrongful conduct.

Section 975 of the Dodd-Frank Act amended the Securities Exchange Act of 1934 to now require the Municipal Securities Rulemaking Board (MSRB) to adopt and impose on financial professionals rules "designed to prevent fraudulent and manipulative acts and practices... and, in general, to protect investors, municipal entities, obligated persons, and the public

155

interest."[2] In addition to this legal mandate, the Exchange Act gives the SEC and Financial Industry Regulatory Authority (FINRA) broad enforcement and examination authority to implement the "municipal entity protection" mandate.

The SEC has in the past devoted significant attention to municipal securities markets. In 2010-2011, it held multiple field hearings that unearthed significant facts and shed light on serious deficiencies and illegal practices that harmed investors and state and local governments. Importantly, these efforts helped restore the troubled municipalities' access to low-interest, long-term debt. The hearings also informed a report later released by the SEC in 2012 on the state of municipal securities market, which called for far-reaching reforms (some but not all of which have been implemented). These reforms were in addition to what were then-still-new rules mandated by the Dodd-Frank Act requiring municipal advisors to register with the SEC and MSRB and be subject to a series of conflicts of interest, competency, anti-manipulative rules, and, above all, a fiduciary duty towards the issuer. We further ask that you update us on the status of the 2012 recommendations, and whether the SEC needs new authorities to better protect municipal entities in Puerto Rico and elsewhere.

Separate from Congressional efforts to provide a path for Puerto Rico out of its municipal debt crisis, we believe that SEC should immediately commence an investigation into the acts, actions, and activities in connection with the underwriting, sale, distribution and trading of Puerto Rico debt in the years leading up to the present crisis. The SEC should determine whether laws and rules have been broken and whether illegal conduct occurred. Without this, there is a risk that investors will not regain confidence in Puerto Rico's debt markets and Puerto Rico's access to normal credit markets will remain impaired.

Thank you for your prompt attention.

Let's take a look at all the leaders of our regulatory and legal organizations and see what <u>three things</u> they all have in common. Many of the following comments were taken from timely newspaper articles written at the time of the respective events.

Securities and Exchange Chairwoman from *2009-2012*

Senator Schumer *comments on the nomination of* ***Mary L. Schapiro;*** *And I believe by temperament, inclination and experience, you can become that much-needed stronger regulator. You come here with along background in securities regulation, with experience leading many of the major institutions that make up our capital markets regulatory system.*

Mary L. Schapiro <u>now sits on the board of Morgan Stanley.</u>

Securities and Exchange Chairwoman from *2013-2017*

Mary Jo White *is tough. Really, she is. That's the message that* ***Chuck Schumer****, the Democrat who represents New York (and Wall Street) in the Senate, tried to convey as he introduced White during her confirmation hearings before the Senate Banking Committee. White is President Barack Obama's choice to head the Securities and Exchange Commission.*

Mary Jo White *is now a partner with Debevoise & Plimpton. Ms. White, 69 years old, is rejoining Debevoise & Plimpton LLP as a partner in New York and taking on the newly created position of senior chair, the law firm is expected to announce Wednesday. Debevoise, an elite New York firm with close ties to Wall Street.*

Attorney General from 2009-2015

Sen. Chuck Schumer *threw his support behind embattled* ***Attorney General Eric Holder*** *on Sunday, saying he sees no reason for him to resign.*

When Eric Holder Left his position as Attorney General, he went right back to a law firm that played a major role in the 2008 financial collapse.

Attorney General from 2015-2017

*Sen. **Chuck Schumer** introduced fellow New Yorker **Loretta Lynch**, the attorney general nominee, to the Senate Judiciary Committee in January as a public servant who "has earned a reputation for keeping her head down and avoiding the spotlight -- just like me.*

Senate Democratic Leader **Chuck Schumer** of New York said Monday that he believes **Rosenstein** is "independent" and has developed a reputation for integrity.

FBI Director from 2001-2013

Chuck Schumer *affirms Commitment to **Robert Mueller.***

Mueller also joined the law firm WilmerHale as a partner in its Washington office in 2014. WilmerHale is a worldwide leader in securities enforcement defense.

FBI Director from 2013-2017

*"In this account, **James Comey's** actions showcase a duplicitous, secretive schemer whose true loyalties were not to the officials to whom he reported, but to partisan Democrats like **Senate Minority Leader Chuck Schumer** (D-N.Y.)."*

This article was reprinted with permission from the American Thinker, it can be found at americanthinker.com

"It felt to me that Jim's loyalty was more to his friend Preet Bharara and to Chuck Schumer," he wrote.

This article was reprinted with permission from the Federalist; it can be found at thefederalist.com

All of these officials were recommended, supported or promoted by Senator Schumer. All of these individuals failed to prosecute major wall street firms and their executives. All of these officials appeared to use their position, power and authority to protect the alleged criminals on Wall Street. Criminals that committed thousands of alleged serious felonies. Alleged felonies that were responsible for the 2008 Financial Collapse, the Detroit Municipal Bankruptcy and the Puerto Rico Municipal Bankruptcy. In total over ten trillion dollars in alleged theft.

Why isn't Senator Schumer in prison? Why were the heads of the SEC, U.S Attorney's Office and the FBI not charged with criminal conspiracy? Did Wall Street get their money's worth for the one hundred million dollars given to Senator Schumer over the past decade?

Senator Schumer wakes up in the morning to tells the public one thing, and then appears to retreat to the dark corners of his office to do just the opposite. And when Senator Schumer is not helping Wall Street steal from the American people, he is on TV apparently trying to divide the country.

Senator Schumer's Careless Remarks
This article was reprinted with permission from Seeking Alpha found at seekingalpha.com

"By now we've all grown accustomed to the act of congressional "ambulance chasing"; members of Congress who regularly appear on the scene every time there is a problem, pointing fingers at the other party or involved government agency, proclaiming their own innocence to the situation and out of the blue presenting a miraculous solution to the problem. Narcissists by nature, members of Congress use these situations to garner TV time and press coverage, giving their constituents the impression, they are not part of the problem and that instead they are working hard on their behalf to make everything right. Over the years, NY Senator Charles Schumer has become known for just this type of activity."

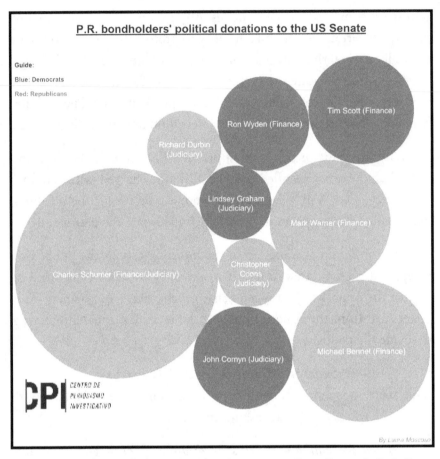

This graph was reprinted with permission from Centro de Periodismo Investigativo; it can be found at periodismoinvestigativo.com

I know it may appear that I am picking on Senator Schumer. Everywhere I looked the trail led me back to Mr. Schumer. I lost my house, my savings, my retirement funds all because of these alleged fraudulent ratings and the political leaders who enabled and protected these alleged criminals. I am not alone; tens of millions of Americans were stolen from. I will not sit back and be a victim. The world needs to know who these people are.

Another noteworthy participant is **Sean Duffy**. Congressman Duffy sponsored the "PROMESA" Legislation that revoked the bond victim's rights and handed control back to many of the same bad actors that participated in the crimes. He did this, to the best of my knowledge, while being fully informed about all the fraud.

Duffy Tops List to Take Over Wall Street Subcommittee
This article was reprinted with permission from Morning Consult; it can be found at "morningconsult.com

"Duffy, who came to Washington as part of the 2010 tea party wave, has chaired the Financial Services Subcommittee on Oversight and Investigations since 2014. He was a key lawmaker in the debate over how Congress should address Puerto Rico's debt crisis, and he was the lead sponsor on the debt restructuring legislation that President Obama signed into law in June.

Like most of his Republican colleagues, Duffy is a critic of the 2010 Dodd-Frank Act." Other headlines shouted out:

Representative Duffy sponsored Puerto Rico Bankruptcy Legislation

Think Wall Street Should Secretly Bribe Foreign Governments? Sean Duffy Does.
This article was reprinted with permission from the Democratic Party of Wisconsin, it can be found at wisdems.org

You can find numerous articles on the web that claim Sean Duffy is in Wall Street's Pocket

Sean Duffy (R-WI) took $658,754 from Wall Street interests during the last election.

This article was reprinted with permission from Allied Progress, it can be found at ***alliedprogress.org***

Truth be told, I took a deep dive into the Washington D.C. Political mess. I looked at about fifty career politicians. Based on that, I could write a three-thousand-page book on all the immoral, unethical and likely criminal acts they are all involved in. To keep the book to three thousand pages, I would have to limit my scope to just those immoral, unethical and likely criminal acts relating to this specific Criminal Organization I am writing about.

Here are some articles that speak to motivations:

"91% of the time the better-financed candidate wins. Don't act surprised."
This article was reprinted with permission from the Washington Post found at washingtonpost.com

According to an article posted on Our Future Dot Org back in September of 2010, the articles author Zach Carter stated that ninety members of congress voted to bail out Wall Street in 2008 and failed to vote for any financial reform measures. These very same politicians received almost two hundred million dollars from Wall Street during their careers.

The Obama Administration

Chicago has a well-earned reputation as having the most corrupt political machine and corrupt city government in all of America. Headlines informed me:

According to various articles available on the web, In 2015
Chicago was considered the most corrupt city in the United States.

Tuesday, May 15, 2018
Report: Chicago most corrupt city in U.S
This video report appeared on the ABC Eyewitness News website found at abc7chicago.com

President Obama (2009-2017) was trained in politics in Chicago and brought his values, or lack of values, to the White House. He sought out like-minded politicians and bureaucrats and stacked the Federal Government with these individuals.

Rahm Emanuel, another Chicago Politician was appointed President Obama's Chief of Staff. Rahm Emanuel most famous quote; "You never want a serious crisis to go to waste."

The 2008 financial crisis brought this country to its knees. In 2009 when government officials were starting to figure out what caused it, President Obama and his team appeared to have figured out how to personally benefit from it. The 2008 crisis was followed up with the Detroit municipal bankruptcy and finally the Puerto Rico municipal bankruptcy. Respectively, the largest municipal bankruptcy in U.S. History.

No one should say President Obama and his team caused the 2008 financial crisis nor would I agree with anyone that would blame President Obama for the Detroit or Puerto Rico bankruptcies. As far as I can tell, the President and most of his team played no role in the original crimes.

The ratings agencies allegedly fabricated thousands of fraudulent credit ratings and the major Wall Street Banks then knowingly sold those bonds. Thousands upon thousands of easy-to-detect financial felonies took place. Evidence was everywhere.

Wall Street executives were looking for political and legal cover and the Obama administration appeared to be looking for money and influence. By stacking the Department of Justice (FBI, U.S. Attorney's Office) and the Securities and Exchange Commission with like-minded political appointees, President Obama and his small team were able to destroy our justice system and our regulatory agencies. This allowed the Obama administration and their allies to provide protection (protection racket). They profited massively using this strategy.

Here are some headlines suggesting FBI and U.S. Attorney corruption:

Obama's DOJ And FBI Conspired to Knife America In the Heart
This article was reprinted with permission from News with Views found at newswithviews.com

This article was reprinted with permission from the American Thinker found at americanthinker.com

Why aren't the Democrats horrified by the corruption at the FBI and DOJ?
This article was reprinted with permission from American Thinker found at americanthinker.com

Federal abuses on Obama's watch represent a growing blight on his legacy
This article was reprinted with permission from The Hill; it can be found at thehill.com

"In all of the discussions about the political weaponization of the Department of Justice (DOJ) and the FBI, alleged corruption at the highest echelons of those agencies and serial abuse of the secret FISA process surrounding the 2016 election, one name has been conspicuously absent: President Barack Obama.

High-ranking officials and other major players in those agencies — which Obama oversaw — are increasingly embroiled in the growing scandal: James Comey, Loretta Lynch, Andrew McCabe, Andrew Weissmann, Sally Yates, Peter Strzok, Lisa Page, Bruce Ohr.

Given the tight control Obama exercised over every part of his administration and agenda, the idea that any of these appointees and loyalists freelanced their activities without at least his tacit approval or that of his White House strains credulity.

The financial crisis actually happened at the end of the **Bush Presidency**. President Bush could theoretically be blamed for the 2008 financial crisis; it did happen on his watch. If he was not participating in it, President Bush was at least asleep at the wheel. For the purposes of this book, it did not appear to make sense to go back fifteen years to explore that administration's role in all of this. It was and is a "protection racket," and that protection started in 2009.

The reasons for the 2008 financial collapse were not well known until President Obama was in office. President Obama, his Attorney General, his FBI Director and their Leadership Teams at the Securities and Exchange Commission appeared to <u>make sure there were no investigations and no prosecutions</u>.

Check out this quote from President Obama:

Obama to Occupy Wall Street Protestors
"You are the reason I ran for office"
From a 2011 Campaign Speech made by President Obama

Then President Obama puts in **Eric Holder as Attorney General** and **Robert Mueller as FBI Director**. The two of them were swimming in evidence regarding Wall Street. How disingenuous was our President? It takes a special kind of person to present himself as a Wall Street Crusader and then appoint people with apparent instructions to protect Wall Street.

The financial crisis brought us to our knees but the wholesale destruction of the Department of Justice and the Securities and Exchange Commission, may destroy our Country.

Tens of trillions of dollars in wealth was stolen or destroyed, much of it during the Obama Administration, and only one person was ever investigated or charged with a crime. Much of the stolen money was laundered in countries that were hostile to the United States. Giving our enemy's resources to use against us. You saw how easy it is to determine if fraudulent ratings were issued and if banks knowingly sold those fraudulent bonds. No Wall Street Executives went to jail.

What do you think a jury of American citizens would do to Eric Holder and Robert Mueller?

Check out this "policy" that Attorney General Eric Holder came up with:

"The Holder Doctrine was the name given to a June 1999 memorandum written by Eric H. Holder Jr., then the deputy attorney general of the United States, whom President Obama nominated in 2009 to become attorney general, a position he held until his retirement this year. Mr. Holder's argument essentially was that big financial institutions are "too big to jail" because the potential for "collateral consequences" from prosecutions — including corporate instability or collapse — had to be considered when deciding whether to bring a case against them, or apparently, against anyone who worked there and engaged in bad behavior."

You can find this in a memo that was widely distributed to DOJ personnel

In other words, do not prosecute anyone from Wall Street's major firms. The Department of Justice didn't, and Wall Street harmed the American people again and again: the 2008 financial crisis (alleged fabricated credit ratings, Detroit, alleged fabricated credit ratings, Puerto Rico, alleged fabricated credit ratings). By mailing letters to the credit rating agencies and the banks, I have given the DOJ and the SEC all the evidence they need to prosecute. The board members and executives can't deny knowledge of this anymore. But will the SEC and DOJ do anything, or will Senator Schumer and others continue to protect them?

NYT's William Cohan Blasts "Holder Doctrine" of Headfake Bank Settlements" With No Prosecutions

This article was reprinted with permission from Naked Capitalism found at nakedcapitalism.com

"What is revealing here is that the Administration seems to think that the public buys this sort of enforcement theater. The public has lost interest in these deals. They know the banks got away with murder and pacts that are cost-of-doing business level fines don't get their attention. They want to see managers and executives prosecuted."

When Eric Holder left his position as Attorney General, he went right back to a law firm that played a major role in the 2008 financial collapse.

Why Eric Holder's new job is an insult to the American public

This article first appeared in Salon.com.
An online version remains in the Salon archives.
Reprinted with permission

"If we had a more aggressive media, this would be an enormous scandal, more than the decamping of former Obama Administration officials to places like Uber and Amazon. That's because practically no law firm

has done more to protect Wall Street executives from the consequences of their criminal activities than Covington & Burling. Their roster of clients includes every mega-bank in America: JPMorgan Chase, Wells Fargo, Citigroup, Bank of America. Yet **Holder has joined several of his ex-employees there***, creating a shadow Justice Department and an unquestionable conflict of interest. In fact, given the pathetic fashion in which DOJ limited punishment for those who caused the greatest economic meltdown in 80 years, Holder's new job looks a lot like his old job." [Underlining and bold by author.]*

"My three years in politics was very instructive about the way in which the appetite for political power can destroy a human mind, destroy principles and values, and transform people into little monsters." Mario Vargas Llosa

This famous quote is available widely and can be found at brainyquote.com

The Trump Administration

Some people claim that the Obama Administration holdovers still control the Department of Justice and the Securities and Exchange Commission.

Obama Holdovers at DOJ Still Run the Show
This article was reprinted with permission from
The Hill found at thehill.com

"President Donald Trump may sit in the White House, and Attorney General Jeff Sessions occupy the leading spot at the Department of Justice — but it's Barack Obama-era holdovers who are really calling some of America's law enforcement shots.

That's according to J. Christian Adams, a former DOJ lawyer who has

the inside scoop on who's running what at this all-too-important Cabinet-level spot."

But regardless of what people believe, the person currently in power is the person responsible to the American people. Many of the same career politicians will continue to have their say when it comes to any new political appointees. When Preet Bharara left the DOJ, Geoffrey S. Berman was appointed as the United States Attorney for the Southern District of New York by a group of judges. President Trump has the option of replacing him with another political appointee. There have been zero prosecutions related to this alleged criminal organization by Mr. Berman. He either independently believes Wall Street executives can break any law without fear of prosecution or he is once again following instructions from his political allies.

It is too soon to tell if President Trump will be any different then President Obama on this issue. At the current time, he probably does not yield the control he needs with the Department of Justice to force any changes. He has, however, supported the roll-back of the Dodd-Frank Legislation, a strong indication that he may not be any different then President Obama on Wall Street and Political corruption. The appointment of Jeff Sessions as the Attorney General is another indication the President wants to keep the status quo. Mr. Sessions has been swimming in Washington politics for decades and is likely to maintain the status quo.

Recent appointments to the Securities and Exchange Commission are also not encouraging:

Jay Clayton's SEC Protects Wall Street Racketeering
This article was reprinted with permission from Activist Post found at
activistpost.com

By Aaron Kesel

"Empirical evidence indicates policy changes appear to be crippling watchdog organizations from addressing and arresting those on Wall Street committing fraud.

Many questionable legal provisions are transpiring within the federal system of justice, which victims of white-collar-crimes are crying foul about making fraud easier to get away with.

White collar offenders aren't being called criminals, in some ways due to the repeal of Acts such as Glass Steagall.

According to various reports by mainstream media organizations like the Wall Street Journal, Politico and Bloomberg, fines upon Wall Street shenanigans are down this year, considerably; which means Senators Elizabeth Warren and Bernie Sanders, two outspoken critics of Wall Street, were correct to be critical of Trump's nomination of Jay Clayton to head the SEC.

As a matter of fact, SEC fines are the lowest they have been since 2013, according to Bloomberg. Such reductions in penalties for misdeeds are even more alarming, considering the fact that entities like Wells Fargo are getting caught doing schemes resulting in the firing of thousands of employees for ripping off millions of customers.

Compounding the dynamics of weakening the laws meant to hold Wall Street in check are the more recent guttings of Dodd Frank Act, and putting Mick Mulvaney in charge of the Consumer Financial Protection Bureau (CFPB) who is on the record hating the CFPB.

There is also the fun fact that Congress and Trump have made it harder for victims of misdeeds to sue financial institutions by voting to end arbitration clauses that protect average Americans, The Wall Street Journal reported.

Now there is evidence that Jay Clayton, as Chairman of the SEC, is guilty of covering up Goldman Sachs & Bain Capital misdeeds.

Wall Street victims, like eToys shareholders and eToys court-appointed fiduciary Laser Haas, have complained repeatedly about Goldman Sachs partnership with Bain Capital in racketeering crimes (please see this reporter's previous articles on Mattel, eToys, Fingerhut and Paul Traub frauds here and here).

Visibly, the SEC is covering up massive crimes by Sachs, Bain Capital and their bad faith lawyers ignoring Haas's pleas in federal court for justice against bankruptcy rings.

It just so happens, that Jay Clayton was partners with the Sullivan & Cromwell law firm, which the eToys parties are accusing of being duplicitous in the deliberate destruction of the eToys public company, according to The Wall Street Journal. (archived)

Additionally, prior to Jay Clayton's resume being yanked down all over the Web, Clayton boasted about being invested in Mitt Romney's Bain Capital.

Furthermore, Jay Clayton and his Sullivan & Cromwell law firm represented Goldman Sachs, which Fortune magazine documents.

On top of all those glaring conflicts of interest issues, Jay Clayton's wife (Greta Clayton) was a VP at Goldman Sachs, purportedly working the very mergers and acquisitions division the eToys victims claim has defrauded eToys.

Jay Clayton promised his wife Gretchen would resign from Goldman

Sachs once he was confirmed as Chairman of the SEC. Yet, to this reporter's knowledge, that doesn't appear to be the case looking at her LinkedIn.

Speaking of confirmation, eToys usurped fiduciary, Laser Haas, attempted to block Jay Clayton's nomination as Commissioner of the SEC because of these glaring conflict of interests issues, according to the lawsuit.

Whistleblower Laser Haas sued Donald Trump, Jeff Sessions, the SEC, the FBI, the United States Trustee program and Assistant United States Attorney, Ellen Slights, for their connections; refusal to prosecute Goldman Sachs, Bain Capital and seditious lawyers who rip off victims in the billions of dollars.

It is so commonly known that Wall Street is actually protected, rather than investigated and prosecuted, by our federal systems of justice, there's a recent book by ProPublica's Jesse Eisinger entitled The Chickenshit Club.

Corroborating the fact that Washington, D.C., is hell-bent on protecting Wall Street, on March 22, 2017, the Federal District Court in Washington's District of Columbia received Laser's lawsuit seeking a Restraining Order until the Senate was made aware of the Goldman Sachs/ Bain Capital enterprising and the plethora of Jay Clayton's glaring conflicts of interests.

Inexplicably and intolerably, the Federal Clerk of Court, in violation of the law flatly refused to docket Laser's litigation about Jay Clayton's SEC nomination until 3 weeks after the Senate confirmed the nomination of Jay Clayton to be the new Chairman of the SEC.

The law states in Rule 79 that a clerk of the court is required to docket a case upon receiving; in this instance they say the case was filed May 9th. But this is contradicted by the court's docket that notes the papers were received March 22nd. Further, as Laser himself documented, they refused to docket the case until 5/24/17 after the order to dismiss on 5/5/17.

It's not as if Goldman Sachs is least likely to wind up on the SEC's radar. Truth be told, Goldman Sachs is involved in so many aspects of Wall Street endeavors, from Treasury Bills, Public Offerings and more; which – in a legitimate era of justice – would mandate a task force dedicated to watchdogging just Goldman Sachs alone.

However, from the dynamics of what Fed investigator Carmen Segarra's reports revealed, America is already well aware of the staunch refusal to investigate (properly) – much less dare to have the guts to prosecute – the likes of Goldman Sachs.

See a few of the cases this reporter has remarked upon (here) on how the federal watchdog agencies have refused to investigate and prosecute many cases. These include, but are not limited to, many billions of dollars of questionable acts in the cases of KB Toys, Stage Stores, Fingerhut, TerraStar, the 1.5 million domain names ripped off from Jeff Baron, how Ritchie Capital was fleeced of its $100 million-plus Polaroid deal, RedTag/Ibid, multi-billion-dollar rip off of Mattel, Okun 1031 Tax Group, Playco and eToys cases and many more.

Staunch refusals to prosecute create above-the-law fraudsters such as the recently discussed New York Attorney at Law, Paul Traub (see my previous article "Meet Mitt Romney's Frank Nitti: Paul Traub").

With Goldman Sachs/Bain Capital's "guy" – Jay Clayton – now in charge of the top Wall Street watchdog agency, the SEC, it is far worse than mere issues as willfully blind prosecutors, as noted in Eisinger's recent book The Chickenshit Club!

It appears it has long been open season for Wall Street to hunt for victims; and under Jay Clayton's friendship with Wall Street, it's going to get much worse.

Knowing they are free to rob without remorse or relent, they simply steal faster, bigger and from as many as they can.

Including the open season that expanded after the untimely demises of victims Marty Lackner, Anna Schaeffer, Jack Wheeler and eToys shareholder Robert Alber.

Alber was warned that "people like you who turns down a bribe – usually wakes up dead."

Subsequently, after eToys shareholder Robert Alber was forced to shoot and kill would-be assassin Michael Sesseyoff in self-defense, Alber "woke up dead" like he was previously threatened.

Just days after Alber died, the Delaware Assistant United States Attorney Ellen Slights had the FBI contact Laser Haas and threaten Laser with federal prosecution – unless Haas immediately redacted certain names.

Who's next? Will it be this last remaining whistleblower who dares to ignore threats of federal prosecution and those against his life seeking justice? Or will people finally wake up and understand what is going on as has been documented over and over again throughout this series?

If our tax-paid public servants have escalated their willful blindness to the point of being outright tools for Wall Street racketeering – then it is completely open season upon the American citizenry and as a result the economy.

U.S. President Donald Trump promised to "drain the swamp" and criticized his opponent Hillary Clinton's cozy relationship with Goldman Sachs. But he broke that promise, along with many others, putting Sachs executives all throughout his cabinet including National Security Adviser Dina Powell, Top Economic Advisor Gary Cohn, and Treasury Secretary Steve Mnuchin, The Intercept reported.

All of which is compounded by the appointment of the much-conflicted Jay Clayton who has brought in two of his former colleagues at Goldman Sachs and his law firm Sullivan & Cromwell – Steven Peikin and Sean Memon – to help deregulate Wall Street.

This impotency of Jay Clayton concerning Goldman Sachs, and his participating in the deregulating of Wall Street, enables Goldman Sachs to continue its victimizing and also Sachs lawyers open season of perpetrating frauds on the courts."

I have shared this story with President Trump via a number of tweets. He seems to get it! The president appears to understand what is going on. He replied to me with this tweet:

"Hold Wall St and our Politicians accountable"

Donald J. Trump @ realDonald_bot 20 Feb 2017

More
Replying to @ lawless61
The politicians can't
11:54 AM – 20 Feb 2017

I believe what he was telling me is that money controls our congressmen and senators. To stay in power and have the money to win reelection, they must engage in these alleged criminal activities while protecting their financial contributors. If our politicians ever came up with the courage and character to take action, they would be at risk of implicating themselves. I just don't think there are enough good people in public office to change any of this. I hope I am wrong. Short of the American people taking to the street, these elected officials need to be voted out of office.

I didn't want to pretend to speak for our president, but I believe that is what he was trying to tell me. If I got that wrong, my sincerest apologies Mr. President.

The damage done to innocent Americans, and our country as a whole, is not a consideration for most of our career politicians. They believe they are untouchable and so far, they are right! Short of cleaning house at the FBI, U.S. Attorney's Office and the SEC, there is no one left to prosecute these folks.

> "In politics, nothing happens by accident.
> If it happens, you can bet it was planned that way."
> **Franklin D. Roosevelt**

This is a widely available quote and can be found at brainyquote.com

The alleged corruption continues today in the **Trump Administration**. Some of the political leaders have changed and the mind-boggling, record breaking, trillion-dollar alleged thefts have temporarily subsided. I fear that until we change our voting patterns or vote for term limits, eventually our politicians will fully destroy this country. America will become a second or third world country. <u>There is only so much wealth that can be stolen until there is nothing left to steal.</u>

> *In the meantime, it would be best not to trust any ratings coming out of Moody's, Fitch or S&P. It may also make a lot of sense to **avoid all municipal bond investments** until this house of cards explodes and the rating agencies, banks and politicians move on to another type of financial fraud.*

If you don't believe in God, imagine for a moment that God existed and woke up this morning deciding to fix things. God waves His hand and fifty of our worse, most corrupt, most immoral career politicians disappear. Next God waves His other hand and all of the political appointees in the FBI and U.S Attorney's office also disappear. God thinks for a bit, waves His hand again and makes all the Commissioners at the Securities and Exchange Commission disappear. Finally, God faces Wall Street, waves both hands and 600 corrupt Wall Street Executives disappear. With this change, a change effecting less than 1000 people, do you think our country would be better off?

Instead of relying on God, let's pretend that we vote fifty career politicians out of office -- you know them, the guys and gals you see on TV every day trying to spike up people's emotions and convince you a certain event is a life or death issue. Isn't it possible that, with fifty new congressman and senators and the some of the remaining "good politicians," Congress could clean house at the Department of Justice and the Securities and Exchange Commission? If they could do that, then the DOJ and SEC could properly prosecute those Wall Street executives.

Would it really be that hard to make these small changes? Less than one thousand people could change this country in ways we can't imagine right now. You just have to come to grips with the fact that it is "your politician," "your guy or gal," that is part of the problem. And yes, oh my God, you might have to vote for a Liberal Republican or a Conservative Democrat just one time, to make this happen. It could make all the difference; it's up to you.

What do we do now? In my opinion we just need to ask a few pointed questions. Did serious financial fraud take place in the billions and trillions of dollars? Did the participants know about the fraud? Normally this would be enough to prosecute and convict. We could continue to ask questions. Did they use their respective positions to hide the fraud or protect the perpetrators? Did they receive a career enhancement or compensation of some type for their role?

We can't count on the law enforcement agencies (FBI) to investigate. We can't count of the Attorney General (DOJ) to prosecute. We can file a private RICO lawsuit proving this criminal activity and the cooperation between all parties. We can file hundreds of private civil actions to recover money damages. We will be up against a corrupt Department of Justice and judges appointed by the same Politicians that participated in criminal activity. But it can be done. To combat their unlimited use of tax dollars and political campaign monies, we will need to raise tens of millions of dollars. The evidence is overwhelming and the outcome could help drain the swamp of hundreds of bad actors.

The ratings agency Board of Directors and Executives will be looking at serious charges, many will opt to cooperate to avoid spending the remainder of their lives in prison. The same is true with the SEC Commissioners and Executives and the Department of Justice Officals. Based on available evidence it is likely that more than half of our Congressmen and Senators have earned their day in court. It is now up to the American people to determine if any of them are held accountable.

If you believe there are serious crimes taking place that are either encouraged and or protected by our government officials, I hope you will support the fundraising efforts that will be in place once the book is published. Check the books website for further details.

CHAPTER SIX

THE GRAND DISTRACTION

No criminal enterprise can survive in the light of day. To run a successful criminal operation, one must keep the activities of the Wall Street executives and our politicians out of the news and out of the sight on the American people. The best way to accomplish this is to keep the general public focused on other issues and keep them divided.

Our politicians understand this and have identified a number of great emotion-filled issues. Issues if left unsolved by the Congress that will effectively distract the voting public and the press.

Do you really think our congressmen and senators can't solve our immigration challenges and gun control? Do you think the politicians really care about Russian influence on our elections? Or, is it possible that these issues are used to distract the public, raise more campaign dollars and most importantly, allow the career politicians to get on with the business of trading protection for money?

Take a quick look at the topics covered most by the newspapers, television news and cable news networks.

Russian influence on our elections
Russian collusion
Children separated from parents at border
Another mass shooting
More Hillary corruption
Racist comments by famous people

You get my point. Whenever the news cycles start to dry up, our politicians will come up with some new emotion-filled topic to eat up all the oxygen in the press. Attempting to convince the American people into believing these issues are "life or death" issues. The politicians need to keep the public arguing about Democrat vs Republican, Conservative vs Liberal, so their alleged criminal activities can go on unabated and unnoticed. It really is the "Great Distraction".

If you want your wife to stop talking about your infidelity, just clean out your joint bank accounts; your wife's focus and your conversations will change quickly. The infidelity will become a minor point of discussion.

"The whole aim of practical politics is to keep the populace alarmed (and hence clamorous to be led to safety) by menacing it with an endless series of hobgoblins, all of them imaginary."

--H. L. Mencken

This is a widely available quote and can be found at brainyquote.com

Let's face it: our political leaders could easily solve these issues but do not want to. They are great fund-raising tools and great distractions.

If the politicians really hate each other so much and can't agree on anything, how is it possible that 68% of these individuals can come together in agreement to vote for a law (PROMESA) that revokes the legal rights of U.S. Citizens? Citizens that were likely victims of Wall Street crimes. How is it that all 435 Congressman and 100 Senators have shown no interest in prosecuting Wall Street executives or municipal executives for their crimes? They are in 100% agreement on that!

One of the politicians' favorite strategies is to pitch Democrats against Republicans. Senator Schumer and many others wake up every morning hoping to get on the news to dish out, to serve up, another hurtful, disingenuous, news story to help divide our country and ultimately, I believe, destroy our system of government. You have heard it all before:

"They want our seniors to eat dogfood"
"They will force everyone into backstreet abortions"
"These Nazi's will take away all your rights"
"They will tax and spend us into bankruptcy"
"They want to kill our children"

Let's think about the logic here. How many politicians think they will win more supporters by hurting children, let alone killing them? Logic would suggest none. Common sense goes out the window for so many low IQ political activists. Well I shouldn't say low IQ; many of them are likely smarter than me. But nevertheless, they take to the streets and chant: "They want to kill our children." More surprisingly, the cable news outlets are all over it and their commentators are trying to convince you it is all true. An unbiased honest press would have reported the story like this:

Today the X party held a caucus focusing on broad budget cuts in an attempt to balance the budget. It appears that one of the programs buried in one of the appropriations that are to be cut was a school lunch program. The X party leader recently held a press conference claiming the cuts to the school lunch program were unacceptable. After speaking with a number of caucus members it appears that it was an unintentional oversite that will hopefully be addressed shortly. How does this news story equate to, "They want to kill our children"?

The politicians have been so successful that most voters would rather reelect a corrupt Republican than vote for an "evil" Democrat. Equally, most Democrats will set aside almost any criminal or moral violation concerning their elected officials rather than have an "evil" Republican in office. This division has been a very effective tool in preventing any consensus by the voters on the most despicable behaviors by our politicians.

This strategy has also been very effective dividing the press into camps. Their reporting is often limited to covering "bad acts" by the "other party officials" while their favorite politician's transgressions never make it on air.

A big reason this criminal enterprise has been so successful is that it would require the press and the voters to "agree" <u>both parties are thoroughly corrupt</u>. Honest reporting about this "Criminal Underground" would risk incriminating "their guy." Keep the hate between the Liberals and Conservatives at a fever pitch and people will put up with increasingly bad behavior by their respective parties. After all, "my guy" might be a murderer and rapist but at least he is not a (fill in the space) Democrat/Republican.

This is a well thought out and purposely executed strategy, created and practiced by our most senior politicians. All done without any concern about what it is doing to our country and the American people!

Take a look at Nancy Pelosi's contributions

House Minority Leader Nancy Pelosi on Thursday referred to President Donald Trump's chief strategist, Steve Bannon, as a "White Supremacist." This article was reprinted with permission from CBS News found at cbsnews.com

Pelosi flat-out defended the rapists and murderers that make up MS-13
from the President's harsh rhetoric saying,
"Calling people animals is not a good thing."
This article was reprinted with permission from Conservative Angle
found at conservativeangle.com

I recall newspaper articles covering a local meeting on healthcare where
Nancy Pelosi tried to infer that the participants were Nazi's and were car-
rying swastikas and similar symbols.

'So Inhumane': Pelosi Scolds Trump, Claims
He Called Undocumented Immigrants 'Animals'
This article appeared in a Web Blog called Political Conundrum found at
www.tapatalk.com

Hoyer: Pelosi's Comment About 'Five White Guys'
Negotiating DACA Is 'Offensive'
This article was reprinted with permission from The Washington Free
Beacon found at freebeacon.com

Last Thursday Rep. Nancy Pelosi (D-Rich Off Hubby's Money) held a
<u>rambling press conference</u> in which she characterized the bonuses corpora-
tions are giving their rank-and-file employees as "crumbs."
This article was reprinted with permission from RedState found at
redstate.com

"Those who seek to reverse the remarkable progress we've made continue to
seek justification for their flagrant, hateful discrimination."
Nancy Pelosi Tweet

Is Nancy Pelosi trying to unite or divide American? You decide.

Nancy Patricia Pelosi net worth is
$140 Million
Nancy Patricia Pelosi salary is
$193,000

In 2009, Nancy Pelosi's net worth was about $20 Million;
in 2018 it was about $140 Million.
Any questions?

Do you think the theft of $10 TRILLION DOLLARS is news? Where is it in in the press? If you believe the press is biased, as most people do, why would they run a story that implicates both the Democrats and the Republicans in a criminal enterprise?

Shawn Hannity at Fox News will not likely cover this topic because it makes Republican Paul Ryan look like a crook. Rachel Maddow at MSNBC will likely not cover this topic because it makes Democrat Chuck Schumer look like a crook.

I sent evidence of all this to the *Wall Street Journal* over a dozen times. I sent it to their executive editors, their news editors and their most well-known reporters. They all refused to report on this alleged criminal organization. A financial newspaper that will not report the theft of trillions of dollars by Wall Street firms! I sent this information to the *New York Times* at least a dozen times. I contacted their news editors and public editors. I sent this information to the *Bond Buyer*, the largest municipal bond publication I am aware of. I also called them and emailed them. They did touch superficially on this in some articles but never told the whole story.

I sent this to *The Hill,* a widely read on-line publication. They were kind enough to print a number of my editorials covering small pieces of this alleged criminal empire. I am sincerely grateful to them for that. But when it came to telling the whole story, they were unreceptive.

I also contacted, CNN, Hannity, Fox News, Dateline, ABC News, NBC News and MSNBC, and they all neglected to cover the story or simply ignored all the evidence I sent them.

The *New York Observer* was courageous enough to report on one of the most explosive aspects of this story: the CIA recorded phone conversations on money laundering, DOJ bribes and political payoffs. For that, I am really grateful. When it came down to telling the whole story, the paper showed little interest.

The real hero in the press was a relatively small on-line news publication called *Caribbean NewsNow*. The editor at the paper was willing to tell the whole story and even investigated some of the issues himself. For that, I hope one day he will get a Pulitzer Prize.

At the end of the day, I wrote over fifty newspaper articles. Each article covered a small piece of this very large story. About half of the articles were printed in some sort of news publication or website. I want to send out a sincere thank you to those publications and websites that were willing to take that risk.

In the final chapter, I will share newspaper articles that have touched on small parts of this explosive story and explore why the publications didn't do more?

CHAPTER SEVEN
HOW MANY OTHERS KNEW AND DID NOTHING?

I am somewhat familiar with Robert Slavin at the *Bond Buyer*. What surprises me about this article is that I would have guessed that by September 7th of 2016, Mr. Slavin and the *Bond Buyer* knew that the seventy billion in Puerto Rico Bonds were likely fraudulent. They neglected to mention that in this article. Why would experts on municipal debt exclude that fact in an article about Puerto Rico Corruption? First, we must take a look at who the bond buyer is.

The Bond Buyer is the only independent information resource serving the entire municipal finance community. Its comprehensive paid-subscription package of news, analysis and data is unique in the industry, serving a complete spectrum of senior industry professionals, through its website, e-newsletters and alerts, and daily print edition.

The Bond Buyer reaches more than 75,000 municipal finance professionals: issuers, government officials, investors — all players on the "deal team." The Bond Buyer also offers in-depth education about cutting-edge public-finance topics to Executive & Senior Management decision makers.

Was the *Bond Buyer* doing what was in its own best interest? Given their customer base, is it possible they withheld that information to best serve their target readers, professionals who issue and sell these bonds? Was the *Bond Buyer* a co-conspirator, given they likely knew and withheld that information? Maybe the *Bond Buyer* called the FBI or SEC and told them? Not likely. To be fair, the *Bond Buyer* did touch on a few problems with Puerto Rico Bonds in other articles but appeared to withhold the size and scope of the alleged fraud from the public. I don't know, maybe I missed it? Take a look at the article and see if you can spot anything on municipal bond fraud.

Puerto Rico Corruption and Why it Matters
This article was reprinted with permission from The Bond Buyer found at bondbuyer.com

By
Robert Slavin
Published
September 07 2016, 2:39pm EDT

Center for a New Economy chief economist Gustavo Bobonis said corruption is perceived to be worse in Puerto Rico than in the 50 states.

Puerto Rico's debt crisis has its roots in a number of factors, not the least of which is government corruption.

As the latest corruption case went to trial Puerto Ricans have been transfixed this summer by the testimony. The case has produced pay-to-play allegations against at least one government official, a claim that the current governor's campaign manager illegally solicited cash donations and led to the resignation of the president of the Puerto Rico House of Representatives from that post. Along with producing scandal and causing leadership changes, analysts say corruption over the years also has taken a toll on the island's finances. Puerto Rico's government now faces the restructuring of $70 billion of public debt, under the oversight of a federal control board *named last month by President Obama.*

Government corruption has been a key factor in leading the Puerto Rico's gross national product to contract eight of the last nine years, said Zulma Rosario Vega, executive director of the Puerto Rico Office of Ethics.

Gustavo Bobonis, chief economist at the Center for a New Economy, said corruption affected the island's economic development, though it was probably not the chief factor.

Luis Cámara Fuertes, a professor of political science at the University of Puerto Rico, said corruption reduces competitiveness. If the government only entertains corrupt offers, then it accepts more expensive bids.

A common complaint about Puerto Rico government contracts is that "the system is very closed," he said. One needs to have connections to do business with the government.

By hurting the island's economy, corruption leads to reduced funds flowing into government coffers. Corruption also leads to inefficient use of public sector funds, which can undermine public corporation financial strength and divert government spending from potentially useful projects to wasteful ones.

Unfortunately for Puerto Rico these possibilities have been more than academic.

Starting with the administration of Puerto Rico Gov. Pedro Rossell-, who held office from the start of 1993 to the start of 2001, Puerto Rican governments have used bonds to finance "mega public works projects," wrote Emilio Pantojas García, professor of Sociology at University of Puerto Rico.

"Examples of major projects undertaken with bond issues guaranteed with future income to be realized from the fees of [the Puerto Rico Electric Power Authority and the Puerto Rico Aqueduct and Sewer Authority]

include the 'Super Aqueduct' of the PRASA and two natural gas pipelines ... of PREPA, which were intended to deliver natural gas from port to various power plants. Other projects included the 'Urban Train' subway, a multi-purpose coliseum, and various municipal projects.

"Of these the 'Super Aqueduct' was the only functional project. The urban train operates with a large deficit, and the two gas pipelines were never completed, although the materials were bought and contracts to develop them were issued, as a rule to party donors and affiliates," Pantojas García wrote in "Is Puerto Rico Greece in the Caribbean?" published in Winter 2016 in The Fletcher Forum of World Affairs.

"As a result, 33 members of the Rossell- administration were later indicted and convicted of corruption by the U.S. Federal Prosecutors in Puerto Rico," Pantojas García continued. "In general, these projects established a 'pay-for-play' scheme, requiring contractors to kick back 10% of the contracts to the ruling party, a practice that became known as 'tithing' (el diezmo)."

In 2006 the government introduced a sales and use tax to, among other things, refinance existing debt and thus lower government expenditure on the existing debt. However, money from the tax was used in part to purchase land for conservation at triple the assessed value of the properties. "The sellers were developers linked to the governing Acevedo Vilá administration (2005-2008)," Pantojas García wrote.

Corruption took a still different form in the Luis Fortuño administration. While the governor laid off many government workers, he also increased spending on service and consulting contracts. Some of these contracts and construction contracts were awarded to professionals who had just resigned from office. Though not necessarily illegal, the solicitation and awarding of the contracts may have been unethical, Pantojas García said in a phone interview.

Corruption in Puerto Rico has generally been on a big scale, Cámara Fuertes said. It has been more likely to entail big businesses offering contributions when they seek contracts than government officials seeking bribes for minor permits.

Though corruption has already harmed bondholder recoveries on all bonds through leading to economic contraction and government inefficiency, they may not do so in the future on particular bonds connected to corrupt projects. Executive director of Backyard Bondholders Jorge Irizarry said, "I don't see how the internal corruption [on a government project] could be a liability to the bondholders."

There has been no systematic study done in recent years comparing the level of corruption in Puerto Rico to that in the 50 U.S. states. However, most indicators are that there is more government corruption on the island than on the mainland.

For 2013, Transparency International ranked Puerto Rico 33rd in study of corruption perception of 177 countries and territories. This was worse than the 19th place that the United States achieved. Its score of 62 was higher than the global average of 43, but worse than the U.S. score of 73.

Transparency International constructs the corruption perception survey based on other groups' surveys of people who have experience with the countries and territories.

According to the World Economic Forum's Global Competitiveness Report for 2013-2014, Puerto Rico ranked 44th out of 144 polities in both diversion of public funds and irregular payments and bribes. By comparison the USA ranked 30th in the former and 36th in the latter categories. The higher one ranks the less corruption the forum believes there is.

Bobonis said corruption is perceived to be worse in Puerto Rico than in the states and offered explanations for the greater corruption. He cited the island's comparatively low-income levels, greater needs, and more intense political polarization as factors. The polarization has given governments an incentive to use corruption to maintain political power, he said.

Bobonis also noted that Puerto Rico's local and commonwealth governments get a large portion of their revenue from the federal government. In this context residents may not be as perturbed by the misuse of government money, when much of the money doesn't come from them.

As for whether corruption has been increasing or decreasing, Rosario Vega said the 50 active complaints that her Office of Ethics was working on currently was fairly typical. Valdivieso said the 24 investigations that her office was pursuing compares with the 15-20 investigations that the office had been doing in the last three to four years. She indicated that the increase was partly due to changes in the leaders of the collaborating agencies. More of them are working with the office, she said.

Puerto Ricans do have some concerns about government corruption. How to handle it was the dominant topic in the first debate among Puerto Rican gubernatorial candidates in early September. When Puerto Ricans are polled, they name corruption as one of their top concerns, professor Cámara Fuertes said.

Puerto Rico has several bodies that investigate corruption in its government. The Office of Ethics and Office of the Comptroller look at possible cases in the central and local governments and the public corporations. Exceptions to this are for the Puerto Rico Senate and House of Representatives and the judicial branch. The ethics committees of the Puerto Rico Senate and House of Representatives look at the legislature. The Puerto Rico Supreme Court oversees ethics in the commonwealth's judicial branch.

Rosario Vega said her office had 1600 active investigations. The office has 10 attorneys doing these investigations. If they follow the normal path, many will be dismissed for lack of evidence.

If there is enough evidence the Office of Ethics will take an investigation and file a complaint. The office's 50 active complaints will ultimately be considered by the office's administrative judges, who will make recommendations. Rosario Vega will make the ultimate decision on penalties.

The number of investigations that the office has done since Rosario Vega took office in 2009 has grown substantially, she said. This was because the office has been more visible and people trust that it will investigate, she said. Puerto Ricans can complain to the office anonymously.

Valdivieso said the increase in the comptroller's office's investigations was partly because of the increased collaboration of Puerto Rico Secretary of Justice César Miranda in prosecuting the cases. Previous secretaries prosecuted fewer cases.

"Other secretaries often found that cases were either not important, not material, or not enough competent evidence was found," she said. "We have been very fortunate that the current secretary of justice has been such a believer in this office."

She added, "I think our office could be very helpful to the [Puerto Rico oversight] board, so I hope they do consult us."

The Office of Ethics penalties are usually monetary, Rosario Vega said. The office can ask government agencies to discipline their employees.

If the Office of Ethics finds that the infraction was made with criminal intention, it will refer the case to the Puerto Rico Department of Justice, United States Department of Justice through the FBI, or a special prosecutor's office. The last body is only used to prosecute very prominent individuals, Rosario Vega said.

The cases referred for criminal prosecution usually involve money, she said. The comptroller's office specializes in financial improprieties. "We investigate corruption, fraud, ill/wrong/incorrect use of public funds anywhere we find it," Valdivieso said in an email.

In addition, the comptroller's office is required by law "to do full audits of municipalities every two years and although there is not always corruption, we do have many findings of noncompliance with the law, fraud, etcetera."

The comptroller and the director of the Office of Ethics are appointed by the governor subject to the legislature's approval. The appointments are made for 10-year terms to prevent political influence, Rosario Vega said.

The governor and legislature still affect the ethics office because they approve its budget each year. Despite its heavy workload, the office recently had its budget cut to $9.2 million from $10.3 million, she said.

Rosario Vega said she hoped the prosecution of corrupt people would prevent other government employees from following their paths.

In addition, the Office of Ethics does a range of other actions to prevent malfeasance and corruption. Employees in the executive branch are required to take 20 hours of training a year from the office on topics concerning professional wrongdoing. The government requires major officials before they start employment and all candidates early in their campaigns to take 7.5 hours of training with the office.

The office also demands from officials and candidates that before they take any possibly questionable actions, they get the office's opinions. In unusual cases the office can also provide dispensations to do what may need to be done, Rosario Vega said.

Here is an article from the *Wall Street Journal* on Puerto Rico. This is just one of many articles the *WSJ* wrote about Puerto Rico. I first went to the paper in 2015 and over a dozen times since. I sent the paper evidence of the alleged massive municipal bond fraud in Puerto Rico. I did all the hard work for them; they just needed to confirm it. I even gave them Web Links to confirm what I was saying. They neglected to tell the story. What was their motivation to hide such a blockbuster story? Political relationships, advertiser revenue or individual political bias? They had to have a reason! Let's look at who the *Wall Street Journal* serves:

The Wall Street Journal is a U.S. business-focused, English-language international daily newspaper based in New York City. The Journal, along with its Asian and European editions, is published six days a week by Dow Jones & Company, a division of News Corp. The newspaper is published in the broadsheet format and online.

The Wall Street Journal is the largest newspaper in the United States by circulation. According to News Corp, in its June 2017 10-K filing with the Securities and Exchange Commission, the Journal had a circulation of about 2.277 million copies (including nearly 1,270,000 digital subscriptions) as of June 2017,[2] compared with USA Today's 1.7 million.

The newspaper, which has won 40 Pulitzer Prizes through 2017[3], derives its name from Wall Street in the heart of the Financial District of Lower Manhattan. The Journal has been printed continuously since its inception on July 8, 1889, by Charles Dow, Edward Jones, and Charles Bergstresser. [underline by author.]

To be honest, I am still not sure why the *Wall Street Journal* wanted to kill a great story about Wall Street and Washington Corruption. I will have to leave that up to you to figure out. I can tell you that they knew and made a choice not to share it with the American people.

Aaron Kuriloff oversees the bonds and currencies teams at The Wall Street Journal in New York. He previously worked as a reporter at Bloomberg News in New York and The Times-Picayune in New Orleans. The Philadelphia native graduated from Brown University and the Columbia University Graduate School of Journalism.

In an email to me, Aaron did not challenge the veracity of my story; he just wanted to know why I care so much. Strange? I am delivering a story that is bigger than Watergate or Russian Collusion, a Pulitzer Prize winning story! <u>Trillions of dollars</u> stolen, government is involved, CIA wiretaps, and he wants to know why I care? I care because their actions resulted in the loss of everything I had, my home, my retirement, my savings and my good credit. I care because I am only one of millions. I care because it is destroying this country. I never heard from Aaron again. Aaron never wrote the story.

Check out the article below. Could you imagine any better opportunity to disclose the massive bond fraud? Not a word about it.

How Big Are Mutual Funds' Puerto Rico Losses? $5.4 Billion
To calculate the red ink, the Journal analyzed mutual-fund holdings and municipal-bond trades
This article was reprinted with permission from The Wall Street Journal found at wsj.com

By Heather Gillers and Tom McGinty
Updated May 14, 2017 6:38 p.m. ET

The losses from sour investments in Puerto Rico bonds are coming into focus for some of the world's biggest mutual funds, and it is a brutal reckoning.

The total red ink for mutual funds that invested in debt issued by the troubled island commonwealth is as much as $5.4 billion over the past five years, according to a Wall Street Journal analysis of mutual-fund holdings and municipal-bond trades.

Those losses, which are both actual and unrealized, were tucked inside a wide range of funds managed by Franklin Resources Inc., BEN 0.19% OppenheimerFunds Inc., Vanguard Group, Goldman Sachs Asset Management, Western Asset Management Co., Lord, Abbett & Co.,

AllianceBernstein Holding AB 1.22% LP and Dreyfus Corp., which is part of BNY Mellon Investment Management.

The damage done to mutual-fund bets is one reason why a court-supervised restructuring of Puerto Rico's debt that starts this week with a hearing in San Juan is expected to become such a lengthy battle. A diverse group of creditors will be competing for a limited pot of money and allocating Puerto Rico's resources will be complex because of the competing interests at stake.

Many mutual-fund firms have greater incentive to agitate for maximum recovery—and have greater potential for losses—because they purchased debt closer to par values. Mutual funds as a group still hold about $14.6 billion of Puerto Rico's $73 billion in outstanding bonds after selling off more than $9 billion over the past five years, according to research firm Morningstar Inc.

Two companies, Franklin and Oppenheimer, hold most of the mutual-fund debt, according to Morningstar. Oppenheimer's paper and actual losses are as much as $2.1 billion, and Franklin's are as much as $1.6 billion, according to the Journal's analysis. Franklin has $741 billion in assets under management, while Oppenheimer has $230 billion.

"We are considering all appropriate legal remedies to protect and preserve the rights of our fund shareholders," said Oppenheimer spokeswoman Kimberly Weinrick in a recent statement.

Another six fund families——managed by Vanguard, Goldman, Western Asset, Lord Abbett, AllianceBernstein Holding and Dreyfus—sustained actual and paper losses of up to between $100 million and $200 million on their Puerto Rico holdings, according to the Journal's analysis.

The losses are relatively small for those firms, all of which have at least $100 billion apiece in municipal-bond assets under management. "It's a tiny portion of the muni assets that we hold and has little impact on our *returns," said Freddy Martino, a spokesman for Vanguard.*

"We have lost money, but the portfolio is very well diversified so overall shareholders have had very attractive returns over that time," said Dan Solender, director of tax-free fixed income for Lord Abbett.

Guy Davidson, director of municipal investments at AllianceBernstein Holding, said he is relieved the firm sold off most of its Puerto Rico debt in 2014. "No matter how you cut it, Puerto Rico's been a bad investment for most investors," he said.

For mutual funds, Puerto Rico's debt has long had a special appeal because the bonds are tax-exempt nationwide. Most municipal bonds are exempt from state taxes only in the state they are issued. The commonwealth's ballooning debt load appealed to state-specific mutual funds in places where local government bonds were scarce or expensive.

About 45% of the Puerto Rico debt mutual funds currently hold is in funds designated by Morningstar as single-state funds.

When Puerto Rico last tapped the bond market in March 2014, offering 8% interest, underwriters were flooded with orders from hedge funds and mutual funds for the junk-rated debt. Twenty mutual-fund families bought a combined $263 million that quarter, according to Morningstar data.

Most funds that stocked up on the island's debt before prices began to slide have fallen behind their benchmarks, according to the Journal's analysis. That includes 13 of 15 funds that had at least 15% of their assets in uninsured Puerto Rico bonds in the first quarter of 2013. Most of these are single-state funds spanning the U.S., from New York to Arizona. Two of those lagging funds closed in 2013 and 2016.

Many funds that had less than 15% of their assets invested in Puerto Rico debt in early 2013 also underperformed their benchmarks during the same period.

How much mutual funds and other creditors in Puerto Rico get back will depend in large part on which securities they own. For example, general-obligation bonds carry some of the commonwealth's strongest legal pledges, and holders of those bonds may fare better than many other investors.

Detroit paid an average of 81 cents on the dollar on its bonds in bankruptcy, while Stockton, Calif., and San Bernardino, Calif., paid an average of 60 cents, according to research firm Municipal Market Analytics. Many Puerto Rico bondholders are likely to suffer steeper losses, said Matt Fabian, a partner at the firm.

Bondholder recoveries are expected to be significantly lower than the total dollar value of the bonds' current market prices unless the federal control board overseeing Puerto Rico allocates more than it has so far, according to analysts, mutual-fund managers and the commonwealth's former adviser.

In March, the board approved spending $800 million a year to pay debt over the next decade, about one-quarter of what is owed.

"The math is pretty straightforward," said Jim Millstein, adviser to the commonwealth for three years until the new governor took office in January.

Write to *Heather Gillers at heather.gillers@wsj.com and Tom McGinty at tom.mcginty@wsj.com*

I contacted the New York Times dozens of times. I even worked closely with one of their major reporters over the course of months. I told the reporter all of the deepest, darkest secrets about the alleged bond fraud, wiretaps etc. Finally, the reporter said something to the affect that the paper will never allow her to tell this story. What was the *New York Times* agenda? Not even the "Public Editor" was willing to consider printing any of this story. Millions would continue to buy fraudulent bond's; the *NYT's* didn't care.

Take a look at the article below, could you see any better opportunity to talk about all this fraud?

Hurricane Aid Has Eased Puerto Rico's Finances. It May Not Be Enough.
This article was reprinted with permission from The New York Times, it can be found at nytimes.com

<u>*Mary Williams Walsh*</u>

Billions of dollars of disaster aid flowing into Puerto Rico since last fall's devastating hurricane have boosted the bankrupt island's finances, but the island's federal overseers said Thursday that it would take still more austerity to translate those temporary gains into a lasting recovery.

At a meeting in San Juan of the territory's federal oversight board, members called on Puerto Rico to reform its labor laws and fix its insolvent government pension system quickly, while it still had the benefit of both the disaster money and court protection from creditors under a special new bankruptcy law for United States territories.

Retired government workers would see their pensions, already less than $25,000 a year for many workers, cut by an average of 10 percent; current government workers would be shifted into a 401(k) plan; and workers in Puerto Rico's private sector would lose mandatory perks like a holiday bonus, usually $300 to $600 a year.

The top Puerto Rican financial official at the meeting, Gerardo Portela, called the oversight board's insistence on more cutbacks "inhumane," coming so soon after a catastrophic natural disaster. And Gov. Ricardo Rosselló, who has sought to avoid painful cuts to pensions and compensation, accused the board of overstepping the limits of its legal authority and said he did not intend to do its bidding.

"Our position has always been clear," he said in a statement on

Thursday. "*Issues that are not in line with my government's public policy will not be carried out. Period.*"

Even before Puerto Rico was raked by Hurricane Maria last September, its finances were in disarray. For many years, it had borrowed money to plug holes in its budget and to repay previous borrowings, building up a debt of more than $70 billion that it could not repay. Today its debt and unfunded pension obligations total more than $120 billion, or twice the size of its economy. And the economy has been shrinking, as residents leave for better prospects on the United States mainland.

However, the hurricane has led to a big influx of disaster relief and private insurance payments, a bonanza that led Mr. Rosselló to project that the island could end the next five years with a cumulative surplus of $6.3 billion.

But the oversight board warned that without significant fiscal and economic reforms, Puerto Rico would be left, after the current flurry of storm-related activity, back where it started — with an unproductive economy and too much debt.

The board meeting was called to certify Puerto Rico's new fiscal plan, a document intended to chart the way forward. Six of the seven voting members voted in favor of an amended plan that includes the new austerity measures.

Since 2016 the island has been functioning under a federal law called Promesa, which gives it legal powers that are normally found only in bankruptcy — in particular, protection from creditors. That means that for the time being, Puerto Rico does not have to make payments on its bond debt, for a savings of about $3 billion to $3.5 billion a year.

In exchange for those extraordinary powers, Congress required the island to submit to a federal oversight board. The law gives the governor of Puerto Rico the right to develop the all-important fiscal plan, but the board must certify it. If it does not find the governor's fiscal plan credible, it has the authority to impose its own version.

But Mr. Rosselló has clashed repeatedly with the board, saying that as Puerto Rico's elected leader, he has the final say over economic policy.

"Our position has always been clear," he said in a statement on Thursday. "Issues that are not in line with my government's public policy will not be carried out. Period."

Puerto Rico has already been through the process once, certifying a fiscal plan in March 2017. But it soon became clear that the governor was not carrying out the parts he disagreed with, and the oversight board took him to court. Before the lawsuit could be adjudicated, Hurricanes Irma and Maria struck, leaving all financial planning in a shamble.

The two biggest flash points over the new plan now under review on Thursday appeared to be labor law reform and the cost of the pensions due to Puerto Rico's retired government workers. On many other elements of the fiscal plan — reducing health care spending and subsidies to cities; lowering tax rates while improving collections; and cutting red tape for businesses — the oversight board and the governor appear to be in agreement.

But board members said none of that would be enough unless Puerto Rico also softened labor laws that make it harder than anywhere else in the United States to lay off workers, which in turn makes employers on the island reluctant to hire people. Employers are also required to provide extensive paid vacations and annual holiday bonuses.

"Obviously this is an extremely difficult issue politically," said one board member, Andrew Biggs, an economist with the conservative American Enterprise Institute. "But there's a risk of doing too little to increase Puerto Rico's labor force participation rate, which is one of the lowest in the world." The current rate of people either employed or looking for work in Puerto Rico is 40.6 percent, compared with 62.9 percent for the United States as a whole.

Other board members noted that since the hurricane, young Puerto Ricans have been fleeing the island to look for work in the 50 states, even those with much less protective labor laws.

But the board does not have direct authority over the island's labor laws, only its fiscal policies. Amending the labor laws would require an act of the Puerto Rican Legislature, and Mr. Rosselló said he would "not propose any bill that reduces vacation and/or sick leave, nor will we eliminate the Christmas bonus."

By contrast, fixing the government's insolvent pension system is a matter of fiscal policy. Retired government workers are counting on future monthly payments worth more than $50 billion in today's dollars — and the pension funds already are essentially penniless. The money appears to have been spent on other things.

Puerto Rico is planning to revert to a pay-as-you-go pension plan, in which the government will pay retirees their monthly benefits directly from its general fund. That will severely strain the general fund, so the oversight board is calling for 10 percent average cuts in the pensions — people with the biggest pensions would get the biggest cuts.

"The board wants to make sure they'll get their pensions, even though there's no money," Natalie Jaresko, executive director of the oversight board, said at Thursday's meeting. But the pain of bankruptcy, she said, had to be fairly shared with all other government creditors, along with younger residents who rely on government services.

Mr. Portela, the chairman of Puerto Rico's Fiscal Agency and Financial Advisory Authority, disagreed with that, calling governmental retirees "the most vulnerable of Puerto Rican society." He reminded the oversight board that teachers in Puerto Rico, like those in many of the 50 states, do not participate in Social Security.

And the governor said he had no intention of cutting anybody's pension.

"Our position regarding pensions has always been crystal clear," he said. "We will not allow for a vulnerable sector of our population to be attacked. It is wrong and immoral to reduce the benefits for those that have contributed to the economy."

Correction: *April 19, 2018*

*An earlier version of this article misstated the amount of debt built up by Puerto Rico. It was more than **$70 billion**, not more than $70 million. [Underline and bold by author.]*

The editors at *New York Daily News* were contacted by us at least a half of dozen times. They wrote extensively about Puerto Rico. The paper never mentioned that billions have been drained out the Puerto Rico Electric Power Authority or that most of the country's seventy billion dollars in debt was likely fraudulent.

The article below would suggest the writers at the paper care about Puerto Ricans corruption. Take a look -- not a mention of any of this. What was their motivation? They were hammering Trump on Puerto Rico; maybe they thought the truth would interfere with their political agenda? I just don't know?

Puerto Rican mayor, two other gov officials arrested on corruption charges

JUL 07, 2018 | 1:10 AM

This article was reprinted with permission from The New York Daily News, it can be found at nydailynews.com

SAN JUAN, Puerto Rico — A mayor and two former government officials in Puerto Rico face public corruption charges in separate cases that involve a total of $8 million in federal and local funds, authorities said Thursday.

The suspects are the mayor of the southwest town of Sabana Grande and the former directors of finance for the northern town of Toa Baja, which has struggled to pay its employees amid an 11-year recession.

U.S. Attorney Rosa Emilia Rodriguez told reporters that the former officials from Toa Baja are accused of using nearly $5 million worth of federal funds to pay the town's public employees and municipal contractors. "Not only is that illegal, it's immoral," she said.

Officials said former finance director Victor Cruz Quintero deposited some $2.5 million worth of funds from the U.S. Department of Housing and Urban Development into the town's general and payroll accounts in October 2014.

He also is accused of making similar deposits and transfers of more than $1.75 million in funds from HUD and the Department of Health and Human Services from September 2014 to February 2016.

Toa Baja's former interim finance director, Angle Roberto Santos Garcia, is accused of making similar transactions worth $650,000 using funds from those two federal agencies.

It was not immediately clear if Cruz and Santos had attorneys.

Rodriguez said the investigation into alleged corruption in Toa Baja is ongoing because officials believe other people are involved.

Federal authorities said that Mayor Miguel Ortiz is accused of defrauding the federal government of nearly $3 million in a separate scheme that began in 2013 and ended in 2016. Officials said he is accused of financing projects without prior approval from Puerto Rico's Department of Education and obtaining funds after misrepresenting the projects' cost. Authorities said contracted companies and the municipality then received amounts much higher than what was outlined.

Ortiz also is accused of receiving nearly $33,000 in cash from one of the companies and its owner. A spokeswoman for Ortiz could not be immediately reached for comment.

The arrests come as Puerto Rico struggles to recuperate from Hurricane Maria and tries to restructure a portion of its $70 billion public debt load.

It was the same story with the *New York Post*. We contacted the paper five or six times and gave their editors all they would need to verify the alleged fraudulent bonds. Take a look at this article, a perfect opportunity to tell their readers the truth and they didn't. [Underline by author.}

Puerto Rico's bonds tumble after Trump comments on debt
By Kevin Dugan and Carleton English
October 4, 2017 | 11:49am Updated

This article was reprinted with permission from The New York Post, it can be found at nypost.com

The price of Puerto Rico's general obligation bonds plummeted as much as 25 percent on Wednesday after President Trump said investors in the US territory's debt will have to "wave goodbye" to ever getting repaid.

"We're going to have to wipe that out," Trump told Fox News after he toured some of the devastation on the island wrought by Hurricane Maria. "That's going to have to be — you know, you can say goodbye to that. I don't know if it's Goldman Sachs but whoever it is, you can wave goodbye to that."

Puerto Rico is suffering under a massive $74 billion pile of debt and its governor last year said it had no means to repay it.

"You know they owe a lot of money to your friends on Wall Street," Trump told a Fox News reporter late Tuesday after the market had closed.

The comments sent GO bonds due in 2035 down as much as 25 percent, to 33 cents, in Wednesday morning trading, its biggest one-day drop ever.

That's less than half the 73 1/2-cent price the bonds were worth on Feb. 28. By the end of trading on Wednesday, the bonds recovered a bit, to 38 cents, a 13.2 percent drop for the day.

Even though President Trump called out Wall Street, most of the bonds are in mutual funds held by mom-and-pop investors.

The three largest holders are Franklin Templeton, Loomis Sayles, and Blackrock, who together own 16.3 percent of the bonds that mature in 18 years. Some bondholders got "dose of reality," David Tawil of Maglan Capital told The Post, noting that prices fell to where they should have been six to nine months ago. Tawil, who has not held Puerto Rican bonds since 2013, said he was "seriously looking at [buying them] now."

The bond's insurers also felt the pain of Trump's comments. MBIA saw its shares fall 8.4 percent Wednesday. Ambac dropped 5.5 percent, and Assured Guaranty fell 2.9 percent.

The White House tried to tamp down any investor fear.

Mick Mulvaney, director of the Office of Management and Budget, said in a CNN interview that investors shouldn't take Trump "word for word." He promised that there would be no Washington bailout of Puerto Rico.

Hedge funds like Monarch and Aurelius, have been waging court battles to get the country to pay them first in a restructuring. Other big investors like Jeff Gundlach, CEO of DoubleLine Capital, have held the bonds but haven't taken part in legal proceedings.

It's not just hedge funds holding Puerto Rican debt. Popular mutual funds — including ones that are managed by Franklin Templeton, Oppenheimer, and Wells Fargo — are also creditors.

Some on Wall street questioned whether Washington had the legal authority to cancel Puerto Rico's debt.

"The federal government has very little authority over these proceedings," Tawil said. [Underline by author.]

If there is a special place in hell for people like Senator Chuck Schumer, the same could be said for the editors of the *Washington Post*. Let's face it, the *Washington Post* is the "Big Daddy" when it comes to reporting on political corruption, almost exclusively aimed at Republicans and Conservatives. This is a bi-partisan criminal empire and a story about this may be inconsistent with the paper's business and political agenda. I always felt that the *Wall Street Journal* and the *Washington Post* both had an obligation to the American people. The largest Wall Street theft in history with the most corrupt politicians supporting it all. I guess I was wrong.

I sent the paper editorials with supporting documents, and I wrote the editors. No interest whatsoever. They couldn't care less about the trillions that were being stolen from the American people, possibly because if it implicated their friends on Capitol Hill. I wonder if a jury would see them as co-conspirators in this "RICO" type" criminal empire? I told them there was a murder and dragged the dead body into their offices, so to speak. Then they intentionally withheld this information from the public.

If this book is a success, I can see all the newspaper editors strategizing on how to discredit me to save their reputations. There is no honor in journalism. Journalism for the most part has been overrun with political bias and personal agendas. Here is a recent *Washington Post* article. A perfect time to shine the light on all of this. I can't find anything about the alleged massive financial fraud, or political corruption in Washington, can you?

No more excuses. Puerto Rico needs help.
This article was reprinted with permission from The Washington Post found at washingtonpost.com

by Editorial Board January 5

IN THE more than three months since Hurricane Maria made landfall in Puerto Rico, a lot of excuses have been offered to explain the failure to restore power and provide other critical services to American citizens who live on the island. Like the enormity of the devastation. Or the complexity of the work. Or the difficulty of getting workers and supplies to a place surrounded by water. Yadda yadda yadda.

The real reasons for the deplorable response to conditions in Puerto Rico are clear: the island's lack of political muscle and the mainland's lack of political will. As a U.S. territory, Puerto Rico has no U.S. senator, no vote in the House and no electoral votes in presidential elections — and so it is all too easy for the White House and Congress to turn a blind eye to the needs of its vulnerable population.

More than 100 days after Maria swept the island on Sept. 20, nearly half of its residents — more than 1.5 million people — remain in the dark, and officials are now saying it will take to the end of February to restore most power. Hard-to-reach rural areas will not get power until the end of May — "just in time," the New York Times notes, "for the 2018 hurricane season." Lack of power is seen as a major factor in the higher death rates that occurred after the storm passed, and it continues to pose a danger as Puerto Rico struggles with limited resources, strained health-care services and the worsening of an already-poor economy.

If this were happening in any state — including another group of islands, Hawaii — there would be uninterrupted media attention and demands for action. As Sen. Chris Murphy (D-Conn) put it following a visit this week to Puerto Rico: "If this were happening in Connecticut, there would be riots in the streets."

Some of the blame for the prolonged power outage — which energy experts say is unprecedented in modern U.S. history — falls on the island's electric power authority and its questionable decision to entrust restoration work to a tiny Montana company. That, though, does not let the federal government off the hook for a delayed response, bungled coordination and insufficient resources. Adding insult to injury was Congress's enactment of a sweeping tax plan that punishes Puerto Rico with new business taxes even as a stalemate developed over disaster relief.

It is time to stop shortchanging Puerto Rico. President Trump needs to acknowledge that more needs to be done and done sooner. Congress needs to allocate the resources sufficient to help Puerto Rico get back on its feet, including ensuring Medicaid costs will be covered. If not, there will be a further exodus of Puerto Ricans from the ravaged island to the mainland, where — need we remind the White House and lawmakers — their votes will count.

The *Boston Globe* is a great case study. Senator Elizabeth Warren was the very first politician who proposed legislation to take away the victims' rights by limiting their ability to file a lawsuit against Puerto Rico. I wrote the editors at the *Boston Globe* and told them that Elizabeth Warren was likely fully aware that the fraud on Wall Street caused the collapse of Puerto Rico. Rather than run to the aid of the victims, Senator Warren ran to the aid of the alleged criminals and Wall Street. The *Boston Globe* would have none of it. The leadership at the paper is "all in" for Mrs. Warren apparently no matter what she does. To the best of my knowledge, they never printed a word about any of her complicity. Wall Street money rolled into her reelection coffers.

HUGE NEWS: The Boston Globe Calls on Elizabeth Warren to Run for President!

This article was reprinted with permission from Move On Dot Org found at front.moveon.org

By Ben O'Keef. Monday, March 23 2015

Over the weekend, The Boston Globe's became the first major newspaper to come out in support of Elizabeth Warren running for president. In a two-page spread penned by the editorial board, The Globe made the case for why Elizabeth Warren's causes would be best championed from the presidential campaign trail and the White House.

The Sunday edition also included three opinion pieces in support of an Elizabeth Warren candidacy—including one by MoveOn.org Civic Action Executive Director, Anna Galland.i

The Globes support is exciting and speaks to the growing support for Senator Elizabeth Warren, but that support is not a new concept. More than 300,000 Americans have already signed a petition urging the senator to run, thousands of people have attended over 400 events across every state in the country, over 500 people have left voicemails for Senator Warren calling on her to run for office, and everyday there is more momentum for Run Warren Run. The message is clear: There is a massive groundswell of support for Elizabeth Warren, and if she chooses to run she has the potential to win.

"If she puts her causes and goals front and center, as Democrats gather their forces for the crucial 2016 campaign, Warren could enrich the political process for years to come."—The Boston Globe [Underline by author.]

Wisconsin's largest newspaper, the *Journal Sentinel,* was not any different than the *Boston Globe.* I sent the *Journal* editorials with supporting evidence and wrote to the *Journal* editors. The paper was fully aware that Speaker Ryan likely knew about the financial fraud in

Puerto Rico. He was initially against any action, met with Treasury Secretary Lew, accepted a bunch of Wall Street money and then turned on the American people. The *Journal* knew everything and to the best of my knowledge, reported nothing.

Paul Ryan raises $11 million in first quarter of 2018
This article was reprinted with permission from Journal Sentinel found at jsonline.com

House Speaker Paul Ryan raked in more than $11 million in the latest fundraising period, his campaign announced Monday.

*Team Ryan said that with the latest $11.1 million haul during the first quarter of 2018, it has raised more than **$54 million during this election cycle.***

"Thanks to the speaker's tireless efforts, our members and candidates across the country will have the resources they need this fall to tout how our agenda is allowing the economy to grow and families to keep more of what they earn," said Kevin Seifert, executive director of Team Ryan.

The Ryan campaign also reported transferring more than $40 million to the National Republican Congressional Committee (NRCC).

Ryan, of Janesville, is facing challenges from Democrats Randy Bryce and Cathy Myers and Republican Paul Nehlen. [Bold by author.]

"The press should be not only a <u>collective propagandist</u> and a <u>collective agitator,</u> but also, a collective organizer of the masses." **Vladimir Lenin** This is a famous quote that can be found reprinted in many places; you can find it at answers.yahoo.com

CHAPTER EIGHT

LOOK AT THE DAMAGE THESE BASTARDS DID!

It is really difficult to put into words all the damage done by the 2008 financial crisis, the Detroit bankruptcy and the Puerto Rico bankruptcy. And you can bet the list of tragedies will grow rapidly as the credit rating agencies continue to issue alleged fraudulent ratings, the banks continue to sell alleged fraudulent bonds and the Department of Justice and our politicians continue to protect them all.

In my case, I lost my savings, my retirement, the kids' college savings, my home and my good credit. But those are just things. How did it impact my relationship with my family, my friends, my grandchildren, grandchildren yet to be born? What did it do the quality of all our lives? Will there be one less doctor in our family because we can't help pay for college? What if that child would have found a cure for cancer? Now we will never know if it were even possible. They robbed not only me of my dreams but the dreams of my family members for possible generations.

What does it do to a person's psychological make-up when he realizes he may never own a home of his own again, never take a vacation overseas, never buy the medical care that could have prolonged their life? What does it do to you when your child or grandchild is sick or hurt and you no longer have any resources to help him? These are results of the actions of less than one thousand bad actors in our government and on Wall Street. People we have no control over and whose criminal acts we cannot punish.

We know who they are; we can name them; we can look at their pictures. But unfortunately, our government has made sure we cannot hold them accountable; they are untouchable unless you are willing to take the law into your own hands. Yes, we know them: Robert Mueller and James Comey, FBI Directors, Mary L. Schapiro and Mary Jo White, SEC Commissioners, Eric Holder and Lorretta Lynch, Attorney Generals, Senator Chuck Schumer, Congressmen Paul Ryan and all the directors and executives at a dozen Wall Street firms. We can see them; we can find them. We know what they did.

The 2008 Financial Crisis was so bad that millions of people lost their homes. Many will never own a home again.

Here's how the US housing market has been impacted by the 2008 crash
This article was reprinted with permission from the Business Insider found at businessinsider.com

"Older millennials, minorities, especially Hispanics, men and the wealthy in overheated housing markets were most likely to be displaced from homeowners to renters.

*The financial crisis of 2008 created the **biggest disruption to the U.S. housing market since the Great Depression.** From the top of the housing bubble roughly a decade ago until just recently, there's been a five* *percentage-point increase in the number of renters to owners to 43.3% from 38.5%." [Bold by author.]*

This quote was found on the blog site "Zero Hedge," and the author claims NBC reported this.

*Already some **5 million** homes have been lost to foreclosure; estimates of future foreclosures range widely. [Moody's Analytics chief economist Mark Zandi], who has followed the mortgage mess since the housing market began to crack in 2006, figures foreclosures will strike **another three million homes** in the next three or four years. [Bold by author.]*

If you take these experts at their word, the number is close to eight million. Eight million people lost their homes. How do you think they feel? Their kids? Their grandchildren? How many will never own a home again? How many family events will they hold in their new two-bedroom apartments? How much less will they see their kids and grandchildren because there is no room to play, no backyard, no extra bedrooms to stay in? I can tell you from personal experience -- too many to count!

Our leaders in Washington D.C. simply don't care about us and what they have done. The politicians got their money from Wall Street and they are happy. Do you think Chuck Schumer was focused on these eight million people when he killed legislation that would have prevented this? Or was Senator Schumer focused on the additional ten million he was likely to get from Wall Street? Do you think Robert Mueller or James Comey, FBI Directors, went home at night to worry about you? Not a chance!

More likely than not, these government servants were at a political fund raiser with Chuck Schumer, other politicians and the SEC commissioners celebrating how successful they have been in delivering protection for their Wall Street friends. The country was a mess, people were suffering, and they managed to prevent any investigations or prosecutions. You can't make this stuff up -- it all really happened. A few days ago, the kids were going to an amusement park, I suggested I had commitments, and I couldn't go. The truth is, I couldn't afford to go. How many tens of millions of Americans had to do something similar because of our leaders?

How many people lost their jobs because of the on-going Wall Street fraud? According to an article by --- in *CNN Money*, the numbers were staggering;

Worst year for jobs since '45
This article was reprinted with permission from the Money, CNN, it can be found at money.cnn.com

The hemorrhaging of American jobs accelerated at a record pace at the end of 2008, bringing the year's total job losses to 2.6 million or the highest level in more than six decades.

A sobering U.S. Labor Department jobs report Friday showed the economy lost 524,000 jobs in December and 1.9 million in the year's final four months, after the credit crisis began in September.

The unemployment rate rose to 7.2% last month from 6.7% in November - its highest rate since January 1993.

The steep annual drop in jobs marked the highest yearly job-loss total since 1945, the year in which World War II ended.

"We're seeing a complete unraveling of the labor market and are on track for getting beyond 10% unemployment," said Lawrence Mishel, president of the Economic Policy Institute.

How many politicians, FBI officials, U.S. Attorney's and Securities and Exchange Commission employees lost their jobs because of all this alleged criminal fraud? The answer appears to be -- none! The better question is how many of them got promoted for their roles in all of this? How many locked up their next career moves with their friends on Wall Street? Were the new contributions from Wall Street enough to pay for the next Presidential Library? How many politicians' children got unexpected job offers from Wall Street firms? You know how it all works.

Do you know what it does to someone when he can no longer provide for himself or his family?

The Mental-Health Consequences of Unemployment
This article was reprinted with permission from the Atlantic Monthly Group found at theatlantic.com

Those who have been looking for work for half a year or more are more than three times as likely to be suffering from depression as those with jobs.

Your whole life your job defines who you are," Yundra Thomas told The New York Times two summers ago. "All of the sudden that's gone, and you don't know what to take pride in anymore." Unemployment is commonly understood as an economic problem, and inquiries into its nature tend to come from that perspective. Why do people struggle to find work even when jobs are available? What are the job prospects for those who have been unemployed for a long time? What policies, if any, can Washington enact to help?

But, as Thomas is saying, unemployment often exacts a toll that goes beyond economic concerns to psychological ones. Humans, after all, are not robots, and the loss of a job is not merely the loss of a paycheck but the loss of a routine, security, and connection to other people.

A new poll from Gallup attempts to gauge the consequences of those losses and finds that "unemployed Americans are more than twice as likely as those with full-time jobs to say they currently have or are being treated for depression—12.4 percent vs. 5.6 percent, respectively." Moreover, for those who have been unemployed for 27 weeks or more (the "long-term unemployed," currently numbering 3.4 million people) the depression rate is 18 percent, nearly one in five.

Rutgers' study found much higher rates of reporting "feeling ashamed or embarrassed" or "strain in family relations" for those for whom a loss of a job had devastating financial consequences. As one reader wrote to the Atlantic 2011, "I look at my peers who are getting married and having children and generally living life and it's depressing. They've got jobs, health insurance, relationships, homes; I don't even have a real bed to sleep on."

None of this happened by accident. It was planned out. Great effort was made by certain people to fill the ranks of the Department of Justice and the SEC with people that would likely participate. The leaders of this alleged criminal empire had clearly defined goals and objectives. When they met those goals, they were rewarded greatly. This was and is an active criminal organization and those members that fail to defraud, steal, lie, intimidate and coerce, are replaced.

There were and will be many other impacts from all this on-going criminal behavior. How many people lost their pensions when the municipal agencies collapsed? What do you think it feels like to never be able to retire? To live in fear that you will be too sick and weak to pay for your rent? Do you think our politicians really care, the executives on Wall Street, the FBI agents? They likely don't; they did this all on purpose, for personal gain.

The most amazing part of this is all of the bad actors got to see what their actions (Wall Street) or lack of actions (FBI, SEC) did to this country. It brought us to our knees. They didn't care. They continued to support the illegal activities on Wall Street, and it got even worse when President Obama took office. Not only did it appear that President Obama continue to support and protect Wall Street, but he took a page out of his *Chicago Political Training Handbook*. He appeared to participate. When Detroit collapsed, President Obama twisted the law and ignored decades of creditors' legal rights by redirecting what little was left in Detroit bond money to his voting base, the auto workers' pensions. President Obama may have suspected the bond money was stolen, and instead of giving what was left back to the victims, he redirected it to others.

By the time Puerto Rico came around, everyone in Congress was ready to remove all the legal rights of the victims. Why not, President Obama did it and almost no one blinked. Criminals don't get kinder over time; they get more emboldened.

What about all the government bailouts that have to be paid back through higher taxes? Who will pay for that? Your children who can no longer afford to go to college? It can't be you: you lost your job, your home, your savings. Do you think it's likely that the federal government debt will also default? People who are honest about it not only see it as likely but very probable. Isn't the federal government also running a Ponzi scheme? The debt can only be paid back from future tax payers, not from current government revenues.

All of this was avoidable, all preventable, were it not for the one thousand or so corrupt participants. I am beside myself trying to understand why there are simply not enough good people in the U.S. Government to stop all this. Why aren't there enough good people on cable news and talk shows to force the issue on the American people? Why aren't there enough real journalists screaming about all this in their articles? Where are the real men (and women)?

CHAPTER NINE

NOW WHAT?

Today I received a letter from the IRS. It appears they are notifying the State Department that I owe substantial taxes and that my passport should not be renewed!

I feel I need to pay what I owe. But the same government I owe this money to has made that impossible by running an obvious protection racket. A protection racket that supports and protects the exact same financial fraud I was a victim of. Seems ironic doesn't it?

Can you recall the analogies from the start of the book? "John," our fictitious victim, was first defrauded by his contractor and engineer. As if that wasn't enough, "John's" home was robbed by a policeman. "John" really got screwed over!

As bad as it was for "John," tens of millions of Americans were damaged far more than "John." Millions lost their homes; millions more, lost their jobs, their life savings, their retirement and in some cases, their families. All of this was made possible by the politicians we voted into office and paid.

Let's recap all the criminal acts and all the evidence that exists and see what we can do about it.

1. The government officials running the "government owned" electric utility in Puerto Rico (PREPA), knowingly issued almost nine billion dollars in bonds that they couldn't repay. The utility lacked cash flow, collateral and character (three C's). The debt was issued using misleading financials and disclosures. PREPA committed fraud. Specific government employees working for PREPA likely committed fraud. The Government of Puerto Rico admitted all this.

2. The Puerto Rico Electric Utility had its audited financials prepared by Ernst & Young, the National Accounting Firm. The lead auditor for Ernst & Young admitted under oath that he knew PREPA has been technically bankrupt since 2010. Ernst & Young likely committed fraud. Executives and auditors at Ernst and Young likely committed fraud.

3. The consulting firm of Alixpartners was hired by PREPA to help them regain credibility in the marketplace. Alixpartners, to the best of my knowledge, knew about the financial fraud within PREPA and other criminal acts. Alixpartners, to the best of my knowledge, did not disclose this information to new funding source's or the authorities. Letters were sent to Alixpartners executives by the author of this book. The letters detailed the criminal activity at PREPA and were sent to aid in Alixpartners future prosecution. Alixpartners likely broke numerous laws. The individual Officers and Executives at Alixpartners likely broke numerous laws.

4. Moody's, Fitch and S&P have a long history of issuing fraudulent and misleading credit ratings for a fee. Many experts have repeatedly sighted the three credit rating agencies as the major

cause of the 2008 financial crisis. Based on the credit rating agencies history and their current internal policies, it would be difficult for the credit rating agencies to argue it was anything other than a deliberate act. Testimony has been given that the employees at the credit rating agencies knew PREPA to be bankrupt when the agencies issued good ratings. This book's author also notified all the board members and executives of the three ratings companies about the fraud. This was done to help prosecute those responsible at-a-later-date. The three agencies are also likely responsible for the Detroit Bankruptcy and the entire seventy billion-dollar Puerto Rico bankruptcy. Moody's, Fitch and S&P likely committed fraud. Executives and Board Members at Moody's, Fitch and S&P likely committed fraud.

5. The book's author sent notifications to all the stock analysis's that cover Moody's and S&P stock. The letters explained that the ratings agencies were involved in the issuance of likely fraudulent ratings. Exposing the rating agencies shareholders to major liabilities. To the best of my knowledge, the Stock Analysis did not act on these disclosures. The major Wall Street firms that employ these Analysis's did not act on these disclosures. Both the analysts and their firms likely broke any number of securities and or criminal laws. They may have exposed their firms to massive civil litigation in the future.

6. According to PREPA executives, dozens of major Wall Street banks knew PREPA to be bankrupt but agreed to sell the bonds for a fee. Internal policies at the banks would limit any argument that the sale of these worthless bonds was anything but intentional. The book's author sent letters to many of these banks notifying their management of this likely fraud and to aid in future prosecution. Banks like B of A, Wells Fargo,

Citibank and many others likely committed fraud. Individual executives and officers at these banks and many other banks, likely committed fraud.

7. Ample evidence exists to suggest PREPA was also involved in an oil scheme where they would burn sludge oil and bill their customers for high grade oil. A class action lawsuit claiming just that was filed against PREPA under the RICO codes. The lawsuit has been repeatedly upheld by the courts. Equipment on site at PREPA and EPA violations also support this claim. The total money unaccounted for over the past decade is in-excess-of <u>fifteen billion dollars</u>. According to verified sources at the CIA and one unverified source within British Intelligence, massive wire transfers have been leaving the island. The wires were being sent to Venezuela and other Countries hostile to the United States. The money would be laundered and find its way back to PREPA management, politicians and to Puerto Rico, U.S. Attorney and FBI officials. PREPA employees likely committed theft. The Puerto Rico FBI and U.S. Attorneys likely broke many laws and possibly committed treason by aiding and abetting the enemies of the United States. The evidence is overwhelming!

8. PREPA's financial records reflect hundreds of millions of dollars each year that are missing and unaccounted for. These missing funds were allocated to construction and maintenance projects over the past decade. PREPA Officials and possibly PREPA contractors appeared to have colluded with one another to make these series of alleged thefts possible. Evidence is strong, investigation is on-going.

9. A cursory review of all of Puerto Rico's municipal debt appears to indicate widespread fraud, lack of cash flow, lack of

collateral, questionable financial statements and strong indications of theft at almost all the municipal agencies. There is a strong likelihood that all of Puerto Rico's debt was likely fraudulent as were their bonds credit ratings.

10. A very preliminary review of municipal debt on a national scale indicates that municipal debt carrying ratings in the BBB to B categories may incorporated fraudulent and/or misleading credit ratings. It appears the credit rating agencies and banks may be extending their alleged criminal activities well beyond Puerto Rico and Detroit.

Total losses due to fraudulent credit ratings on Mortgage Bonds: 8-12 trillion dollars!

Total losses due to fraudulent credit ratings on Detroit Bonds: 18 billion dollars!

Total losses due to fraudulent credit ratings on Puerto Rico Bonds: 70 billion dollars!

Number of prosecutions, zero U.S. bankers, zero U.S government ment employees: zero politicians!

11. Many hedge funds and vulture funds purchased Puerto Rico bonds for pennies on the dollar. Most of the funds likely knew that the bonds were issued fraudulently. The funds intend to re-sell these bonds at-a-later-date. The Hedge Funds and Vulture Funds will be participating in this fraud if they do not disclose all the bond issues to future buyers. Any bonds already sold by them would likely constitute fraud.

12. The former and current FBI "Agents in Charge" of the Puerto Rico Office were fully aware of all this fraud and failed to take any meaningful action. The intentional inaction of these FBI

Agents would suggest they were participating and/or supporting this alleged criminal activity, possibly accepting bribes and participating in actions that aid countries that are hostile to the United States.

13. The U.S. Attorney in charge of the Puerto Rico Office was fully aware of all this criminal activity and to the best of my knowledge, failed to take any action. The Puerto Rico U.S. Attorney appears to have been either participating or supporting all this alleged criminal activity, accepting bribes and participating in actions that aid Countries that are hostile to the United States.

14. Letters were sent, and numerous complaints were filed with many departments within the FBI. All FBI Agents that were in charge of the various field offices were notified. All, to the best of my knowledge failed to take action. The FBI as a whole appears to be supporting and or protecting all the criminals responsible for this activity.

15. All U.S. Attorney's in charge of field offices have been notified about this criminal activity. The Attorney General was notified about this criminal activity. All, to the best of my knowledge, failed to take any action. It appears that the U.S. Attorney's office is participating and or protecting the criminals responsible for all this alleged massive theft.

16. The Inspector General for the Department of Justice was notified about all this alleged criminal activity and claimed there was no evidence to justify an investigation. It appears the entire Department of Justice is either participating or protecting those responsible for all this theft.

17. The Securities and Exchange Commission and its leadership has been fully aware of this alleged criminal activity for a very

long time. The SEC failed to warn the American public about the fraudulent bonds, nor did they take any action to stop it. The SEC appears to be either participating in or protecting those engaged in all this alleged criminal activity.

18. All four hundred and thirty-five Congressmen and all one hundred Senators were faxed and emailed information about all this criminal activity. The majority of our representatives continued to propose and vote for legislation that makes it harder to prosecute those responsible. The majority of our representatives voted for legislation that revoked the legal rights of the innocent victims. It appears our elected officials are participating in and or protecting all those responsible for this alleged criminal activity in exchange for money (contributions).

19. Powerful career politicians appear to have made a concerted effort to fill the ranks of the Department of Justice and the Securities and Exchange Commission with "their" political appointees. Appointees that all appear to have one thing in common: a strong reluctance to investigate or prosecute any of those involved in all this alleged criminal activity. It appears that in exchange for these efforts, tens of millions of dollars were paid (contributed) to specific politicians.

20. The Executive Branch (President and his Cabinet) in past administrations and the current administration were likely aware of some of this criminal activity. The actions taken by past administrations as well as the current administration suggest that the presidents and their staff either participated in this alleged criminal activity or have used the power of their office to protect those responsible.

21. Our most senior judges are often appointed by politicians. Many of the appointments include Judges that have worked

for or worked within certain politician's offices. To achieve the most coveted senior judgeships, judicial candidates often have to spend significant time winning the support of key politicians. To date, the judges appointed to the bankruptcy cases in Detroit and Puerto Rico have refused to make any findings of fraud. It is likely that our judiciary system and its individual judges are more focused on pleasing their political benefactors then serving the American people.

> According to the Caribbean Business Website, Judge Swain will not allow access to Puerto Rico's debt documents!

With members of the Executive, Legislative and Judiciary either participating in or protecting those responsible what can the American people do?

I only see two courses of action!

The most obvious is to vote these career politicians out of office. Hopefully there are enough ethical and honest congressional and senatorial candidates out there to make a difference. In the same vein, term limit legislation, if passed, would likely change things over time.

In the absence of the above, the only option left is to take to the streets. If the government no longer serves the interest of its constituents, it needs to be replaced. When our leadership fears for its own safety, they will act in their own best interests and move to accommodate the masses. I would not recommend this course of action nor do I support any such action.

It is my belief that we should us the system to change the system. Vote these corrupt bastards out of office!

"When they call the roll in the Senate, the Senators do not know
whether to answer
'Present' or 'Not Guilty'."
— **Theodore Roosevelt**

This is a famous quote that has been widely reprinted;
you can find it at brainyquote.com

I often wonder if I was meant to be caught up in all of this. I have worked hard all my life. I went to college at night for sixteen years in an effort to make my family's life better. Maybe I should have been focused on contributing something less material? Something that can make a bigger difference. Maybe, this book is my legacy; maybe it will make a difference. I have to believe that something good will come from all this pain and loss.

I have done my best to tell this story, and I hope that you feel this was a story worth reading. Next time someone brings up the Italian Mafia or the Russian Mafia, have a good laugh and tell them all about the "Capitol Hill's Criminal Underground" -- after all, they voted for them.

In this next and final chapter, I will reprint some of the most damning evidence. Evidence that is impossible to ignore. The book's website will also have links to the TV commercial that was run by us regarding all this fraud and a video of the sixty minutes of testimony I gave to the SEC and FBI. I hope that these disclosures will motivate you to take action. If you don't, who will?

CHAPTER TEN
THE EVIDENCE

The following is an English translation of the original Puerto Rico Senate Investigative Report. Unfortunately, much is lost in this translation from the documents original Spanish. There is enough here though to leave you stunned by the FBI and SEC 's inaction.

TRANSLATION 7/15 MIP
COMMONWEALTH OF PUERTO RICO

17th Legislative 5th Ordinary Assembly Session

HOUSE OF REPRESENTATIVES FINAL REPORT

H. R. 1049

(House of Representatives Resolution 1049)

JUNE 24, 2015

TO THE PUERTO RICO HOUSE OF REPRESENTATIVES:

Your Small and Medium Businesses, Commerce, Industry and Telecommunications Commission of the Commonwealth of Puerto Rico House of Representatives, having previously studied and taken into consideration the

H.R. *1049, has the honor of presenting before this Legislative Body a Final Report on said Resolution, including findings, recommendations and conclusions.*

SCOPE OF THE MEASURE

House Resolution 1049 warrants Small and Medium Businesses, Commerce, Industry and Telecommunications Commission to carry out an investigation with regard to the operational energy expenses of several industries, pymes and businesses located in the Island, taking into account recent decisions made by Small and Medium Business, Commerce, Industry and Telecommunications Commission the Puerto Rico Electric Power Authority ("PREPA"); evaluate different alternatives in the current energy market and would portend to mitigate the economic impact they represent; and analyze the liquidity and financial claims of bondholders, and how decisions made thereof translated into energy rates/tariff increases.

In accordance with provisions stated in the Exposition of Motives of House Resolution 1049, PREPA's finances management must be part of the study and investigation such that the conclusions arrived at could be made public to the people of Puerto Rico. Likewise, it should investigate prospective effects of the new energy reform implemented thereof to the operational energy costs of diverse industries, pymes and businesses working in the Island, and evaluate alternatives in the energy market.

To achieve the objectives established in Resolution 1049, the Small and Medium Businesses, Commerce, Industry and Telecommunications Commission conducted public hearings and analyzed extensive documentation which allowed it to arrive at the conclusions and recommendations set forth in this document.

ANALYSIS OF THE MEASURE

The Small and Medium Business, Commerce, Industry and Telecommunications Commission of the House of Representatives, in accordance with its ministerial duty of analyzing measures referred by the House of Representatives, carried out an ample process of collecting data and essential documents which PREPA provided during the first investigative phase of this legislative measure. The Commission, after compiling all the information, held public hearings on May 12, 22 and 28 of 2015; and on June 4 and 16 of 2015. In addition, it held an executive meeting on June 4, 2015. The following individuals appeared in those public hearings and executive meetings:

May 12, 2015:

1. *Eng. Edwin Rivera Serrano, PR Power Authority Executive Director from 2005 to 2007;*
2. *Mr. Otoniel Crux Carrillo, PR Power Authority Executive Director from 2011 to 2012; and*
3. *Eng. Josue Colon Ortiz, PR Power Authority Executive Director from 2012 to 2013.*

May 22, 2015:

1. *Eng. Luis Garcia Passalacqua, Ex-President of the PREPA Government Board; and*
2. *Eng. Jose Del Valle Vazquez, Ex-President of the PREPA Government Board.*

May 28, 2015:

1. *CPA Luis Figueroa Baez, Finance Director of the PREPA; and*
2. *Eng. Sonia Miranda Vega, PREPA Environmental Protection and Planning Division Director.*

June 4, 2015:

1. *Eng. Luis Garcia Passalacqua, Ex-President of the PRPA Government Board; and*

2. *Atty. Luis Aviles Pagan, Ex-President of the PRPA Government Board.*

June 4, 2015 (Executive Meeting):

1. *CPA Arturo Ondina, Ernst & Young Consulting Partner.*

June16, 2015:

1. *Mrs. Lisa Donahue, PREPA Principal Restructuring Officer*

FINDINGS

*According to the Restructuring Officer, Lisa Donahue, PREPA currently has a debt approximating $8.3 billion. To understand how PREPA incurred in such debt, this Commission analyzed the prospectus and financial statements regarding bonds issued between the years 2000 and 2012, as well as the engineering reports issued in accordance with the **1974 Trust Agreement**, as amended, (from here on "Trust Agreement") which regulates PREPA and its relationship with the representatives of the bondholders and, of course, with the latter.*

Article 4 of the Trust Agreement establishes the application that would be given to the issued bonds, namely:

"ARTICLE IV CUSTODY APPLICATION OF PROCEEDS OF BONDS.

Section 401. A special fund is hereby created and designated "Puerto Rico Water Resources Authority Power System Construction Fund" (herein sometimes called the "Construction Fund"), to the credit of which such deposits shall be made as are required by the provisions of Section 208 of this Agreement. There shall also be deposited to the credit of the Construction Fund any moneys received from any other source for paying any portion of the cost of any Improvements. One or more separate accounts may be created for the Construction Fund for use for specific projects.

The moneys in the Construction Fund shall be held by the Authority in trust, separate and apart from all other funds of the Authority, and shall be applied to the payment of the cost of any Improvements and, except for any moneys in separate accounts, in the Construction Fund received from the United States Government or any agency thereof or from the Commonwealth of Puerto Rico or any agency thereof, pending such application, shall be subject to a lien and charge in favor of the holders of the bonds issued and outstanding under this Agreement and for the further security of such holders until paid out or transferred as herein provided"

Section 402. Payment of the cost of any Improvements shall be made from the Construction Fund as herein provided. Moneys in the Construction Fund shall be disbursed by check, voucher, order, draft, certificate or warrant signed by the Executive Director or by any officer of the Authority designated by him for such purpose."

On the other hand, *Section 208 of the Trust Agreement establishes that the issued bonds would finance the Capital Improvement Plan, including repayment of moneys advanced for paying refinancing costs, together with their accrued interest:*

"Section 208. Revenue bonds of the Authority may be issued under and secured by this Agreement, subject to the conditions hereafter provided in this Section, from time to time for the purpose of paying all or any part of the cost of any Improvements, including the repayment of moneys advanced for paying such cost and, if deemed necessary by the Board, the payment of the interest to accrue on such money advances to the day of such payment and for the providing moneys for deposit to the credit of the Reserve Account.

Before any bonds shall be issued under the provisions of this Section, the Board shall adopt a resolution or resolutions authorizing the issuance of such bonds, fixing the amount and the details thereof, describing in brief and general terms Improvements which are to be acquired or constructed or which were acquired or constructed from any moneys to be repaid from the proceeds of such bonds, and specifying the mount, if any, of the proceeds of such bonds to be deposited to the credit of the Reserve Account."

According to the Trust Agreement and to statements from former Executive Directors and Government Board Presidents, <u>financing for PREPA operations has to come from money collected from the rates imposed to the public corporation subscribers</u>. After having been asked some questions, these former functionaries indicated that the operations of the corporation could never be financed through issuance of debt as long as said practice would constitute an ultra vires action against the Trust Agreement itself.

Likewise, the Trust Agreement stipulates in Section 702 of Article 7 that consulting engineers, as said term is defined in Section 101, page 15, shall approve the improvements to be carried out with the bonds issued by PREPA:

"Section 702.

The authority further covenants that it will construct all Improvements for the construction for which bonds shall be issued under the provisions of this Agreement, or for which moneys repairable from the proceeds of bonds issued under the provisions of this Agreement shall have been advanced to the Authority, in accordance with plans theretofore adopted by the Board and approved by the Consulting Engineers and that upon the completion of such Improvements, it will operate and maintain the same as a part of the System..."

Likewise, and in accordance with Section 706, Article 7 of the Trust Agreement, the consulting engineers appointed by PREPA have the duty to recommend to the Board the need to revise rates/tariffs, yet it has not been done since 1989:

"Section 706. It shall be the duty of the Consulting Engineers to prepare

and file with the Authority and with the Trustees on or before the 1ˢᵗ day of May in each year a report setting forth the recommendations as to any necessary or advisable revisions of rates and changes and such other advices and recommendations as they may deem desirable. After the outstanding 1947 Indentured Bonds have been paid or provision has been made for their payment and the release of the 1947 Indenture, it shall be the duty of the Consulting Engineers to include in such report their recommendations as to the amount that should be deposited monthly during the ensuing fiscal year to the credit of the Reserve Maintenance Fund for the purposes set forth in Section 512 of this Agreement." This Commission did not find a single instance from 1989 to the present whereby the consulting engineers recommended a revision of the rates, as required in Section706.

Between the years of 2000 and 2012, PREPA Government Board authorized an issuance of bonds that raised said corporation the sum of $11,449,840,000, of which $2,720,441,711 were used for capital works while $164,649,287 were used to pay financial consultants and advisors who worked for PREPA. The remaining $8,564,749,002 was used for the prepayment of interests, as well as to refinance previous capital investments, and to capitalize their respective interests, thereby circularly refinancing its debts and interests, with complete disregard for the amortization of the original debt.

The information contained in the paragraph above arises from the content of the issued bond prospectus for the time period indicated above. However, the information with regard to the capital improvements for which the financing by way of the issuance of bonds was being solicited was not defined in each particular work. This Commission could only obtain detailed evidence of works for the 2013-1014 fiscal year from PREPA personnel, which included only energy transmission and fuel distribution projects, but not energy generating projects which certainly comprise a considerably larger expense with amounts, as estimated by this Commission, falling in the millions. With regard to previous years, this Commission's

President visited PREPA's headquarters, and despite requesting that same data for the years between 2000 and 2012, it was never provided. However, with the evidence at hand, we detected that PREPA repeatedly underestimated the costs of these improvements and capital investments for each project, which amount to 200% in excess from the budgeted amount, without reaching a 100% project completion. There are instances within the 12-month period evaluated, where PREPA incurred in costs exceeding the budget, construction was not finished and the project was abandoned.

A sample of this economic imbalance and disaster, which should have been denounced by the consulting engineers and the bondholders themselves before agreeing to their loans is as follows, based on 22 out of 265 projects analyzed for the 2013-1014 fiscal year, that is, a sample of 8% of projects analyzed:

2013-2014 FISCAL YEAR

Project	Region	Estimate	Spent	Percentage of Incurred Costs	Percentage of Completion
9793	San Juan	$ 4,692,684	$ 5,721,299	122%	76%
16987	San Juan	38,054,201	36,145,082	95%	65%
18653	San Juan	250,000	509,753	204%	100%
19647	Carolina	200,000	435,176	218%	100%
9793	Carolina	4,692,684	5,721,299	122%	76%
36701	Carolina	200,000	182,123	91%	Cancelled
19647	Carolina	2,000,000	435,176	218%	100%
14897	Bayamon	22,317	102,974	461.42%	95%

8581	Bayamon	18,225,000	25,548,043	140.18%	27%
17118	Bayamon	4,633,000	8,494,949	183.36%	?
14896	Bayamon	22,317	102,974	461.42%	95%
19455	Caguas	175,000	350,665	200.38%	?
17072	Caguas	455,841	875,590	192.00%	?
07885	Caguas	530,000	690,271	130.24%	100%
19445	Caguas	175,000	350,665	200.38%	?
17072	Caguas	455,841	875,590	192.00%	?
13536	Ponce	450,000	761,107	169.13%	70%
16515	Ponce	15,592,087	21,733,319	139.39%	90%
18609	Mayaguez	200,000	434,819	217.41%	27%
18630	Arecibo	225,000	513,879	228.39%	100%
15636	Arecibo	325,000	280,719	86.38%	15%
786	Arecibo	2,485,197	3,309,174	133.16%	only purchased equipment
TOTALS		**$94,061,169**	**$113,574,646**	**120.75%**	

PREPA, in one year, as seen in the table above, has had a deficit in its estimates of 22 of approximately 265 projects, excluding power generating costs, which are the most costly. It is this Commission's understanding that these alarming instances should have been registered several years ago. But as previously pointed out, PREPA did not provide the information requested.

Errors calculating estimated costs versus actual costs incurred may be attributed to flaws in project estimates; excessive equipment, goods and materials purchasing costs; and excesses in the required labor work forces in charge. But it must be undoubtedly attributed to a faulty and unhealthy administration of public funds. Bondholders must have been aware of the above because in their determination analysis made prior to decide on the issuance of bonds to the PREPA, this information was available, and no false representations were made. The numbers were available and, more importantly, the consulting engineer, appointed by the bondholders and PREPA, had to personally approve any such investment with his signature. No engineering report informing about or denouncing the excessive costs being annually registered for fuel distribution and energy transmission in-frastructure projects were included in any of the issued bonds.

With regard to this matter, this Commission also analyzed how PREPA capital improvement plans decreased following the 2000-2004-year period when 46% of the moneys, that is almost half of what was issued in the debt, was spent either in the Construction Fund or to finance the Capital Improvement Plan. During 2004-2008 only 15% of the capital raised by the issuance of debt was used to finance the Capital Improvement Plan, the rest was used to refinance the debt, according to Mr. Luis Figueroa Baez, PREPA Finance Director. <u>However, from 2009 to 2012 only 18% of the debt was used to finance the Capital Improvement Plan, while the remainder was used to refinance the existing debt, capitalize interest and issue advanced notes to pay future interest.</u>

With regard to Article 7 and the performance of the consulting engineers, this Commission found that for the last 20 years the same person has been executing or subscribing the Engineer Report, which has to be submitted pursuant to the Trust Agreement. The subscriber is Eng. George Romano Jr., who has worked for different firms. This Commission believes this is not synonymous to a healthy administration, and that it should have been questioned by PREPA's highest administrative body, something that

237

did not happen until this Commission brought forth the anomaly to the attention of the current PREPA officials. It was also found that consulting engineers signed for approval, under different names, and have carried out construction work for PREPA, which is contradictory per se with Section 706 of the Trust Agreement. Said provision of the agreement demands that those external consultants, chosen between the bondholders and the public corporation itself, must be independent contractors. Within that parallel appointment practice process, they ceased to be independent because they had to evaluate the same infrastructure projects they were supposed to build.

This Commission also found that the consulting engineers were negligent and failed in the obligation imposed to them by the Trust Agreement (Section 706) when they allowed PREPA's energy-generating stations and the whole system in general to become obsolete; in violation of federal regulation established by the Mercury and Airborne Toxic Emissions Standards (MATS).

Another finding was that the consulting engineers were not impartial to PREPA's refinancing scheme; because while knowing that the electric power authority did not have sufficient income to comply with its financial obligations, they allowed the use of funds allocated for capital improvements to be used in the maintenance of an infrastructure they knew was soon to become obsolete.

PREPA's current economic insolvency was the product of, among other factors, <u>negligent acts on the part of its creditors, who in spite of knowing that PREPA's financial and competitive situation was weak, and knowing that its infrastructure was obsolete, they negligently granted PREPA a good credit rating; disregarding that by 2010, PREPA was technically bankrupt.</u> This fact was corroborated by Arturo Ondina, CPA and consulting partner of Ernst & Young, firm who has audited PREPA for the past 12 years. This occurred while the financial consultants and consulting engineers indicated in their reports that the PREPA financial condition allowed it to issue more

bonds, when the fiscal reality was that PREPA *was not generating suf-*
ficient income to repay the debt.

Those individuals and/or consulting firms knew that any funds grant-
ed to PREPA would be used to pay fees, underwriters and commissions to
the financial intermediaries who issued the debt, from $40 to $60 million
dollars per four-year period, as well as to refinance the outstanding debt,
and not for any works plans and improvements to generator plants. Mr.
Figueroa Baez mentioned this fact in one of the hearings this Commission
conducted.

This Commission realized that PREPA paid previous bondholders
with capital received from new investors, to the point that owed interests
were capitalized and re-grouped whenever a new debt was issued. The
abovementioned was done to benefit the financial community that issued
the debt and who today is collecting same, without any moneys having
been invested in improvements to infrastructure, all to the detriment of the
best interest of the people of Puerto Rico. We believe that the actions and
circumstances mentioned above caused the economic insolvency which has
plagued PREPA in the past years. Said debt was sold at discount, a large
quantity of it between .60 to less than .50 cents to the dollar with the agree-
ment to pay to the dollar in full upon its maturity. Plus, the annual return
yield was agreed to set high interest rates, and the principal and return are
three-fold exempt from payment of local and federal taxes, in accordance
with the Jones Act. When Mrs. Lisa Donahue was asked whether she knew
of any other issuances of debt with characteristics so benefitting to investors,
she replied that she did not know of any other investment tool or instru-
ment that is three-fold tax exempt. This goes to show that the financial
intermediaries and the institutional holders, despite being fully aware of
PREPA's fiscal situation, had no qualms with Unjustly Enriching them-
selves and with having the consequences of their negligent acts be paid for
by the people of Puerto Rico.

Meanwhile, and fully aware that PREPA did not have the resources to repay the debt, investment firms, banks, credit houses, consulting engineers, and PREPA itself failed to bring out into public light the need to make adjustments to the rates charged by PREPA, an act contrary to what the holders were bound to do pursuant to the last paragraph of Section 502 of the Trust Agreement. Bondholders had the contractual obligation to commit PREPA to increase tariffs and rates in an adequate and timely manner in order to avoid the situation this public corporation has to bear today. This act is known as a laches or negligent act ("acto de incuria"). They did not act in time, yet now they demand strict compliance.

PREPA, in an act out of the scope of its own standard procedure of annual issuance of debt, which usually occurred no more than twice a year, in 2010 carried out 8 issuances in a row whereby it reduced its capital improvement plans in order to justify the issuances and then were used for prepayment of interests and to finance PREPA operations without ever recommending a rate increase to the Board. Officials called to appear at the hearings coincided that the aforementioned issuances were carried out with the bondholders' consent every time presentations were held in New York with the financial intermediaries, underwriters and others, with the consulting engineer's endorsement, prior to the issuance of said debts. Therefore, the institutional bondholders bought this debt with the knowledge and with consent of what was going on financially in the corporation, which was ailed with technical insolvency or bankruptcy.

Investors allowed PREPA to issue bonds, then, PREPA borrowed from private banks to pay the bond's interests; then, borrowed from the Government Development Bank (from herein "GDB") to pay back the private bank loans, and the GDB, in turn, issued more bonds to refinance all. Afterwards, PREPA would issue a new debt to pay GDB's outstanding interests, pay principal and pre-pay the new bonds' interests for several years -a cycle that is repeated over and over- and in which the original debt is never paid. This practice could constitute a fraud scheme for which the federal agencies that regulate financial instruments and the Security Exchange Commission could take action against and/or pursue civil suits against these institutions. That is the reason why we are referring this Report and its findings to those entities, so that they may assume the appropriate jurisdiction over these acts.

PREPA's current administration has recognized that it does not know of any corporation who has issued this type of debt and maintained good Investment Credit Rating before credit institutions, while issuing, as PREPA did, a $4,000,000,000 debt in one year.

All surmised herein has been occurring for years and has proven to be an excessive and onerous burden on the operational costs of thousands of small and medium businesses throughout the Island. Due to rates that have gone unrevised for decades and a fuel adjustment clause questioned by many, hundreds of businesses have already closed, and others are in the process of doing so faced with the lack of capital to invest in energy generating mechanisms which would allow them total independence from the system PREPA provides. That is why this Commission has determined its own recommendations and conclusions, and they are the following:

RECOMMENDATIONS

In order to prevent what we have described in this Report from happening again, and to keep control of PREPA's treasury and its operations, we recommend:

1. *That this Report be forwarded to the Justice Department of the Commonwealth of Puerto Rico and the United States of America for their corresponding actions;*

2. *That this Report be forwarded to the United States Securities Exchange Commission for its corresponding action;*

3. *The annulment of the current agreement with the consulting engineer's firm and initiation of a claim against its underwriters of the last 20 years and request restitution of the moneys paid to them;*

4. *An investigation of PREPA projects estimates department for possible judgement flaws in the past years;*

5. *An investigation of purchasing costs for equipment, goods, and other services from PREPA's suppliers, under a presumption of possible overbilling for construction works in the past years;*

6. *An investigation of costs incurred for construction projects workforce in the past years;*

7. *Adoption of a rate adjustment process that no longer has the detrimental effect it has had until now for small and medium business owners in Puerto Rico; and*

8. *That the necessary guidelines and norms be defined by an audit so that events that led PREPA to its current economic situation are not allowed to happen again.*

CONCLUSION

The people of Puerto Rico shall not be held responsible for nor be guarantors of inadequate, negligent and/or speculative financial decisions taken by professionals, investors and financial groups on behalf of PREPA. Our fellow citizens granted that group the terms and conditions they needed to benefit from the production of energy in Puerto Rico in order to safeguard their investment, namely, the following:

- *A prospectus under SEC regulations;*

- *Intervention from external auditors*

- *A Trust Agreement that provided said professionals the tools they needed, including the right to name a contractor to foresee and monitor PREPA, requesting, if necessary, rate adjustments, and giving him access to PREPA's records and facilities, as well as soliciting funds to create capital improvements;*

- *Unequaled tax exemptions;*

- *Contracts with credit house financed by our government;*

- *Recurrent issuance of bonds;*

- *Legal opinions for every issuance;*

- *A stable, democratic government;*

- *Shut down of the government during a particular four-year period where payment of the debt continued over payroll and other obligations, just as our Constitution demands; and*

- *A just, accessible and expeditious state and federal judicial system. Investors and administrators' unilateral decision not to use the aforementioned tools adequately to safeguard their own interest is the reason why PREPA arrived at the deep technical insolvency ailing it today, which, in 2010 was eliminated for accounting purposes and which a year later was confirmed, when a two hundred-million-dollar debt was already in existence. The public corporation's financing by way of 8 simultaneous issuances of debt of over $4,000 million with the consent of the financing intermediaries and consulting engineering firm had the effect of plunging the corporation into deep insolvency. Noteworthy is the fact that the aforementioned took place in the face of the credit houses, whom, knowing this, and therefore PREPA's technical insolvency, allowed this public corporation, and thus the people of Puerto Rico, to continue running into debt. It is necessary for the PREPA to*

*expunge itself from the fiscal situation it is in and adopt the rec-
ommendations expressed herein, as well as those made by PREPA's
current administration. All without it translating into additional
costs to the people of Puerto Rico and putting forth the aforementioned findings for the consideration of the Puerto Rico Justice
Department to conduct an investigation with regard to the matter.
Based on all the findings included in this Report, the Small and
Medium Businesses, Commerce, Industry and Telecommunications
Commission of the House of Representatives of the Commonwealth
of Puerto Rico, having previously studied and taken into consideration House Chamber Resolution 1049, is honored to submit
before this Honorable Legislative Body the Final Report on this
measure, including findings, recommendations, and conclusions.*

Respectfully submitted,
(Illegible signature)
Hon. Javier Aponte Dalmau President
*Small and Medium Businesses, Commerce, Industry and Telecommunications
Commission [Bold and underline by author.]*

It was late 2015, and I wasn't aware at the time that the Securities
and Exchange Commission and the Department of Justice were members of this alleged criminal organization. I was simply dismayed that
the Senior Attorney I was working with at the SEC did not see the
seriousness of all this alleged fraud. Maybe she is a great attorney and
couldn't connect the dots? Stranger things have happened.

And although I was frustrated by the non-response of the FBI and
U.S. Attorneys, these guys went to law school, not finance school.
They may be the best and brightest but might not be "finance experts."
I put this audit together and sent it to them and all our congressmen
and senators.

December 18th, 2015

Forensic Accounting Review
The Government of Puerto Rico

Offering Memorandum

The authority has issued these bonds based on the utilities ability to pay for them from company revenues.

Page 11
"The Power Revenue Bonds are payable solely from the Revenues of the System after payment of Current Expenses of the Authority and any reserve therefor."

The Authority went on to state that based on their revenues the bonds will have debt service coverage of 1.38:1. More specifically, that the Authority will have $1.38 in revenue for each dollar needed for the bonds' repayment. 1.38 debt service coverage is considered moderate to good debt service coverage (DSC).

Page 5	*2009*	*2010*	*2011*	*2012*	*2013*
Ratio of Net Revenues	*1.45*	*1.85*	*1.47*	*1.95*	*1.38*
To Principal and Interest					
Requirements, Per Trust					
Agreement.					

Debt Service Coverage (DSC) is the most critical metric one can look at when Revenues are defined as the loans' primary and only defined repayment source. A coverage ratio of less 1 to 1 is consider insufficient DSC because any hiccup in operations of the company may prevent the company from making the required payment. PREPA is asserting that is has a 38% safety reserve with its 1.38 DSC.

Misleading Statements

In this presentation, PREPA included Accounts Receivable in its Revenues that should not have been included. In years 2009 through 2013, the utility had significant accounts receivable that were not collectable and by all accounting standards should have not be used in their Revenue assumptions.

Page 5 (footnote 2)
"Includes revenues attributable to electric energy consumption by municipalities, residential fuel subsidy and hotel subsidy of $224.7 million, $232.4 million, $246.7 million, 282.6 million and $298.3 million for fiscal years 2009, 2010, 2011, 2012 and 2013 respectively."

When it is not reasonable to anticipate collection of accounts receivable it should not be included in revenue. PREPA included these uncollectable accounts and mislead the bond buyers into believing the utility had sufficient revenues to repay this debt. Below are various accounting rules that should have been complied with:

GAAP Accounting Rules

*Accounts receivable are expected income for services performed or goods sold that are unpaid. Report receivables on your books as current assets, **anticipated to turn into cash within the year.** When you perform services or deliver goods before payment, you're usually an unsecured creditor unless your services come under a lien statute in your state. A mechanic's lien, for example, may make you a secured creditor. An unsecured creditor has no security interest in the assets of the debtor, and you'll probably receive nothing if the debtor declares bankruptcy. A small-business owner must expect some write-offs for uncollected debts*

GAAP uses the less optimistic view when two possibilities exist. When using GAAP rules, a business owner uses a conservative estimate of the number of accounts receivable that won't be paid, relying on the principle of conservatism.

Government Accounting Standards

The revenue-generating activities of an agency will frequently result in receivables on the agency's accounting records. If the agency arrives at the conclusion that any of the amounts so established cannot be collected using the criteria in the Collectible section of this fiscal policy and procedure (FPP), reduce the amount of the receivable. The USAS transaction entry to specifically write off a revenue receivable bad debt, regardless of appropriation year

PREPA went on to say:

> Page 24
> "The Projections of Net Revenues prepared by the Authority for the five fiscal year period from 2014 through 2018 are also premised in part on the inclusion in Revenues of the municipalities consumption of electric energy and certain other revenues that the Authority does not collect."

PREPA went on to say:

The Authority has not collected these receivables in almost a decade and admits to such but elects to include them in the Revenue stream used to calculate repayment of these bonds.

Below is the actual debt service coverage without the non-existent (accounts receivable) revenue

Page 5	2009	2010	2011	2012	2013
Ratio of Actual Revenues To Principal and Interest Requirements, Per Trust Agreement.	.92	1.25	.95	1.07	.82

You can see clearly that the utility never had sufficient revenues to pay its new bond debt.

<u>Unbelievably, the credit rating agencies issued the following ratings:</u>

Baa3 - Moody's
A credit rating used by Moody's credit agency for long-term bonds and some other investments. A Baa3 rating represents a relatively low-risk bond or investment; banks are allowed to invest in Baa3 rated bonds. However, Baa3 is at the bottom of investment-grade bond ratings, being only one grade above junk bond ratings. Risk-averse investors must therefore exercise caution in Baa3 investments, especially if the rating was recently downgraded. It is a subdivision of a Baa rating.

BBB – S&P
A bond rating assigned to an investment grade debt instrument. A BBB rating reflects an opinion that the issuer has the current capacity to meet its debt obligations

BBB- Fitch
BBB Ratings indicate the expectations of default risk are currently low. The capacity for payment of financial commitments is considered adequate.

These ratings are incomprehensible. In addition to inadequate DSC (Under 1 to 1), PREPA has a negative net worth and 1.7 billion dollars in unfunded pension obligations. By PREPA's own admission they were meeting their bond payments through the use of short-term debt not revenues. Yet, this was all ignored by the credit rating agencies.

The article below was printed prior to the bond offering, and Bank of America, Merrill Lynch agree with me.

Puerto Rico's Utilities: Big and on the Edge (Bond Buyer)

by _Robert Slavin_
APR 19, 2013 5:51pm ET

Among PREPA's problems is that it has high accounts-receivable levels. The net accounts receivables as a percent of total revenues was 26.7% in fiscal 2011, according to Fitch. That compares to an 11.5% average for Fitch-rated retail electric systems. The other rating agencies and Janney Capital Markets managing director Alan Schankel agree that this is a problem for PREPA.

Though PREPA has not drawn as much money from the Puerto Rican government over last several years as PRASA, in fiscal 2011 it did get subsidies from the government and Government Development Bank of Puerto Rico, Robert Donahue, managing director at Municipal Market Advisors, said in a phone interview.

After adjusting for contributions in lieu of taxes and other related charges, Fitch calculated that for fiscal 2011 funds available for debt service failed to cover debt service. Is this the end?

A Bank of America Merrill Lynch analysis published April 12 calculated that unaudited fiscal 2012 net revenues would provide 1.1 times coverage of maximum annual debt.

"PREPA is very damaged, very distressed," says Lisa Donahue, an expert on fixing utility companies that are in trouble. "PREPA needs a lot of work."

Yet the credit rating agencies say otherwise?

$673,000,000 in bad bond debt was sold to investors. If this bond offering was analyzed and rated correctly it would be fair to say that most of the investors would not have purchased these bonds.

What I have seen in these financials has all the makings of a Ponzi scheme.

A Ponzi scheme is a fraudulent investment operation where the operator, an individual or organization, pays returns to its investors from new capital paid to the operators by new investors, rather than from profit earned by the operator. Operators of Ponzi schemes usually entice new investors by offering higher returns than other investments in the form of short-term returns that are either abnormally high or unusually consistent.

Ponzi schemes occasionally begin as legitimate businesses until the business fails to achieve the returns expected. The business becomes a Ponzi scheme if it then continues under fraudulent terms. Whatever the initial situation, the perpetuation of the high returns requires an ever-increasing flow of money from new investors to sustain the scheme.[1]

To support my conclusions, I have included information on the rapid downgrades by the credit agencies that followed the sale of this bonds.

Moody's

August	2013	Baa3	
February	2014	Baa3 to Ba2	(6 Months later)
June	2014	Ba2 to B2	(10 Months later)
September	2014	Ba2 to Caa3	(13 months later)

Puerto Rico Electric Power ... **Puerto Rico's** debt-laden ...

In addition to the aforementioned debt service coverage issue, the offering memorandum offers other statements that are equally misleading and untrue. All of these statements should have had a material impact on the utilities ability to take these bonds to market.

Litigation

The authority makes the following claim:

Page 89
The Authority is a defendant or codefendant in numerous legal proceedings pertaining to matter incidental to its business and typical for an electrical utility of its size and nature.

In doing a Nexis search I was unable to locate any other major utility that is currently being sued under RICO charges. Racketeering, Influence and Corruption charges are exceedingly difficult to bring in a court of law. The courts are reluctant to allow the use of this powerful law enforcement tool for fear of its abuse. In PREPA's case, the RICO charges were challenged in court and withstood the challenge. A RICO charge also speaks to the character of the company's leadership, a factor that is critical is assessing the quality of the information disclosed by the utility.

The combined potential litigation damages appear to me to be excessive for a utility. Since the printing of this memorandum, additional litigation, possibly amounting to billions in damages, have been filed for activities during this period.

Inexplicitly, this appeared to play no factor in the issuance, rating and sale of these bonds.

Environmental Matters

There is so much here that I quite frankly don't know where to begin. PREPA has a long history of violating EPA rules and regulations, once again speaking to the character of the company's leadership. Indications that should not be ignored by any analysts. PREPA is currently under a variety of legal orders to force compliance. The utility has repeatedly stated they may still be unable to comply with these legal orders resulting in material fines.

Violation of Covenants

To make the sale of these bonds more attractive, the company added a special rate covenant that would require the utility to raise rates to maintain a 1.20 debt service coverage. Once again, speaking to the character of the company's leadership and the misleading nature of this memorandum, the covenant was immediately violated and shortfalls in bonds payments are being made with lines of credit.

Capital Improvement Budget and Construction Budget

PREPA has a long history of raising capital through the issuance of bonds with the promise of using material amounts of the bond funding to up-grade facilities and reduce electricity costs. I went back and looked at previous bond offerings and all offerings included a material amount of the bond funds for capital improvements. This bond offering has $500,000,0000 set aside for that purpose.

Once again, a basic review of the utilities follow-though on these improvements finds that the utility has consistently failed to make the promised improvements.

Given the material nature of these "set asides" and the utilities failure to successful execute the promised up-grades, I am recommending a through audit be done on all these reserve accounts.

Where did that money go? What was it used for? It was not used for up-grades or bond payments. They borrowed more money to make the bond payments.

The larger question is -- why has the utility failed to make the very improvements that would have reduced their cost and saved the utility from a possible financial collapse?

In the addendum of my report, I will use publicly available information to better understand the possible motive for all this dysfunctional behavior.

Over the last few years, the utility has cancelled over 15 billion dollars in alternative energy projects. These projects would have been built by third parties and cost the utility nothing. The savings to the utility would have been over 20% in electricity production costs, far in excess of what the utility needs to return it to financial soundness.

Additionally, the utility has repeatedly been slow or failed to make the promised conversions from oil to natural gas.

Summary

It is clear to me from my experience that I have reviewed the financials of a criminal enterprise. The company made misleading and false statements that resulted in the sale of $673,000,000 in non-performing bonds to the general public. It would be my conclusion that this bond issuance not be supported and that the utility should be put under receivership.

What I have seen indicates the probable commission of a series of felonies and I would have been required to report what I have found to the appropriate authorities for further investigation.

ADDENDUM

This review has made it clear that the utility and its executives are engaging in a number of activities that are inconsistent with the proper management of a large utility. The question is --why would a utility issue bonds that it knew it couldn't pay? Why would the utility consistently fail to make the upgrades that would have solved all of their cash flow and EPA issues? There has to be a reason, because of the intentional nature of the company's activities. What is the motive? This clearly fails outside my area of expertise, but common sense dictates I ask the question.

Typically, when a company is running a Ponzi scheme, it is critical that it never end or it will become visible to the most recent victims pretty quickly. I believe that management undertook this bond offering in an effort to keep the Ponzi scheme alive and postpone the day of reckoning.

By doing some basic web searches, I found out that the law firm of Hagens Bermen filed another RICO lawsuit in February of 2015. I initially did not read the complaint. After a review of the financials, I went back to read the complaint to see if it might have something to do with what I am seeing in these financials. I read the complaint and it did help make sense of this.

A Ponzi scheme almost always requires a company executive who redirects money for his own personal use. The executive then takes money designated for other purposes to replace what was taken. As long as the money keeps flowing, the crime is hard to detect. Hangens Bermen answers part of the question. The complaint alleges that executives at PREPA paid for fuel oil No.2 and took delivery of a lower rated oil (more heavily polluting and less efficient no 6 oil) and were paid kickbacks from the oil companies for the price difference.

As I explored this, I found the alleged kickbacks were staggering: over $500,000,000 a year.

On page 49 of the memorandum the utility listed its fuel oil costs as the following:

	2009	2010	2011	2012	2013
Cost (No 2 oil)	*$1.919.8*	*$2,006.9*	*$2,291.4*	*$2,901.8*	*$2,603.6*

Number 2 fuel oil is a distillate home <u>heating oil</u>.[3] Trucks and some cars use similar <u>diesel fuel</u> with a <u>cetane number</u> limit describing the ignition quality of the fuel. Both are typically obtained from the light gas oil cut. Gas oil refers to the original use of this fraction in the late 19th and early 20th centuries - the gas oil cut was used as an enriching agent for <u>carbureted water gas</u> <u>manufacture</u>.

Number 6 fuel oil is a high-viscosity residual oil requiring preheating to 220 – 260 °F (104 – 127 °C). Residual means the material remaining after the more valuable cuts of crude oil have boiled off. The residue may contain various undesirable impurities including 2 percent water and one-half percent mineral soil. This fuel may be known as residual fuel oil (RFO), by the Navy specification of Bunker C, or by the Pacific Specification of PS-400.

The price difference between No 2 (Quality Oil) and No 6 (Poor Quality Oil) is approximately 30% (We found later the price difference was 54%).

Actual Cost Difference of	2009	2010	2011	2012	2013
Oil Delivered	$575.9	$602.0	$687.4	$870.5	$781.08

This helps explain why PREPA continually failed the EPA tests: No 6 oil is terrible on the environment and on the equipment. It also helps explain why the company wanted to kill all natural gas conversions and all renewable energy projects. If this is true, and there are indications in the paper that it is true, it explains why PREPA management would do almost anything to keep this secret and keep it going.

What it does not explain is why PREPA cannot make its bond payments. I believe the answer to that question would be uncovered in a through audit.

It appears there might be multiple schemes going on at the same time at PREPA. With $575,000 to $781,000 per year to buy silence, it is no wonder this has gone on for over a decade. PREPA corruption may represent *one of the biggest thefts of public money in history and one of the largest municipal bond frauds.*

The **Rico Law Suit** is too long to reprint in its entirety. I have tried to leave out the less important legal boilerplate and repetitive claims. Hopefully this will result in a more enjoyable review.

Case 3:15-cv-01167-JAG Document 1 Filed 02/24/15 Page 1 of 80
UNITED STATES DISTRICT COURT
DISTRICT OF PUERTO RICO

ISMAEL MARRERO ROLÓN, ANNE CATESBY JONES, JORGE VALDES LLAUGER, PUERTO RICO BATHROOM REMODELING, INC., PERFORMANCE CHEMICALS COMPANY, INC., Plaintiffs,

v.

AUTORIDAD DE ENERGÍA ELÉCTRICA A/K/A PUERTO RICO ELECTRIC POWER AUTHORITY; WILLIAM RODNEY CLARK; EDWIN RODRIGUEZ; CÈSAR TORRES MARRERO; INSPECTORATE AMERICA CORPORATION; BUREAU VERITAS HOLDING, INC.; CORE LABORATORIES N.V. D/B/A SAYBOLT; ALTOL CHEMICAL ENVIRONMENTAL LABORATORY INC. D/B/A ALCHEM LABORATORY; ALTOL ENVIRONMENTAL SERVICES, INC. D/B/A ALTOL ENTERPRISES; PETROBRAS AMERICA INC.; PETROLEO BRASILEIRO S.A; CARLOS R. MÈNDEZ & ASSOCIATES; SHELL TRADING (US) COMPANY; PUMA ENERGY CARIBE LLC; PUMA ENERGY INTERNATIONAL, B.V.; TRAFIGURA A.G.; TRAFIGURA BEHEER, B.V.; PETROWEST, INC.; VITOL S.A., INC.; VITOL, INC.; JOHN DOES 1-100,

Defendants.

Civ. No. 15- CLASS ACTION COMPLAINT - JURY DEMAND

OVERVIEW

1. *Plaintiffs and the Class complain of a scheme perpetrated by all Defendants to procure and provide the Puerto Rico Electric Power Authority ("PREPA") (in Spanish, Autoridad de Energía Eléctrica, or "AEE") with millions of barrels of fuel oil for the combustion of electricity under the guise the fuel oil met the specifications of contracts between PREPA and certain of its Fuel Oil Suppliers, as well as specifications set by the Environmental Protection Agency ("EPA") in a 1999 Consent Decree, as amended in 2004 (collectively, "Compliant Fuel Oil"). In fact, Defendant Fuel Oil Suppliers supplied PREPA with fuel oil that did not meet contractual or EPA specifications ("Non-Compliant Fuel Oil"), but was nonetheless accepted by PREPA in exchange for, on information and belief, undisclosed kickbacks or commissions to the PREPA Participants (defined below).*

1. *As a result of this scheme, PREPA overpaid its fuel suppliers for fuel oil and passed through the entire cost of the Non-Compliant Fuel Oil to Plaintiffs and the Class on their regular monthly electricity bills.*

2. *The scheme was perpetuated by the Fuel Oil Cartel Enterprise defined as and comprised of: (i) Defendants PREPA and other employees and agents of PREPA, including, on information and belief, the former Administrator of the Fuel Oil Office, Defendant William Clark, the current Administrator of the Fuel Oil Office, Edwin Rodriguez, the Assistant administrator of the Fuel Oil Office, Cesar Torres Marrero, and other governmental employees or agents, who were or are responsible for all of the activities associated with fuel procurement for PREPA (the "PREPA Participants"); (ii) Defendants Petrobras America Inc. and Petroleo Brasileiro S.A. (collectively, "Petrobras"); Shell Trading (US) Company ("STUSCO"); Carlos R. Méndez & Associates ("Mendez"); Puma Energy Caribe LLC and Puma Energy International, B.V. (collectively "Puma"); Trafigura A.G. and Trafigura Beheer, B.V. (collectively, "Trafigura"); PetroWest, Inc. ("PetroWest"); Vitol S.A., Inc. and Vitol, Inc. (collectively,*

"Vitol"); and other John Does, which contracted with PREPA to provide Compliant Fuel Oil but actually provided cheaper Non-Compliant Fuel Oil at the more expensive prices, in exchange for paying undisclosed commissions or kickbacks to the PREPA Participants ("Fuel Oil Supplier Participants") and (iii) Defendants Inspectorate America Corporation, Bureau Veritas Holding, Inc. (collectively "Inspectorate"), Core Laboratories N.V. d/b/a Saybolt Laboratory ("Saybolt"), Altol Chemical Environmental Laboratory Inc. d/b/a Alchem Laboratory, Altol Environmental Services, Inc. d/b/a Altol Enterprises (collectively "Alchem"), and other John Does, which falsified laboratory test reports to show that Non-Compliant Fuel Oil delivered by the Fuel Oil Supplier Participants was compliant when it was not, in exchange for the continued business of the Fuel Oil Supplier and/or the PREPA Participants.

3. PREPA pays billions of dollars per year for fuel oil. Compliant Fuel Oil, which is supposed to meet specifications in PREPA contracts and the EPA Consent Decree, is more expensive than Non-Compliant Fuel Oil, which is dirtier and more harmful to the environment. Compliant Fuel Oil is more expensive because diesel oil is mixed with No. 6 fuel oil to reduce the percentage of sulfur and other harmful ingredients. Thus, PREPA's acceptance of Non-Compliant Fuel Oil, while charging Plaintiffs and the Class the prices for Compliant Fuel Oil, caused Plaintiffs and the Class to suffer significant out-of-pocket losses as the cost of those overcharges was passed on directly in the form of higher electricity costs. 4. Plaintiffs sue on their behalf and on behalf of all persons and entities who paid for electricity in Puerto Rico during the period January 1, 2002, to the present to recover their out-of-pocket losses, compensatory damages, punitive damages, and attorneys' fees and expenses. 010476-11 760966 V1 under the Racketeer Influenced Corrupt Organizations Act ("RICO") and for the disgorgement of profits under the common law of unjust enrichment.

Puerto Rico Electric Power Authority ("PREPA") (in Spanish, Autoridad de Energía Eléctrica, or "AEE") is a public corporation and government instrumentality organized under the laws of the Commonwealth of Puerto Rico with its principal place of business located in San Juan, Puerto Rico. PREPA is an agency that owns the electric distribution system for the main island, Vieques, and Culebra, as well as all but two generating stations. PREPA began in the 1920s as a government irrigation system, but its responsibilities grew over the years to encompass island electrification.

PREPA is one of the largest public power agencies in the United States. In 2012, PREPA was ranked as first in number of customers served (approximately 1.5 million) and first in revenues ($4.4 billion in FY2011).

William Rodney Clark is a resident of Puerto Rico and a citizen of the United States. Clark was the Administrator of PREPA's Fuel Procurement Office from July 1996 to May 2014, and worked in the office from 1988 to 2014. As Clark states on his own LinkedIn biography, from 1994 to 2014, he was "[r]esponsible for all the activities associated with fuel procurement such as preparation of bid invitations, bid evaluation, management of contracts, scheduling, invoice processing and price assessment. Also, responsible for all administrative aspects of PREPA's Fuel Procurement Office including official representation of PREPA with the US Coast Guard, Puerto Rico Ports Authority, Harbor Pilots and Inspection companies serving as official gaugers for the importation of goods into US territory. These activities represent approximately ... 70% of all operating expenses for the company." 5 In fact, within PREPA, according to a former employee, Clark was referred to as the "Emperor" for his power in the Fuel Oil Cartel Enterprise.

Edwin Rodriguez is a resident of Puerto Rico and a citizen of the United States.

Rodriguez became the Manager of PREPA's Fuel Procurement Office in or about May 2014 when Clark retired. Prior to May 2014, Rodriguez was Clark's right-hand man and was referred to as the "Magician" for his role in the Fuel Oil Cartel Enterprise.

César Torres Marrero is a resident of Puerto Rico and a citizen of the United States. Torres has held the positions of Service Coordinator for the Fuel Oil Office and, on information and belief, became the Assistant Manager of PREPA's Fuel Procurement Office in or about May 2014 when Clark retired, and Rodriguez was promoted.

Petrobras America Inc. and Petroleo Brasileiro S.A. (collectively "Petrobras") supplied PREPA with fuel oil during the Class Period. For example, just for the period August 2012 to November 2014, PREPA paid Petrobras nearly $2 billion for fuel oil supplied or to be supplied during that same period. Petrobras is no stranger to the kickback and fuel oil scheme described below. In late 2014, Petrobras became embroiled in a scandal involving a sprawling kickback scheme that resulted in Brazilian prosecutors filing charges against 35 people including Petrobras executives. Prosecutors allege that a group of as many as 16 contractors formed a cartel to drive up the prices of Petrobras projects. The companies, which include Brazilian multinationals Odebrecht SA, Camargo Corrêa SA, Construtora OASA and others, are suspected of colluding to inflate the cost of work performed for Petrobras. According to an agreement made public in federal court documents, a former Petrobras executive, Roberto Costa, is cooperating with authorities. Videotapes released by the court – which have riveted Brazilians to their TVs – show Mr. Costa telling investigators that for at least seven years he and others siphoned millions in kickbacks from companies to whom Petrobras awarded inflated construction contracts. They then used the money to bribe politicians through intermediaries to guarantee they would vote in line with the ruling party while enriching themselves, according to the tapes. Mr. Costa described the kickbacks from the companies as a "three percent political adjustment" and said he personally raked-off tens of millions of dollars, according to the tapes.

As relates to this case, Mr. Costa was an instrumental player for Petrobras in securing fuel oil contracts with PREPA. In 2006, on behalf of Petrobras, Mr. Costa personally attended a contract signing ceremony with

PREPA, together with PREPA President Luis Aníbal Aviles Pagan (who signed on behalf of PREPA) and PREPA directors Luis F. Jimenez Pagan and Edwin Rivera Serrano.

Shell Trading (US) Company ("STUSCO") is a Delaware corporation with its principal place of business at One Shell Plaza, 910 Louisiana Street, Houston, Texas, and its office in Puerto Rico at Route 901 Km. 2.7, Yabucoa 00967. According to its website, STUSCO "conducts a substantial trading-for-profit business, which includes the buying and selling of crude oil, finished products and feedstocks, as well as trading oil futures. As part of the global Shell Trading network, STUSCO buys and sells more than 5 million barrels of hydrocarbons per day in physical markets, making it one of the largest petroleum supply organizations in North America and the world."7 During the Class Period, STUSCO sometimes served as an intermediary between Petrobras and PREPA, entering into contracts for the supply of fuel oil to PREPA of more than $3 billion and purchasing fuel oil from Petrobras to fulfill the contracts.8 For example, in 2011, PREPA renewed its 7.8 million barrels a year contract with STUSCO, which required STUSCO to deliver 60,000 barrels almost every two to three days to PREPA's Aguirre power plant. Petrobras supplied the fuel oil to STUSCO for this and other contracts.9

Trafigura A.G. is a business organization, similar to a U.S. corporation, with a principal place of business in Lucerne, Switzerland and with a business location at 1401 McKinney Avenue, Suite 2375, Houston, Texas 77010 and in Puerto Rico at Centro Ind. DeMercadeo, Floor 8, Luchetti Ind. Park, Carr. #2 km 2.0, Bayamon 00000. 27. Trafigura Beheer B.V. is a business organization, similar to a U.S. limited liability company, with a principal place of business located at Gustav Mahlerplein 102 1082 MA Amsterdam, Netherlands. (Trafigura A.G. and Trafigura Beheer B.V. are collectively referred to as "Trafigura").

Recently, one publication in Brazil reported that Trafigura paid bribes or kickbacks to Mr. Costa while he worked for Petrobras in 2013, depositing *at least $446,800 in a secret account maintained on Mr. Costa's behalf at the Bank Lombard Odier in Switzerland. 10*

PetroWest, Inc. ("PetroWest") is a Puerto Rican corporation with its principal place of business located at Carr 345 KM 1.5, Parque Industrial, Hormigueros 00660. PetroWest supplied PREPA with fuel oil during the Class Period. For example, just for the period 2010 to 2014, PREPA agreed to pay PetroWest more than $3.7 billion for fuel oil supplied. Trafigura and Petrobras supplied the fuel oil to PetroWest to fulfill the contracts with PREPA.

Puma Energy Caribe LLC ("Puma Energy Caribe") is a Puerto Rico limited liability company with a principal place of business at Centro Internacional de Mercadeo Torre 1 #100 Carr 165, Suite 804, Guaynabo Puerto Rico 00968. 31. Puma Energy International, B.V. ("Puma Energy International") is a business organization, similar to a U.S. limited liability company, with a principal place of business at 2 Qual de la Poste, 1204, Geneva, Switzerland. Vitol and Trafigura have supplied fuel oil to Puma Energy Caribe and Puma Energy International (collectively "Puma") during the Class Period to fulfill contracts with PREPA.

Trafigura purchased the rights to the Puma brand in 1997.11 Trafigura also owned nearly 50% of Puma through 2013. Trafigura supplied fuel oil to Puma to fulfill Puma's contracts with PREPA for fuel oil during the Class Period. For example, for the period 2011 to 2014, PREPA agreed to pay Puma nearly $1 billion for fuel oil supplied.

Trafigura is also not a stranger to the how the scheme to defraud worked in Puerto Rico. For example, Trafigura Beheer B.V. paid $31 million in bribes to the People's National Party ("PNP") in Jamaica. 12 Trafigura claimed the bribes to the Prime Minister, PNP chairman, Energy Minister, and Information Minister, among others, were payments on a commercial agreement relating to the procurement of oil, while the PNP claimed the payments were donations.

Vitol, S.A. is a Swiss "société anonyme," similar to a U.S. corporation, with its principal place of business at Boulevard du Pont d'Arve 28, in Geneva, Switzerland, and with an office in Puerto Rico located at 3108 Ave Julio Monagas, Ponce, Puerto Rico, 00717-2200. 35. Vitol, Inc. is a Delaware corporation with a principal place of business at 1100 Louisiana, Suite 5500 in Houston, Texas, and an office in Puerto Rico located at 3108 Ave Julio Monagas, Ponce 00717-2200. Vitol, S.A. and Vitol, Inc. (collectively, "Vitol") supplied PREPA with fuel oil during the Class Period. For example, just for the period 2005 to 2013, PREPA agreed to pay Vitol more than $3.3 billion for fuel oil supplied. 36.

Vitol is also familiar with the scheme to defraud used by the Fuel Oil Cartel Enterprise. For example, Vitol S.A., Inc. pled guilty in November 2007 to the crime of Grand Larceny in the First Degree in the State of New York for paying approximately $13,000,000 in "surcharges" or illegal kickbacks to Iraqi government officials in exchange for Iraqi crude oil, when all monies paid for Iraqi crude oil were supposed to be paid into a United Nations trust account under the United Nations Oil-For-Food Programme.14

Carlos R. Mendez & Associates ("Mendez") is a Puerto Rico corporation with its principal place of business located at 3108 Avenue Julio E Monagas, Ponce, PR 00717-2200. Mendez has represented Fuel Oil Supplier Participants, including, but not limited to, Petrobras and Vitol, in Puerto Rico to, inter alia, ensure that (i) the Laboratory Participants submitted test results showing the fuel oil delivered by the Fuel Oil Supplier Participants was compliant when it was Non-Compliant Fuel Oil, and (ii) PREPA accepted the delivery of Non-Compliant Fuel Oil from the Fuel Oil Supplier Participants based on the falsified test results from the Laboratory Participants.

The Energy Information Administration notes, in 2012, "65% of Puerto Rico's electricity came from petroleum, 18% from natural gas, 16%

*from coal, and 1% from renewable energy." The Fuel Oil Cartel Enterprise
has worked to prevent renewable energy projects from replacing the use of
fuel oil to combust for electricity.*

*Fuel Oil Cartel Enterprise, dubbed by the media and government rep-
resentatives in Puerto Rico as the "Cartel de Petroleo," has been defined to
include "various interest groups, such as suppliers – including oil smugglers
– political parties, grantees, [PREPA] employees, bondholders and bankers,
and individuals with political ambition and connections."*

*The Fuel Oil Cartel Enterprise constitutes an association-in-fact enter-
prise within the meaning of § 1961(4) of RICO. 71. PREPA and/or the
Fuel Oil Supplier Participants hired the Laboratory Participants thousands
of times (every time a delivery of fuel oil arrived) via phone calls or emails
pursuant to which the Defendant Laboratory Participants provided fuel
testing services for millions of barrels of fuel oil purchased by PREPA annually from the Fuel Oil Supplier Participants.*

*The testing services provided by the Laboratory Participants includ-
ed tests of fuel oil to be delivered to PREPA from the Fuel Oil Supplier
Participant, and were conducted on behalf of PREPA and the Fuel Oil
Supplier Participants. The Laboratory Participants performed tests to
verify the quality of fuel oil delivered and the minimum and maximum
allowable levels of certain fuel compounds, including, but not limited to,
sulfur, vanadium, asphaltenes, and BTU content. The results of these tests
were supposed to enable PREPA to determine whether fuel to be delivered
to PREPA met contractual specifications and the EPA Consent Decree, i.e.,
whether it was Compliant Fuel Oil.*

The PREPA Participants directed and participated in the scheme,
agreeing to accept and pay full price for Non-Compliant Fuel because
the Fuel Oil Supplier Participants agreed to pay the PREPA Participants
undisclosed kickbacks, including lavish trips and parties. The Fuel Oil
Supplier Participants were incentivized to participate in the scheme to

defraud, and to pay kickbacks, in order to ensure that they received billions of dollars in contracts for the supply of fuel oil to PREPA at higher prices than for the Non-Compliant Fuel Oil being delivered.

According to a referendum brought by Representative Rodriguez Miranda of the Puerto Rico House of representatives and referred to the Committee of Internal Affairs, the PREPA Participants and other "'middlemen' involved in the sale of the fuel," including "mid-level officials," received commissions, or kickbacks, valued at over $100 million.

The Senate President, Eduardo Bhatia, was interviewed for a special television program entitled "¿Por qué pagamos tanto? En su totalidad," which aired in Puerto Rico on or about May 12, 2014. Senator Bhatia explained that PREPA purchases more than $3 billion a year in fuel oil from the Fuel Oil Supplier Participants, and "the one in charge of making those purchases in Puerto Rico," i.e., the PREPA Participants, "receives a commission for the sale of about 10 per cent, which means, in Puerto Rico there is a group of people that gets close to 300 million dollars per year in commissions," and who "would do the unspeakable to keep the current model within the Authority unchanged."

By 2014, PREPA was financially strapped, and creditors were worried that PREPA would eventually default on part of its $8.3 billion in outstanding bonds. Thus, as part of a forbearance agreement with its creditors allowing PREPA to extend its line of credit, PREPA was required to agree to restructure.

The scheme is still going on today. For example, on August 14, 2014, a controversy erupted regarding a fuel oil delivery by Petrobras at the Aguierre plant on the Energy 8001 barge, because Alchem reported to PREPA that the BTUs were noncompliant.

As a result of Alchem's report, PREPA should have rejected the fuel oil; instead PREPA told Alchem to stop testing. On information and belief, in 2014, PREPA agreed to let Petrobras control all aspects of the Fuel Oil Enterprise. Petrobras was able to gain control as a result of the severe financial restraints under which PREPA is currently operating. While Petrobras cut off PREPA's fuel oil credit line in May 2014 unless PREPA became current, Petrobras "relented" so long as future contracts were entered on its terms. One such term required that PREPA allow Petrobras to select the laboratories to be used by both the supplier and PREPA to verify fuel oil content, rather than to have competing or conflicting Certificates of Analysis from sample analyses.

On September 30, 2014, PREPA and Petrobras signed a contract for the delivery of Compliant Fuel Oil in exchange for the payment of $680,000,000 through August 15, 2015. The contract solidified Petrobras' control of the Fuel Oil Cartel Enterprise and the choice of Laboratory Participants.

Defendants used thousands of mail and interstate wire communications to create and manage the fraudulent scheme and RICO enterprise. Defendants' scheme involved national and multi-national companies' contracting for and procurement of fuel oil from states and nations outside Puerto Rico, marketing and sales plans and programs, and encompassed governmental agents and employees, laboratories, and Fuel Oil Suppliers across and outside the country.

End of law suit document.

NOTES

[1] Mark Gongloff, HUFFPOST, Financial Crisis Cost U.S. $12.8 Trillion Or More: Study, Web based article, posted 9-12-12, Web Link: **huffingtonpost.com/mark-gongloff/financial-crisis-cost-128-trillion_b_1878857.html**, verified article 8-29-18

[2] Edwin Meléndez, Víctor R. Martínez, Center for Puerto Rico Studies-Hunter, Conflict of Interest Shadows Members of the FOB, Web based article, posted on 04-15-17, Web Link: **centropr.hunter.cuny.edu/events-news/puerto-rico-news/fiscal-oversight-board/conflict-interest-shadows-members-fob**, verified 08-31-18

[3] Raul M. Grijalva quote, Mr. Grijalva's website, Everything needs to be suspended, there needs to be loan forgiveness including and or suspension of any repayment, Web based quote, posting date is unknown, Web Link: **grijalva.house.gov/in-the-news/**, verified 08-31-18

[4] Richard Lawless, The Daily Caller, What does it cost to buy a Paul Ryan vote?, Web based article, posted on 07-11-16, Web Link: **dailycaller.com/2016/07/11/what-does-it-cost-to-buy-a-paul-ryan-vote/**, verified 08-31-18

[5] Benjamin Weiser, New York Times, Schumer Aide Is Confirmed as United States Attorney, Web based article, posted on 08-08-09, Web Link: **nytimes.com/2009/08/08/nyregion/08bharara.html**, verified 08-31-18

[6] Willian D. Cohan, The Atlantic Business, How Wall Street's Bankers Stayed Out of Jail, Web based article, posted in September 2015 Issue, Web Link: **theatlantic.com/magazine/archive/2015/09/how-wall-streets-bankers-stayed-out-of-jail/399368/**, verified 08-31-18

[7] Larry Doyle, Sense on Cents, Preet Bharara On "Too Big to Prosecute", Web based article, posted on 07-27-12, Web Link: **senseoncents.com/2012/07/preet-bharara-on-too-big-to-prosecute/**, verified 08-31-18

[8] Elizabeth Warren Press Release, Senators Warren, Blumenthal, Reid, Schumer Introduce Puerto Rico Emergency Financial Stability Act, Web based article, posted 12-18-15, Web Link: **warren.senate.gov/newsroom/press-releases/senators-warren-blumenthal-reid-schumer-introduce-puerto-rico-emergency-financial-stability-act**, verified 08-31-18

[9] Brian Montopoli, CBS News, Charles Schumer's Wall Street Dance, Web based article, posted on 06-29-11, Web Link: **cbsnews.com/news/charles-schumers-wall-street-dance/**, verified 08-31-18

[10] Eric Lipton and Raymond Hernandez, New York Times Business Day, A Champion of Wall Street Reaps Benefits, Web based article, posted on 12-13-08, Web Link: **nytimes.com/2008/12/14/business/14schumer.html**, verified 08-31-18

[11] Zaid Jilani, Alternet, Chuck Schumer, Friend of Wall Street and War-Ready to be anointed head of the Senate Democrats, Web based article, posted on 03-28-15, Web Link: **alternet.org/**

chuck-schumer-friend-wall-street-and-war-ready-be-anointed-head-senate-democrats, verified 08-31-18

[12] DaShanne Stokes, goodreads, Leadership by deception isn't leadership. It's fraud, Web based quote, posting date is unknown, Web Link: **goodreads.com/quotes/8423626-leadership-by-deception-isn-t-leadership-it-s-fraud**, verified 08-31-18

[13] Jan LaRue, American Thinker, James Comey: The Cowering Inferno, In this account, James Comey's actions showcase a duplicitous, Web based article, posted on 06-11-17, Web Link: **americanthinker.com/articles/2017/06/james_comey_the_cowering_inferno.html**, verified on 08-31-18

[14] Sean Davis, The Federalist, Former Bush AG On Comey's 2007 Brush With Scandal: 'Jim's Loyalty Was More To Chuck Schumer', Web based article, posted on 05-17-17, Web Link: **thefederalist.com/2017/05/17/former-attorney-general-on-comeys-integrity-jims-loyalty-was-more-to-chuck-schumer/**, verified 08-31-18

[15] Dave Davidson, Seeking Alpha, Senator Schumer's Careless Remarks Result in IndyMac's Early Demise, Web based article, posted on 07-13-08, Web Link: **seekingalpha.com/article/84766-senator-schumers-careless-remarks-result-in-indymacs-early-demise**, verified 08-31-18

[16] Joel Cintrón Arbasetti, Centro De Periodismo Investigative, The crisis in Puerto Rico fills politicians and lobbyists' pockets in the United States, Puerto Rico Bondholders Political Contributions Graph, Web based article, posted on 12-19-15, Web Link: **periodismoinvestiga-tivo.com/2015/12/the-crisis-in-puerto-rico-fills-politicians-and-lobbyists-pockets-in-the-united-states/**, verified 08-31-18

¹⁷ Ryan Rainey, Morning Consult, Duffy Tops List to Take Over Wall Street Subcommittee, Web based article, posted on 11-29-16, Web Link: **morningconsult.com/2016/11/29/rep-duffy-tops-list-take-wall-street-subcommittee/**, verified 08-31-18

¹⁸ Democratic Party of Wisconsin Staff Writer, Democratic Party of Wisconsin Press Release, Think Wall Street Should Secretly Bribe Foreign Governments? Sean Duffy Does, Web based article, posted on 02-02-17, Web Link: **wisdems.org/news/think-wall-street-should-secretly-bribe-foreign-governments-sean-duffy-does**, verified 09-01-18

¹⁹ Staff writer, Allied Progress, GOP Congressman reimagines "Wall Street Titans" as huge fans of Dodd-Frank wall street reform, Sean Duffy (R-WI) took $658,754 from Wall Street interests during the last election, Web based article, posted on 04-26-17, Web Link: **alliedprogress.org/research/wisconsin-congressman-reimagines-wall-street-titans-huge-dodd-frank-wall-street-reform-fans/**, verified 09-01-18

²⁰ Wesley Lowery, The Washington Post, 91% of the time the better-financed candidate wins. Don't act surprised, Web based article, posted on 04-04-14, Web Link: **washingtonpost.com/news/the-fix/wp/2014/04/04/think-money-doesnt-matter-in-elections-this-chart-says-youre-wrong/?noredirect=on&utm_term=.9d897572d0af**, verified 09-01-18

²¹ Craig Wall, Eyewitness News Channel Seven, Report: Chicago most corrupt city in U.S., Web based video clip, posted on 05-15-18, Web Link: **abc7chicago.com/politics/report-chicago-most-corrupt-city-in-us/3478310/**, verified on 09-01-18

²² Kelleigh Nelson, News with Views, Obama's DOJ And FBI Conspired To Knife America In The Heart, Web based article, posted on 02-06-18, Web Link: **newswithviews.com/obamas-doj-and-fbi-conspired-to-knife-america-in-the-heart/**, verified 09-01-18

[23] Thomas Lifson, American Thinker, Do we need to destroy the FBI in order to save it?, Web based article, posted on 02-22-18, Web Link: **americanthinker.com/blog/2018/02/do we need to destroy the fbi in order to save it.html**, verified 09-01-18

[24] Patricia McCarthy, American Thinker, Why aren't the Democrats horrified by the corruption at the FBI and DOJ?, Web based article, posted on 01-29-18, Web Link: **americanthinker.com/blog/2018/01/ why arent the democrats horrified by the corruption at the fbi and doj.html**, verified 09-01-18

[25] MONICA CROWLEY, THE HILL, Federal abuses on Obama's watch represent a growing blight on his legacy, Web based article, posted on 02-12-18, Web Link: **thehill.com/opinion/white-house/373379-federal-abuses-a-growing-blight-on-obamas-legacy**, verified 09-01-018

[26] Yves Smith, naked capitalism, NYT's William Cohan Blasts "Holder Doctrine" of Headfake Bank "Settlements" With No Prosecutions, Web based article, posted on 08-20-14, Web Link: **nakedcapitalism. com/2014/08/nyts-william-cohan-blasts-holder-doctrine-head-fake-bank-settlements-prosecutions.html,** verified 09-01-018

[27] David Dayen, Salon, Why Eric Holder's new job is an insult to the American public, Web based article, posted on 07-07-15, Web Link: **salon.com/2015/07/07/why eric holders new job is an insult to the american public/**, verified 09-01-18

[28] Mario Vargas Llosa Quote, BrainyQuote, My three years in politics was very instructive about the way in which the appetite for political power can destroy a human mind, destroy principles and values, and transform people into little monsters, Web based quote, Posting date unknown, Web Link: **brainyquote.com/quotes/mario vargas llosa 851074**, verified 09-01-018

[29] Christian Adams, THE HILL, Obama holdovers at the Justice Department still run the show, Web based article, posted on 02-09-18, Web Link: **thehill.com/opinion/white-house/373051-obama-hold-overs-at-the-justice-department-still-run-the-show**, verified 09-01-18

[30] Aaron Kesel, Activist Post, Jay Clayton's SEC Protects Wall Street Racketeering, Web based article, posted on 09-01-18, Web Link: **activistpost.com/2017/12/jay-claytons-sec-protects-wall-street-racketeering.html**, verified 09-01-18

[31] Franklin D. Roosevelt Quote, Brainy Quote, in politics, nothing happens by accident. If it happens, you can bet it was planned that way, Web based quote, posting date is unknown, Web Link: **brainyquote. com/quotes/franklin_d_roosevelt_164126**, verified 09-01-18

[32] H. L. Mencken, Brainy Quote, The whole aim of practical politics is to keep the populace alarmed (and hence clamorous to be led to safety) by menacing it with an endless series of hobgoblins, all of them imaginary, Web based quote, posting date is unknown, Web Link: **brainyquote.com/quotes/h_l_mencken_101109,** verified 09-01-18

[33] Emily Schultheis, CBS News, Nancy Pelosi calls Steve Bannon a White Supremacist, Web based article, posted on 02-02-17, Web Link: **cbsnews.com/news/nancy-pelosi-calls-steve-bannon-white-supremacist/**, verified 09-02-18

[34] No writer identified, Conservative Angle, Nancy Pelosi Defends MS-13 Gang Members From Trump's 'Animals' Comment, Web based article, posted 05-18-18, Web Link: **conservativeangle.com/community/threads/nancy-pelosi-defends-ms-13-gang-members-from-trump's-'animals'-comment.2414/**, verified 09-02-18

[35] Jenniel, PoliticalCondumdrum Froum, Pelosi Scolds Trump, 'So Inhumane': Pelosi Scolds Trump, Claims He Called Undocumented Immigrants 'Animals', Web based article, posted on 05-19-18, Web

Link: **tapatalk.com/groups/politicalconundrum/pelosi-scolds-trump-t19457389.html**, verified 09-02-18

[36] Jennifer Van Laar, Red State, "School's In: CEO Blasts Nancy Pelosi's "Crumbs" Comment, Last Thursday Rep. Nancy Pelosi (D-Rich Off Hubby's Money) held a <u>rambling press conference</u> in which she characterized the bonuses corporations are giving their rank-and-file employees as "crumbs.", Web based article, posted on 01-16-18, Web Link: **redstate.com/jenvanlaar/2018/01/16/schools-ceo-blasts-nancy-pelosis-crumbs-comment/**, verified 09-02-18

[37] Robert Slavin, The Bond Buyer, Puerto Rico Corruption and Why it Matters, Web based article, posted on 07-07-16, Web Link: **bondbuyer.com/news/puerto-rico-corruption-and-why-it-matters**, verified 09-02-18

[38] Heather Gillers and Tom McGinty, Wall Street Journal, How Big Are Mutual Funds', Puerto Rico Losses?, $5.4 Billion, Web based article, posted on 05-14-17, Web Link: **wsj.com/articles/how-big-are-mutual-funds-puerto-rico-losses-5-4-billion-1494763205**, verified 09-02-18

[39] Mary Williams Walsh, New York Times, Hurricane Aid Has Eased Puerto Rico's Finances. It May Not Be Enough, Web based article, posted on 04-19-18, Web Link: **nytimes.com/2018/04/19/us/puerto-rico-fiscal-plan-hurricane.html**, verified 04-02-18

[40] Associated Press, New York Daily News, Puerto Rican mayor, two other gov officials arrested on corruption charges, Web based article, posted on 07-07-18, Web Link: **nydailynews.com/news/crime/ny-news-puerto-rico-mayor-arrested-corruption-20180707-story.html.** Verified 09-02-18

[41] Kevin Dugan and Carleton English, New York Post, Puerto Rico's bonds tumble after Trump comments on debt, Web based article, posted on

10-04-17, Web Link: **nypost.com/2017/10/04/puerto-ricos-bonds-tumble-after-trump-comments-on-debt/**, verified 09-02-18

[42] Editorial Board, Washington Post, No more excuses. Puerto Rico needs help, Web based article, posted on 01-05-18, Web Link: **washingtonpost.com/opinions/no-more-excuses-puerto-rico-needs-help/2018/01/05/8dd307a8-f245-11e7-b390-a36dc3fa2842_story.html?noredirect=on&utm_term=.6e823ff05bdd**, verified 09-02-18

[43] Ben O'Keefe, The Boston Globe, HUGE NEWS: The Boston Globe Calls on Elizabeth Warren to Run for President!, Web based article, posted on 03-23-15, Web Link: **front.moveon.org/rwrbostonglobe/**, verified 09-02-18

[44] Mary Spicuzza, Journal Sentinel, Paul Ryan raises $11 million in first quarter of 2018, Web based article, posted on 04-11-18, Web Link: **jsonline.com/story/news/politics/2018/04/09/paul-ryan-raises-11-million-first-quarter-2018/499494002/**, verified 09-02-18

[45] Vladimir Lenin, Yahoo Answers, The press should be not only a collective propagandist and a collective agitator, but also a collective organizer of the masses, Web based article, original posting is unknown, Web Link: **answers.yahoo.com/question/index?qid=20100826045702AAhYNdT&guccounter=2**, verified 09-02-18

[46] George Washington, Zero Hedge, More Foreclosures and Suicides than During the Great Depression, Web based article, posted on 05-17-13, Web Link: **zerohedge.com/contributed/2013-05-17/more-foreclosures-and-suicides-during-great-depression**, verified 09-02-18

[47] David Goldman, CNN Money, Worst year for jobs since '45, Web based article, posted on 01-09-09, Web Link: **money.cnn.com/2009/01/09/news/economy/jobs_december/**, verified 09-02-18

[48] Rebecca J Rosen, The Atlantic, The Mental-Health Consequences of Unemployment, Web based article, posted on 06-09-14, Web Link: **theatlantic.com/business/archive/2014/06/the-mental-health-consequences-of-unemployment/372449/**, verified 09-02-18

[49] Theodore Roosevelt, Brainy Quote, When they call the roll in the Senate, the Senators do not know whether to answer 'Present' or 'Not guilty.', Web based quote, original posting date is unknown, Web Link: **brainyquote.com/quotes/theodore_roosevelt_122699**, verified 09-02-18